"'Jesus' parables are like diamonds,' writes Lohfink, held within settings that both preserve and protect. *The Forty Parables of Jesus* presents the content of Jesus' unique sayings mindful of the traditions that preserved, preached, and interpreted those parables. But Lohfink also provides the larger context in which parables, as provocative short stories with a twist, were heard, read, and understood. Lohfink has deftly written a well-exegeted and researched book that is at the same time eminently readable. *The Forty Parables of Jesus* witnesses to the 'unbelievable nearness of God,' and invites us to embrace the implicit Christology of Jesus' parables."

— Laurie Brink, OP, PhD, Catholic Theological Union

"Drawing from his magisterial career and vast publications on Scripture, Father Lohfink invigorates the discussion on parables for scholars and students alike. With perceptive analysis, he marshals a broad range of examples to expand our knowledge of how these stories undermine our expectations of conventions, ultimately reminding us of what was so compelling about Jesus' parables. This book is more than a commentary, but a text much like the parables themselves: an invitation to ponder the Good News, rethink the genius of story, and enlarge the stunning horizon of the proclamation of the Reign of God."

— Guerric DeBona, OSB, St. Meinrad Seminary and School of Theology

"Drawing on his genius for biblical interpretation that is both intelligent and pastoral, profound and accessible, Gerhard Lohfink turns to an exposition of Jesus' parables, forty in all. He begins by noting, through a selection of parables from a variety of sources, how context and structure add meaning to parables, including those of Jesus. His goal is not to pit the possible original meaning of Jesus' parables against the layers of meaning derived from their use in the early church and in the Gospels, but to illustrate the rich and varied layers of meaning these characteristic stories of Jesus hold for us as Christians."

— Donald Senior, CP, Catholic Theological Union, Chicago

*Gerhard Lohfink*

# The Forty Parables of Jesus

Translated by

*Linda M. Maloney*

LITURGICAL PRESS
ACADEMIC

Collegeville, Minnesota
www.litpress.org

Cover design by Ann Blattner and Tara Wiese.
Cover art by Br. Martin Erspamer, OSB, a monk of Saint Meinrad Archabbey, Indiana.

Scripture quotations are from New Revised Standard Version Bible © 1989 National Council of the Churches of Christ in the United States of America. Used by permission. All rights reserved worldwide.

Originally published as *Die vierzig Gleichnisse Jesu* by Gerhard Lohfink © 2020 Verlag Herder GmbH, Freiburg im Breisgau.

© 2021 by Order of Saint Benedict, Collegeville, Minnesota. All rights reserved. No part of this book may be used or reproduced in any manner whatsoever, except brief quotations in reviews, without written permission of Liturgical Press, Saint John's Abbey, PO Box 7500, Collegeville, MN 56321-7500.

ISBN: 978-0-8146-9035-2 (paperback)

**Library of Congress Cataloging-in-Publication Data**

Names: Lohfink, Gerhard, 1934– author. | Maloney, Linda M., translator.
Title: The forty parables of Jesus / Gerhard Lohfink ; translated by Linda M. Maloney.
Other titles: Vierzig Gleichnisse Jesu. English.
Description: Collegeville, Minnesota : Liturgical Press Academic, [2021] | "Originally published as Die vierzig Gleichnisse Jesu by Gerhard Lohfink © 2020 Verlag Herder GmbH, Freiburg im Breisgau." | Includes bibliographical references and index. | Summary: "Reflections and interpretations of the forty parables of Jesus, including a review of scholarship in this area"-- Provided by publisher.
Identifiers: LCCN 2021003115 (print) | LCCN 2021003116 (ebook) | ISBN 9780814685105 (hardcover) | ISBN 9780814685341 (epub) | ISBN 9780814685341 (mobi) | ISBN 9780814685341 (pdf)
Subjects: LCSH: Jesus Christ—Parables.
Classification: LCC BT375.3 .L6413 2021  (print) | LCC BT375.3  (ebook) | DDC 226.8/06—dc23
LC record available at https://lccn.loc.gov/2021003115
LC ebook record available at https://lccn.loc.gov/2021003116

For Peter Stuhlmacher
*in gratitude*

# Contents

Preface xi

## Part One: How Parables Work

1. The Lion, the Bear, and the Snake (Amos 5:18-20) 3
2. The Bramble Becomes King (Judges 9:8-15) 6
3. The Poor Man's Lamb (2 Samuel 12:1-4) 11
4. The Song of the Vineyard (Isaiah 5:1-7) 14
5. The Faithless Wife (Ezekiel 16:1-63) 18
6. The Vine and the Branches (John 15:1-8) 22
7. The Elm and the Vine (Hermas *Similitudes* 2.1-10) 25
8. The King Who Gained a People (*Mekhilta Exodus* 20.2) 27
9. The Man in the Well (Friedrich Rückert) 30
10. The Perfect Swimmer (Martin Buber) 35

## Part Two: Jesus' Forty Parables

1. The Successful Break-in (Luke 12:39) 42
2. Overpowering the "Strong Man" (Mark 3:27) 45
3. The Treasure in the Field and the Pearl (Matthew 13:44-46) 47
4. The Budding Fig Tree (Mark 13:28-29) 54
5. The Mustard Seed (Mark 4:30-32) 56
6. The Leaven (Luke 13:20-21) 61
7. The Seed Growing by Itself (Mark 4:26-29) 63
8. The Abundant Harvest (Mark 4:3-9) 65

9. The Two Debtors (Luke 7:41-42)   73
10. The Lost Sheep (Matthew 18:12-14)   75
11. The Lost Coin (Luke 15:8-10)   77
12. The Lost Son (Luke 15:11-32)   79
13. The Laborers in the Vineyard (Matthew 20:1-16)   89
14. The Judge and the Widow (Luke 18:1-8)   95
15. The Importunate Friend (Luke 11:5-8)   99
16. The Banquet (Luke 14:16-24)   101
17. The Fishnet (Matthew 13:47-50)   106
18. The Weeds in the Wheat (Matthew 13:24-30)   109
19. The Pharisee and the Tax Collector (Luke 18:10-14)   114
20. The Merciful Samaritan (Luke 10:30-35)   118
21. The Two Different Sons (Matthew 21:28-31)   122
22. The Rich Man and the Poor Man (Luke 16:19-31)   126
23. The Ten Virgins (Matthew 25:1-13)   131
24. The Barren Fig Tree (Luke 13:6-9)   136
25. The Quarreling Children (Matthew 11:16-19)   139
26. Going to Court (Matthew 5:25-26)   141
27. The Foolish Wheat Farmer (Luke 12:16-20)   143
28. The Guest without a Festal Garment (Matthew 22:11-13)   145
29. The Unforgiving Servant (Matthew 18:23-34)   147
30. The Vigilant Slaves (Luke 12:35-38)   153
31. The Slave Keeping Watch (Matthew 24:45-51)   159
32. A Slave's Wages (Luke 17:7-10)   162
33. The Money Given in Trust (Matthew 25:14-30)   166
34. The Crooked Manager (Luke 16:1-13)   173
35. The Assassin (*Gospel of Thomas* 98)   178
36. Building a Tower and Making War (Luke 14:28-32)   181
37. Building a House on Rock or on Sand (Matthew 7:24-27)   184
38. The Lamp on the Lampstand (Matthew 5:15)   187
39. The Grain of Wheat Dies (John 12:24)   189
40. The Violent Farmworkers (Mark 12:1-12)   191

## Part Three:
## What Is Different about Jesus' Parables

1. The Material  207
2. The Form  210
3. The Tradition  218
4. The Subject  222
5. The Theme within the Theme  234

Acknowledgments  241
Works Cited  242
Scriptural Index  248
The Parables in the Church Year  255

# Preface

*"The parables not only draw us into the center of Jesus' proclamation; at the same time they point to the person of the proclaimer, the mystery of Jesus himself."*

—Eberhard Jüngel[1]

Jesus' parables were never museum pieces. From the very beginning they were retold, reflected on, explained, relocated into new situations—and in the process they survived as something eternally fresh and blooming. Above all, they were inserted into the text of the gospels, where they were even given their own framework in many cases; the frames were themselves a kind of interpretation. In the process it could well happen that the "point" of a parable shifted.

Obviously it is legitimate to inquire about the oldest form and original meaning of Jesus' parables, but not with the idea that the "overlayer" of church tradition must be removed to get access to the solid original rock. I reject that image. Church tradition is not a field of boulders, and most certainly not a dump. Without the church's tradition as a faithful and sculpted heritage Jesus' parables would no longer exist. It is only because they lived on in the church's preaching that they have survived and are able to develop their power ever anew.

I prefer a different picture: Jesus' parables are like diamonds that were given a setting even in their earliest transmission and then especially in the gospels. Settings for precious stones are not only valuable in themselves; they are necessary. They present the stone, hold

---

[1] Eberhard Jüngel, "Die Problematik der Gleichnisrede Jesu," in *Gleichnisse Jesu. Positionen der Auslegung von Adolf Jülicher bis zur Formgeschichte*, ed. Wolfgang Harnisch, WdF 366 (Darmstadt: Wissenschaftliche Buchgesellschaft, 1982), 283–342.

it fast, preserve and protect it. In the case of Jesus' parables, they have to be included in the interpretation. The church needs both a constant attention to its tradition and historical criticism that inquires about its origins.

In fact, we need to speak in much more radical terms: we receive the true image of Jesus only through the church's proclamation and never apart from it. Peter Stuhlmacher rightly wrote: "Historical criticism is a valuable tool, but in the exegesis of biblical books it must be embedded in the framework of the church's tradition."[2]

That all needed to be said to avoid a wrong understanding of what follows. Now that it has been said I can speak of what this book is about. It is about the origins. It is about the oldest form of Jesus' parables and what they originally said. That is to say, it is about one of the most important questions in the interpretation of the gospels and about problems that have sustained research on Jesus for a long time. In this book I will refer gratefully to the work of many New Testament scholars on Jesus' parables.

Still, I do not intend to offer a review of scholarship, nor am I primarily interested in purely scholarly debate. All that I want to do is to unlock these bold and often surprising texts for my readers. In doing so I have occasionally referred to parable interpretations I have published previously in various places, but I have questioned those interpretations again, thought about them, and often reformulated them.

The book's title speaks of *forty* parables. Please, don't anyone put that number on the scales! For example, is the great speech about the Last Judgment in Matthew 25:31-46 anything like a parable? Does the opening image of a separation of sheep and goats permit us to call it that? At any rate the whole composition is by no means a parable.[3]

---

[2] Peter Stuhlmacher, "Der Kanon und seine Auslegung," in *Biblische Theologie und Evangelium. Gesammelte Aufsätze*, WUNT 146 (Tübingen: Mohr Siebeck, 2002), 167–90, at 179.

[3] Joachim Jeremias, in his book on parables that has gone through many editions, and rightly so, treats forty parables, but he counts the Last Judgment (Matt 25:31-46) and the return of the unclean spirit (Matt 12:43-45) among them. I have not followed him in that. I cannot see a genuine parable in either of those texts. See Joachim Jeremias, *The Parables of Jesus*, trans. S. H. Hooke (New York: Charles Scribner's Sons, 1962; 2nd rev. ed. 1972).

The number *forty* also resulted from my having set aside Jesus' extremely terse and concise "similes." It is true that no clear boundary can be drawn between a parable and those "similes," but in normal parlance they are not regarded as "parables." Under those presuppositions we arrive at about *forty* parables—an astonishingly large number for an ancient author!

It is also striking that all these parables are admirable examples of the storyteller's art. They speak of the coming of the reign of God—the central theme of Jesus' preaching—in a way that only parables can. Finally, they lead us to Jesus. Nearly every parable discloses to us—discreetly and in hidden fashion—the mystery of Jesus himself.

In the summer semester of 1976 Peter Stuhlmacher and I conducted a seminar together at Eberhard-Karls University, Tübingen. It was titled "Basic Problems in the Pastoral Letters." From that time on our conversation about church and theology has never been broken off. I dedicate this book to Peter Stuhlmacher as a sign of my profound gratitude for his faith and his theology.

Gerhard Lohfink<br>
January 2020

# Part One

## How Parables Work

The books on parables and parables research that are now classics begin with a statement of basics: the nature of a parable, how it is linguistically shaped, what life situation it is rooted in, and what kinds or genres of parables there are. A great deal of space was devoted to that last question. How can we catalogue Jesus' parables in clearly-defined types so we can file them correctly?

But that is just what will *not* happen here. In part 1 we will simply look at ten different parables from very different epochs and ask how they are structured and how they work. We will not consider any authentic parables of Jesus. Then, in part 2 of the book, this 360-degree view will help us to deal properly with Jesus' own parables.[1]

## 1. The Lion, the Bear, and the Snake (Amos 5:18-20)

Not long ago I presented a parable to a discussion group that meets regularly to read and discuss selected literary texts. I did not name the author but only asked the participants how they would read and interpret the following:

> A man was attacked by a lion. By sheer accident he was able to save himself, but then a bear ran at him. Again he escaped. With the last of his strength he made it to his house and just barely slammed the heavy door in the bear's face. Gasping for breath, he leaned his hands against the wall—and a snake bit him. The bite was fatal.

I was amazed at the intensity with which the group engaged with this brief text. A seventeen-year-old whose provocative but intelligent remarks often roused the group said spontaneously: "But the meaning is obvious: your worst enemies are not outside; they are in your own house."

---

[1] Translator's note: German scholarship distinguishes between "Gleichnisse" (similitudes) and "Parabeln" (parables). Similitudes, based on real-life situations, are the subject of this book. The author speaks literally of "Jesus' similitudes." But in English usage "parable" is the term we all understand, and so it will be used here.

"What!" said an older woman. "This parable is about death. It means to say that you can't escape dying. It comes inevitably, no matter how much luck you have had in your life."

A middle-aged man, a professor of classical philology, offered: "Certainly you might say that . . . but I would like to modify that last interpretation a little. The parable doesn't just speak about death; it is about fate. You will never escape the fate that hangs over you, no matter how hard you struggle. At any rate, that was how the Greeks thought. You can run as fast as you like; in the end it will get you—even if the gods have to send you a serpent."

Another, a successful psychotherapist, said: "Of course you didn't invent that parable. It is certainly very ancient, and those old parables contain a lot of experience—at depth. The parable is about the shadows that victimize so many people. Most cannot deal with them without therapy; they are repeatedly threatened and even overwhelmed by them, and the shadows continually reappear in new configurations."

"I have a completely different interpretation," said a shrewd young man who had a broad range of interests and was working on a dissertation on seventeenth-century moral theology. "The lion symbolizes a severe temptation. The man who is being tempted succeeds in escaping from it, but then the same temptation reappears in a different form. He manages to escape again. He is happy at having won out and thinks he is finally free, but then the temptation plays its last card and appears in yet another form. And now it conquers the person precisely because he thought he was such a winner."

At last a woman with a very unhappy and painful marriage behind her spoke up: "You all seem to be theoreticians," she said. "The worst part of my marriage was not the really hard blows: the death of our little daughter and my husband's cheap affairs. No, the worst things were the little pinpricks he employed to wound me over and over again, his sarcastic remarks, the stabs he deliberately inflicted. It was those teeny-tiny poison darts that were ultimately the death of our marriage."

Then I told the group where I had found the parable: I read the text from the prophet Amos:

> Alas for you who desire the day of the LORD!
> Why do you want the day of the LORD?

> It is darkness, not light;
>> as if someone fled from a lion,
>> and was met by a bear;
> or went into the house and rested a hand against the wall,
>> and was bitten by a snake.
> Is not the day of the Lord darkness, not light,
>> and gloom with no brightness in it?

Then, of course, I had to say something about the "Day of the Lord," the crucial phrase that frames and dominates the parable. Amos is using the parable to explain to his hearers in the Northern Kingdom of Israel what the "Day of the Lord" means for them. Before war and deportation overtook them the people of the Northern Kingdom lived in a fragile security. Their economic situation was good (Amos 3:15). The rich were getting richer all the time and exploiting the poor (Amos 2:7; 4:1; 8:4). Pompous worship services were celebrated, along with lavish feasts (Amos 5:21-23; 6:4-6). But the political situation was heating up. The people expected God to defeat their enemies, as on the "day of Midian" (Isa 9:3; Judg 7). For them that was a day on which God had intervened, a day when God had rescued Israel from its foes. Now they were longing for such another "Day of the Lord."

But the prophet levels that expectation to the ground. The "Day of the Lord" the people are wishing for will look completely different. It will be an evil day, a day of destruction and death, because community life in the Northern Kingdom of Israel by no means corresponded to God's will.

This little passage from Amos is terse and pithy in the extreme. Its statement is utterly compressed. The historical Amos could really have spoken it. Instead of light, the symbol of salvation and rescue, darkness will come over the land. The hoped-for "Day of the Lord" will prove to be death and decay. Embedded in the prophecy of woe stands the parable of the futile flight. There is no salvation any longer for the people of the Northern Kingdom!

Our discussion group then debated for a long time about how open to a variety of interpretations an isolated parable text standing by itself can be. Only the literary context or oral commentary or the actual situation in which a parable is spoken can establish its meaning without doubt. For that very reason Amos gave his parable a frame—the "Day of the LORD." The frame could, of course, have simply been the contemporary historical situation that everyone knew about: the intensifying military pressure from the East and the people's illusionary ideas about rescue.

Without any framing, and without any knowledge of its historical situation, would Amos's parable be completely open to any and every reading? "Certainly not," said one part of the group. "After all, the various interpretations that have been offered all run in a certain direction: they are all about *inevitability*." "That's not true at all," said the seventeen-year-old. "My interpretation, that the real enemies are always in one's own house, has nothing to do with 'inevitability.'" I had to admit that she was right. Apparently a parable without a frame and a clear historical context can admit of the widest variety of interpretations.

We will encounter that same problem with regard to Jesus' parables. If we regard them as "autonomous aesthetic constructions" that stand by themselves[2] it may help us to investigate their structure more carefully than usual, but we will too easily miss what they have to say. Then we will see them only as general ethical admonitions, acute precepts of wisdom, or the uncovering of the realities of human existence. But Jesus' parables were decidedly more than that: they spoke of the urgent advent of the reign of God and about the "here and now" of the rule of God in Israel. Jesus' parables must never be isolated from the one who spoke them and the situation into which they were uttered.

## 2. The Bramble Becomes King (Judges 9:8-15)

Our second text comes from the book of Judges, where it stands in the following context: Abimelech, the son of Jerubbaal, has become king of Shechem (Judg 9:6). To get there he had to hire a troop of ruffians to kill his seventy half-brothers from his father's harem (9:4-5). Only Jotham, the youngest, survives by hiding just in time (9:5).

---

[2] If I have understood Dan Otto Via correctly this is precisely his position. See esp. his *The Parables: Their Literary and Existential Dimension* (Philadelphia: Fortress Press, 1974), 71–73. However, a little later (pp. 83–84) he relativizes it somewhat. Here we should also mention Wolfgang Harnisch and his book *Die Gleichniserzählungen Jesu* (reprint Darmstadt: Wissenschaftliche Buchgesellschaft, 1963) He deliberately sets aside any inquiry into a historical location of Jesus' parables.

Jotham addresses the citizens of Shechem from the top of Mount Gerizim. He starts his speech with a parable, the famous "Jotham's fable":

> The trees once went out
>   to anoint a king over themselves.
> So they said to the olive tree,
>   "Reign over us."
> The olive tree answered them,
>   "Shall I stop producing my rich oil
>     by which gods and mortals are honored,
>     and go to sway over the trees?'
> Then the trees said to the fig tree,
>   "You come and reign over us."
> But the fig tree answered them,
>   "Shall I stop producing my sweetness
>     and my delicious fruit,
>     and go to sway over the trees?"
> Then the trees said to the vine,
>   "You come and reign over us."
> But the vine said to them,
>   "Shall I stop producing my wine
>     that cheers gods and mortals,
>     and go to sway over the trees?"
> So all the trees said to the bramble,
>   "You come and reign over us."
> And the bramble said to the trees,
>   "If in good faith you are anointing me king over you,
>     then come and take refuge in my shade;
>   but if not, let fire come out of the bramble
>     and devour the cedars of Lebanon." (Judg 9:8-15)

There are animal fables; there are also plant fables. Judges 9:8-15 is a plant fable, but like all fables it casts a sharp and illusion-free light on situations in the human world. The text is carefully constructed: it has four strophes and the first three are nearly identical in their structure. As a result the fourth strophe can stand out all the more clearly, producing a sequence of 3 + 1. Wherever that formula appears in stories, or in parables, the extra part bears special weight. We could also say that the last part is the climax of the whole, just as in every good joke the point appears only at the end.

The imagery for the parable has been carefully chosen: first the olive tree, fig tree, and vine, and then—set apart in the fourth strophe—the bramble. In the Mediterranean world the olive, fig, and vine were fundamentals of life, not only economically but as marks of civilization. By contrast, brambles were considered useless. At most they served as fences or fuel.

The trees represent a whole people, and the people of the trees want a king. As so often in parables a few representatives are chosen from among many possibilities. In a strictly stylized form they are invited, one after the other, to become king over the people. But all three refuse. In fact, they reject the proffered kingship with indignation. They are already serving the people through their gifts—oil, figs, and wine. Should they lay aside their treasures just to "sway" over the other trees?

The Hebrew word here translated "sway" has a basic meaning of "move back and forth," "wander around," even "stagger." It was used for people who had completely lost their orientation: drunkards, for example (Isa 24:20; Ps 107:27). When the olive, the fig, and the vine all say, "Shall I . . . go to sway over the trees?" the kingship is ridiculed with bitter sarcasm.[3] It is the best among the people who refuse to be king, because the king only "waves" over the trees, that is, carries out his bombastic royal rituals that are no use to anyone. Of course we have to ask how the vine can "sway" over the trees: is the imagery losing its logic here? The answer is easy: in Palestine at that period, differently from now, vines were not planted in rows and most certainly not trained on wires. Either they simply grew along the ground (Ps 80:10, 12) or they were stretched onto the boughs of trees (Ps 80:11) and allowed to hang down from there.[4] In that case they certainly could "sway."

---

[3] The English expression "to hold sway" also has pejorative overtones of illegitimacy.—Trans.

[4] The Roman author L. Junius Moderatus Columella, in his twelve-volume standard work *De re rustica*, speaks primarily about Italy (but the provinces as well) in offering the following possibilities for viticulture: (1) The vine itself represents a kind of vertical "stem," with the grape-producing branches hanging from it (5.4); (2) the "stem" is tied to an upright post crowned with a horizontal crosspiece on which the branches of the vine can extend and then hang down from it (4.1, 16); (3) trees (usually elms) can be planted when the vineyard is laid out; later their branches will be trimmed so that the vines can be drawn as "garlands" around them or hang down from them (5.6, 7); (4) the branches of the vines may simply be spread out on the ground (4.1; 5.4).

So we have the same statement repeated three times in succession: the olive, the fig, and the vine reject the royal office dismissively and even mockingly. They don't want to sway back and forth like drunkards. Against this background of a more and more urgent statement, then, the fourth strophe comes to the point: of all the trees (the three named represent all trees) only the bramble remains, and this one, the thorny bush, reacts quite differently from its predecessors: The bramble is delighted and proclaims immediately: "Take refuge in my shade!"

Anyone who has never been in southern climes where the burning south wind blows off the desert—the sirocco or *khamsin*—has no idea what shade really means. But it is especially important to know that in the ancient Near East "giving shade" was a characteristic statement about a king and even about God. It was part of the ancient Near Eastern royal ideology that a king "gives shade." It meant that the sovereign gave the people life, sheltered them, was their refuge (Ps 121:5; Isa 32:2; Lam 4:20).

The bramble—this bush that offers shade to no one because no one can lie beneath it— appropriates that royal metaphor of saving shade immediately and without restraint. But that is not enough! The promise of salvation, "take refuge in my shade," so arrogant in the circumstances, is followed immediately by a deadly threat: "but if not, let fire come out of the bramble and devour the cedars of Lebanon." This sudden challenge reveals what the bramble really wants: a tyranny that does not shy away from violence.

A number of important interpreters[5] reject the final threat as not original to the fable. First of all, the bramble suddenly begins to speak of itself in the third person. Second, it is odd that the cedars—the noblest of all trees, they should have been invited before the olive—suddenly enter the picture. Thus verse 15e-g must not be part of the original parable.

I do not find this line of argument at all persuasive. A first-person speech can very easily shift to the third person. That shift can, in fact, be a highly effective stylistic turn. Moreover, the introduction of the majestic cedar of Lebanon only at this point makes all kinds of sense: precisely here it effectively intensifies the bramble's threat: if even

---

[5] Thus, e.g., Walter Gross, *Richter*, HTKAT (Freiburg: Herder, 2009), 487; cp. also Ansgar Moenikes, *Die grundsätzliche Ablehnung des Königtums in der Hebräischen Bibel*, BBB 99 (Weinheim: Beltz Athenaeum, 1995), 116–18.

the tall, powerful cedar is threatened by the bramble's fire, then all the other trees in the crowd are certainly imperiled! Above all, without verse 15e-g the fourth strophe does not outweigh the first three. It would remain ironic ("in my shade") but relatively harmless. But as it is, the arrogant lust of kings for power emerges, naked and with no ironic camouflage.

It is generally agreed that the Jotham fable does not really fit its current context. It must at some point have existed by itself, serving simply to ridicule the kingship. We can only grasp its full fury if we consider it in the context of Israel's history. The silent ideal in the background is the association of tribes *before* the royal period, that is, the so-called time of the "judges." It was a time of solidarity in freedom. The only unconditional duties lay within the family and the clan. The tribe and the tribal association could not command anything. This association of tribes was not some primitive pre-state form; it was a conscious alternative model over against the monarchically organized Canaanite city-states but especially counter to the "Egyptian slave-state." In spite of all the problems in that nonstate period of Israel it was a time of free will, personal responsibility, and equality. The "judges"—and one of the best-known judge figures was a woman, namely, Deborah—were charismatic personalities who continually regathered the people. Certainly they were not always successful: hence the longing in Israel for a strong king who could protect the people against hostile attacks. Hence also, though, the biting criticism by many insightful persons against the institution of kingship (cp., for example, 1 Sam 8:10-18). Would anybody really want to go back to Egypt?

Did Jotham, the son of Jerubbaal, really speak "Jotham's fable" from the summit of Mount Gerizim to the citizens of Shechem? That is impossible. The fable of the trees that wanted to anoint a king for themselves is a political-theological satire against the institution of kingship—very probably from the later royal period but still with a backward glance at the time of the judges, which was regarded as ideal. Martin Buber rightly called the fable "the most powerful antimonarchical poem in world literature." It was shaped so as to circulate among the people. It had to be structured as clearly as possible and contain a lot of repetition so it could be easily remembered. And, like every good joke, it had to end with an unexpected and sharp point.

It is true that the nub had to be at the end of the parable, but hearers knew from the beginning that this was about the issue of the institution of kingship since, after all, the trees wanted to create a king for themselves. Then in the very first strophe the kingship is refused, and in the second, and in the third as well. Each time the king is painted as a figure of fun because he "sways" over the trees. Still, it is only at the end that the full arrogance and lust for power on the part of kings (or perhaps a particular king?) is disclosed. And—if the parable hit home—the listeners would know that the people of God are not to be ruled by power structures as was the case with the surrounding peoples.

As regards our later examination of Jesus' parables we need to keep in mind that evidently the structure of 3 + 1 can be found in parables, in which case the climax comes at the end. In addition, we must expect that individual parables can be constructed in ways that are extremely like other parables and using stereotypically repeated formulae. But above all: we can never exclude the possibility that parables "argue" in order to persuade their hearers. Oddly enough, that very thing is occasionally denied. Then it is said that Jesus' parables could certainly not have an argumentative character. I have never understood why they could not.

### 3. The Poor Man's Lamb (2 Samuel 12:1-4)

The following parable is also about misuse of power. We can only briefly indicate its biblical context here: King David has taken Bathsheba, the wife of Uriah, into the royal palace and into his bed while Uriah is fighting a war for him. Uriah was one of his best and most faithful officers.[6] The night with Bathsheba has consequences: Uriah's wife becomes pregnant. David orders Uriah back from the front, entertains him at the palace and tries to get him to go home and sleep with his wife Bathsheba. Uriah sees through the king's plan. He does not go home; instead he lies down with the guards at the palace gate. That way he can publicly attest that he has not been with his wife. Then David sends Uriah back to the front and sees to it that he is

---

[6] Uriah was one of the thirty (or thirty-seven) "warriors of David," a seasoned troop especially devoted to David. We could also call them elite soldiers. See 2 Sam 23:8, 39; 1 Kgs 1:8.

killed in the battle for the city of Rabbah, together with other soldiers of David's army. Then the king takes Bathsheba to wife. The way David stages this murder is told with the highest degree of narrative art, but it reaches its climax with the story told by the prophet Nathan when God sends him to David. Nathan relates the following case:

> There were two men in a certain city, the one rich and the other poor. The rich man had very many flocks and herds; but the poor man had nothing but one little ewe lamb, which he had bought. He brought it up, and it grew up with him and with his children; it used to eat of his meager fare, and drink from his cup, and lie in his bosom, and it was like a daughter to him. Now there came a traveler to the rich man, and he was loath to take one of his own flock or herd to prepare for the wayfarer who had come to him, but he took the poor man's lamb, and prepared that for the guest who had come to him. (2 Sam 12:1-4)

When Nathan gets to that point, David breaks out in fury: "As the LORD lives, the man who has done this deserves to die; he shall restore the lamb fourfold, because he did this thing, and because he had no pity." Nathan says to David: "You are the man!" (2 Sam 12:5-7).

Was that the end of the story? At any rate David was enraged, and if there was any more to the story it did not need to be told. It had made its point.

The story of the "poor man's lamb" hits precisely on the baseness of David's treatment of Uriah. David, who by this time has an entire harem,[7] has taken the wife of one of his most faithful soldiers. Even so, David does not notice that the story is aimed at him and reveals his personal character. Why not?

Of course we could say that the David in the story—obviously we are still on the purely narrative level—is completely self-confident throughout the whole business. He is positively blind. He has tripped and fallen into a criminal act that has drawn him ever deeper, step by step. The whole thing starts when David, standing on the roof of his palace, sees a woman at a distance, bathing. He desires her, wants her in his bed, tries to make her husband Uriah seem responsible for her pregnancy, and in the end just gets rid of him. Several more of his soldiers are also killed: "collateral damage." Apparently David is not the least bit aware of his profound guilt. He is completely

---

[7] 2 Sam 3:2-5; 5:13-16.

content with himself, and so it does not occur to him that the story is about him.

It is clear, however, that this rather psychological answer is not really adequate. We are interested in how the parable works. Does it function so well because from the start it is not clear that it is a parable? "There were two men in a certain city, the one rich and the other poor." A concrete legal case might begin that way, and the prophet could be presenting it to the king. The poor man has only a single lamb, and the rich man has whole flocks, yet he takes away the poor man's lamb. That seems clearly to be a legal matter, and indeed one of the most serious kind. At any rate that is how the David of the story sees it, and he reacts accordingly.

But is the form of the narrative really so obviously the presentation of a legal matter? "There were two men in a city" is a "nominative beginning" that will often reappear in Jesus' parables:

> "A man was going down from Jerusalem to Jericho" (Luke 10:30)
> "Someone gave a great dinner" (Luke 14:16)
> "There was a man who had two sons" (Luke 15:11)
> "There was a rich man who had a manager" (Luke 16:1)
> "There was a rich man who was dressed in purple" (Luke 16:19)
> "In a certain city there was a judge" (Luke 18:2)
> "A man planted a vineyard" (Mark 12:1)
> "A man had two sons" (Matt 21:28)
> "Two men went up to the temple to pray" (Luke 18:10)

Were there parables beginning that way at the time when the story of the "poor man's lamb" was formulated? Then it might have dawned on David: "Careful, this is a parable!" But even if that was not the case David should have seen, as the story went on, that what he was hearing was not just some legal matter happening in his kingdom. He ought to have noticed it when he heard how the lamb drank from the man's cup at table and slept on his breast. That was not unrealistic, certainly. Children might bring up a lamb that way, or similarly, as a pet—and yet this is a clear metaphor playing on the subject of Uriah's marriage. On the other hand, the behavior of the rich man is so brutal and misanthropic that the story could, after all, make David think it was a legal matter that the prophet was presenting to him.

Thus there is no doubt: here we are looking at two different narrative genres. On the one hand it sounds like a real "case report," while on the other hand there are some indications that this is a "parable" that calls for deeper consideration. The text oscillates between the two. The extravagant features appear precisely because this is a metaphoric treatment of David's actual behavior. Bread and wine represent the table in Uriah's house, the lamb is his beloved Bathsheba who rests in his arms. Thus the parable is arranged in such a way that it could certainly remind David of his crime—but at the same time it fools him. David is meant to be drawn into the story. He is supposed to pronounce a death sentence on himself without knowing it and only then understand: "I am that man!"

We have to expect that Jesus, too, could tell stories with this kind of double meaning. At first the women and men around him heard only a fascinating, even an exciting story, but they had to realize all of a sudden: "He's talking about us! We are part of the story!" And so they got caught in the parable's net.

## 4. The Song of the Vineyard (Isaiah 5:1-7)

We have seen that the parable of the "poor man's lamb" was told in such a way that at first it fooled the king. The following prophetic text goes even further in leading its audience astray—at least in the beginning! They are invited to let themselves be drawn into a story that will have a very different outcome from what they expect. The text starts out like a love song, and who doesn't like to listen to a love song?

Probably in the early days of his mission, somewhere between the years 740 and 730 BCE, the prophet Isaiah presented a song in Jerusalem that was later called "the song of the vineyard." He sang it in a time of well-being, fullness, and self-satisfaction. He may have sung it in the temple, perhaps even in the festal joy of the feast of Booths:

> Let me sing for my beloved
>     my love-song concerning his vineyard:
> My beloved had a vineyard
>     on a very fertile hill.
> He dug it and cleared it of stones,
>     and planted it with choice vines;
> he built a watchtower in the midst of it,
>     and hewed out a wine vat in it;

he expected it to yield grapes,
> but it yielded wild grapes.
And now, inhabitants of Jerusalem
> and people of Judah,
judge between me
> and my vineyard.
What more was there to do for my vineyard
> that I have not done in it?
When I expected it to yield grapes,
> why did it yield wild grapes?
And now I will tell you
> what I will do to my vineyard.
I will remove its hedge,
> and it shall be devoured;
I will break down its wall,
> and it shall be trampled down.
I will make it a waste;
> it shall not be pruned or hoed,
> and it shall be overgrown with briers and thorns;
I will also command the clouds
> that they rain no rain upon it.
For the vineyard of the LORD of hosts
> is the house of Israel,
and the people of Judah
> are his pleasant planting;
he expected justice,
> but saw bloodshed;
righteousness,
> but heard a cry! (Isa 5:1-7)

Before Isaiah begins, he announces his intention. He will sing a song for his audience—a song about a vineyard that his friend has planted. How would the hearers have understood that introduction? There was a good deal to indicate that they would not have thought of a real vineyard. In the ancient Near East a play with symbols was very common, and a vineyard could symbolize a beautiful woman, a beloved, a bride. In the later Song of Songs the vineyard has clearly erotic connotations (Song 1:6; 2:15; 7:8, 13; 8:11-12).

Besides, Isaiah says explicitly that he is going to sing about his friend's vineyard. The listeners must have thought: had the prophet become a "suitor"? someone's "best man"? At that time direct communication between prospective bride and groom was not permitted, so a man was chosen to be a mediator between them. He was called the "friend of the bridegroom" (cp. John 3:29). So if the prophet is going to sing a song about his friend, and if it is also going to be about his friend's vineyard, the audience's expectation almost inevitably would be that he was about to describe a beautiful bride—but of course the description would be full of metaphors. They must have supposed that he was going to sing of a vineyard as an image for the lovely bride, one that had to be carefully watched and tended because noble, delicious grapes were ripening therein.

At first the expectation is by no means disappointed. The prophet describes in detail how his friend built the vineyard as a model layout on a fruitful height. The ground was deeply tilled and freed of stones. A particularly noble strain of grapes was planted. In the midst of the vineyard he built a tower for the watchers who, at the time of the harvest, would protect the grapes from birds and thieves. At a particular place in the vineyard two rectangular pits with a drain between them were dug in the rocky soil to serve as winepresses; there the wine-treaders would press the juice from the grapes after the harvest.[8] Whatever could be done to establish a model vineyard was done.

The audience would have followed the story enthusiastically, aware that a new vineyard like this one required a lot of initial investment, just as one had to invest quite a bit in a beautiful young woman. Now they anticipate the sweet grapes that love will bring to the bridegroom.

And yet—at just that moment the song reverses itself. Against all expectations, the vineyard bears no plump, delicious grapes but only withered, stinking, sour things. Probably at this point the hearers would have radically altered their thinking: apparently the whole thing was heading toward one of the tales of "the betrayed lover." Stories of that kind were told often and with malicious glee—for example, when someone had paid a steep bride-price for a wife and then was shown to be a fool because, when his bride's veil was removed, she was revealed to be hideous, or she had already betrayed him with another man.

Still, the hearers could only think in that direction for a moment because the second dramatic turn in the song follows immediately.

---

[8] The grapes were trodden underfoot in a trough cut in the rocky soil but slightly elevated, and the juice flowed through a channel into a lower trough where it was clarified and from which it was then drawn out.

Suddenly the prophet is no longer singing the role of "friend of the bridegroom" but portraying the bridegroom himself, and his song becomes a lament, a bitter accusation against the bride. Her punishment is elaborately described in the image of the destruction of the vineyard.

As painstakingly as the construction of the vineyard had been pictured, so now its destruction, and it becomes more and more obvious who the speaker really is. When that speaker proclaims that the bridegroom will forbid the clouds to drop rain on the vineyard it is clear that this bridegroom is God's self, and "the vineyard of the LORD of hosts is the house of Israel." With this Isaiah has finally torn away his mask. Vineyard and vine are not limited to erotic connotations; they are also fixed metaphors for God's people Israel (Hos 10:1; Ps 80:9-17).

God has done everything for this vine, planning for the long term, and still Israel has been unfaithful. The social order given it by God should have been lived as a model for all peoples; instead the poor and those deprived of their rights cry out in the land. The song ends in Hebrew with wordplays that can only be awkwardly rendered in translation: "He looked for justice, but see: injustice; for righteousness, and instead: a cry for help."

The whole text that apparently began as praise of a lovely bride has revealed itself more and more clearly as an accusation against the people of God. The friend about whom Isaiah wanted to sing was revealed, step by step, as God, and what was meant to be God's model gift to the world will become a wasteland. Isaiah's wordplay is highly refined. He renders ordinary language and expected descriptive models alien. He begins like someone playing the zither, a sound everyone likes to listen to, and in the end he suddenly has an axe in his hand with which to finally cut down his audience's icy shield of indifference.

In sum: in the case of biblical parables we must always expect that the addressees will be brought into a situation in which they believe they are going to enjoy a thrilling story—and then all at once everything changes: they are confronted with the will of God or the evil situation in which they are living in God's eyes.

Is the song of the vineyard a parable? Of course it is! But at the same time it is an accusation, in fact an indictment such as is presented in court. Thus those who interpret biblical parables must expect to find not "pure" genres but highly artistic and sometimes even oscillating plays on other genres.

## 5. The Faithless Wife (Ezekiel 16:1-63)

Isaiah's song of the vineyard showed us God as a wrathful lover—one who threatens God's people with judgment. Still, the song of the vineyard is a relatively brief text, and at first the fact that God was the accuser remained concealed. It is altogether different with Ezekiel 16. Here God stands revealed from the beginning as the accuser, and the accusation is sweeping. Despite the parable form, we have here an obvious indictment. That is evident from the very fact that the speech is introduced with: "Mortal, make known to Jerusalem her abominations, and say, Thus says the Lord God to Jerusalem" (Ezek 16:2-3). Then follows immediately:

> Your origin and your birth were in the land of the Canaanites; your father was an Amorite, and your mother a Hittite. As for your birth, on the day you were born your navel cord was not cut, nor were you washed with water to cleanse you, nor rubbed with salt, nor wrapped in cloths. No eye pitied you, to do any of these things for you out of compassion for you; but you were thrown out in the open field, for you were abhorred on the day you were born.
> I passed by you, and saw you flailing about in your blood. As you lay in your blood, I said to you, "Live! and grow up like a plant of the field." You grew up and became tall and arrived at full womanhood; your breasts were formed, and your [pubic][9] hair had grown; yet you were naked and bare.
> I passed by you again and looked on you; you were at the age for love [= puberty]. I spread the edge of my cloak over you, and covered your nakedness: I pledged myself to you and entered into a covenant with you, says the Lord God, and you became mine. Then I bathed you with water and washed off the blood from you, and anointed you with oil. I clothed you with embroidered cloth and with sandals of fine leather; I bound you in fine linen and covered you with rich fabric. I adorned you with ornaments: I put bracelets on your arms, a chain on your neck, a ring on your nose, earrings in your ears, and a beauti-

---

[9] Variations from the NRSV are indicated by brackets and follow the author's translation.

ful crown upon your head. You were adorned with gold and silver, while your clothing was of fine linen, rich fabric, and embroidered cloth. You had choice flour and honey and oil for food. You grew exceedingly beautiful, fit to be a queen. Your fame spread among the nations on account of your beauty, for it was perfect because of my splendor that I had bestowed on you, says the Lord GOD.

But you trusted in your beauty, and played the whore [seduced by] your fame, and lavished your whorings on any passer-by. (Ezek 16:3-15)

Ezekiel's parabolic speech goes on and on. What I have quoted here is not even the first quarter of the whole text. The faithlessness of the city Jerusalem toward its God is depicted with extreme intensity and severity. The city has become a whore. She has given herself over to all the sins of the Canaanites. She has spread her legs for every passerby. She has done worse than Samaria and Sodom. She has forgotten what God has done for her, that she received all her beauty and all her adornments from God alone. Therefore God will gather her lovers against her; they will tear off her clothes, steal all her jewels, and leave her lying naked and bare. Probably the accusatory speech originally ended with those images. It finished as it had begun: Jerusalem again lies naked on the ground, bare and helpless.

> Therefore, O whore, hear the word of the LORD: Thus says the Lord GOD, Because your lust was poured out and your nakedness uncovered in your whoring with your lovers, and because of all your abominable idols, and because of the blood of your children that you gave to them, therefore, I will gather all your lovers, with whom you took pleasure, all those you loved and all those you hated; I will gather them against you from all around, and will uncover your nakedness to them, so that they may see all your nakedness. I will judge you as women who commit adultery and shed blood are judged, and bring blood upon you in wrath and jealousy. I will deliver you into their hands, and they shall throw down your platform and break down your lofty places; they shall strip you of your clothes and take your beautiful objects and leave you naked and bare. (Ezek 16:35-39)

Remember: the question in this first part of the book is "how do parables work?" Here Ezekiel 16 presents us with a new variant on parables: the text before us is longer than anything we have seen before. The basic speech would have consisted more or less of the portions I have quoted. At a later stage this older version of the parable speech would have been expanded even further, especially by verses 44-63.

As we have already seen, in contrast to the song of the vineyard in Isaiah 5 it is clear here from the outset that it is God who is speaking: the one who constantly speaks in the "I"-form can only be God. Also clear from the beginning is the one to whom God is speaking: the city Jerusalem. That is already stated before the speech begins, but even if that indicator were absent it had to be obvious to everyone when it is said that "Your mother was a Hittite and your father an Amorite" (v. 45). The prophet makes his hearers (or readers) aware that Jerusalem was originally a pagan city displaying all the dark sides of paganism.

Certainly Jerusalem here represents the whole people; it is they who are addressed. Jerusalem is only foregrounded because Ezekiel wants to talk about the people of God in the figure of a girl or woman, and in the ancient Near East and in antiquity generally the great cities were symbolically seen as women, especially in laments over cities that had been destroyed. The same is true for the Old Testament, where Jerusalem is addressed as "Daughter Zion" (Lam 2:1), as "Daughter Jerusalem" (Lam 2:13), or as "virgin daughter Zion" (Lam 2:13). That is the only reason why the city of Jerusalem is in the foreground here.

It is also clear from the outset that the speech here is metaphorical, that is, "transferred," and the hearers or readers were certainly in a position to transfer the metaphorical elements into the ongoing real history of the people of God. It was not necessary to interpret the story for them in a separate appendix. They knew: all of this is our history. They were able to internalize what was said, in shock and sorrow—but they could also reject it with outrage and bitterness.

The exposed child is Israel, which would have been lost among the nations—that is, it would never have come into existence—if God had not created it to be God's own. The word "Live!" (v. 6) represents a creative act that calls Israel to life. Then God cares for this people, causing it to grow great and beautiful, letting it grow to adulthood and adorning it. The hearers must think of all that God has done for God's people in order to elevate it above the nations. When they are then told that God takes the young woman to wife they obviously think of the covenant God made with Israel on Sinai. With that, Israel came to life in the fullest sense. And when, finally, God describes to the hearers how this bride has offered herself as a whore to everyone, many of them would have thought not only of the participation of the people in the Canaanite cults but also of the alliance policies of their kings, their pandering to the great powers and becoming subject to them.

Israel's history with God is thus related as a parable with an ongoing series of correspondences between the image-level and the real situation. In technical language it would be called an "allegory." Still, the narrative does not remain entirely on the plane of imagery. At several points the subject itself is mixed directly into the imagery: for example, when the Amorites and Hittites are named as Jerusalem's forebears or when the sacrifice of the firstborn to a pagan god is referred to directly (cp. v. 36).

For us listeners today the parable of the faithless wife is harder to understand than Jotham's fable or Isaiah's song of the vineyard. For example, one needs to know that in the ancient world of paganism the exposure of children in marshes and barren wastes was common practice. Girls especially were simply thrown away soon after birth. One needs to know that a newborn child was rubbed with finely-ground salt and then tightly swaddled, not merely for reasons of hygiene but above all in order to protect it from demons. One must know that even earrings and nose rings had apotropaic significance: they were supposed to barricade the body's orifices so demons could not enter. One must know that Hosea and Jeremiah had previously described God's covenant with Israel in terms of marriage and named participation in the fertility cults of the Canaanites as whoredom and adultery (Hos 1–3; Jer 3:1-13). Indeed, one must know a lot more in order to comprehend the text of Ezekiel 16 in all its details and its full scope.

And yet, even if we cannot immediately comprehend many of these details that were known to hearers at that time, the parable of the faithless wife is, now as then, a deeply moving text applying to the whole people of God, for we ourselves repeatedly break faith with God and too often surrender ourselves to false—sometimes even demonic—models of behavior.

Ezekiel's parable that I have presented here has the audacity to portray God as an unsuccessful lover. God has done everything for the beloved, has waited a long time—much as did the owner of the vineyard in Isaiah 5:1-7. And all these efforts were in vain. God's disappointment turns to wrath. But that wrath is not indifference. Cold indifference would be the end of love, but glowing wrath reveals that love is not dead. It is only wounded—as deeply wounded as only true love can be. At the end of Ezekiel 16 we then hear—in an expansion and continuation of the prophet's original version—the following promise:

> Yes, thus says the Lord God: I will deal with you as you have done, you who have despised the oath, breaking the covenant; yet I will remember my covenant with you in the days of your youth, and I will establish with you an everlasting covenant. (Ezek 16:59-60)

Overall, Ezekiel 16 shows that Israel's prophetic books contain "allegories." They were probably part of the mission and preaching of the prophets themselves, and the people in Israel were apparently able to understand such allegories.

### 6. The Vine and the Branches (John 15:1-8)

Now we jump from the Old to the New Testament, to the Gospel of John. There we find a type of parable different from everything we have seen thus far. New Testament scholars call it "metaphorical speech." Here is a typical example:

> I am the true vine, and my Father is the vinegrower. He removes every branch in me that bears no fruit. Every branch that bears fruit he prunes to make it bear more fruit. You have already been cleansed by the word that I have spoken to you. Abide in me as I abide in you. Just as the branch cannot bear fruit by itself unless it abides in the vine, neither can you unless you abide in me. I am the vine, you are the branches. Those who abide in me and I in them bear much fruit, because apart from me you can do nothing. Whoever does not abide in me is thrown away like a branch and withers; such branches are gathered, thrown into the fire, and burned. If you abide in me, and my words abide in you, ask for whatever you wish, and it will be done for you. My Father is glorified by this, that you bear much fruit and become my disciples. (John 15:1-8)

Many translations of this text fail to make a clear distinction between the two types of cutting. The author of the Fourth Gospel is aware of it because the language chosen distinguishes the two: branches that bear no fruit are "removed," while groups of branches with a lot of blooms are "pruned." The Greek verb the NRSV renders "pruned" is often translated "purify" or "cleanse." That makes sense in the context of John 15:3 ("you have already been cleansed").

It is important to know that our text does not identify the "removal" and the "pruning" with the two ordinary cuttings before and during the time of growth, because in the procedure before growth a good many branches that bore fruit the previous year are removed. This is only about the second cutting in the middle of the growing season.[10] It is at this point that branches on which no fruit is growing are "cut off," while groups of branches with many blooms are "pruned." But that is only a preliminary observation!

If we compare the metaphorical discourse in John 15 with the parable of the faithless wife in Ezekiel 16 we see right away that here we are looking at something altogether different. Ezekiel presented an ongoing narrative beginning with the bloody foundling and ending with the faithless wife lying in her blood. The whole thing was, indeed, "judgment speech" or, more precisely, the "speech of an accuser," but it was a continuous narrative. We do not find anything like that in John 15:1-8. Instead, what we have here is an artful mixture of parabolic speech and instruction, though not the kind of instructive speech in which a series of comparisons and metaphors is scattered throughout. Instead, this instruction conceals a complete, succinct parable within it. That is to say, if we chop off all the instructional elements and preface the remaining text with the introduction to one of the familiar Synoptic parables, then without any particular manipulation we will have the following text, meaningful in itself:

> It is with the reign of God as with a vine. Every one of its branches that does not bear fruit will be cut off, and every branch that yields fruit will be pruned so that it may bear yet more fruit. Branches that do not remain on the vine will be cast aside and wither. They will be collected, thrown on the fire, and burned.

---

[10] Thus correctly Uta Poplutz, "Eine fruchtbare Allianz (Weinstock, Winzer, und Reben, Joh 15,1-8)," in *Kompendium der Gleichnisse Jesu*, ed. Ruben Zimmermann (Gütersloh: Gütersloher Verlagshaus, 2007), 828–39, at 831.

We cannot miss a resemblance between this reconstructed text and Matthew's parable of the fishnet (Matt 13:47-50). There the distinction is between good and bad fish; here between fruitful and useless branches of a vine. The bad fish are thrown away, the cut branches burned.

Of course I have not undertaken this "pruning" of the instructional discourse in John 15:1-8 in order to reveal and reconstruct a genuine Jesus parable. My "pruning" was only a demonstration. I wanted to show how artistically John 15:1-8 is structured: parable material, interpretation of the parable material, admonition, and promise are all intertwined and firmly interwoven.

Our reconstruction has already helped us to recognize the "parable material." The "interpretation" is found at the very beginning of the metaphorical discourse: God is the vintner, Jesus is the vine, the disciples are the branches. The "admonition" runs through the whole text and is especially characterized by the key words "remain" (7x) and "bear fruit" (5x). Then, near the end, we find the great promise: "If you abide in me, and my words abide in you, ask for whatever you wish, and it will be done for you."

With the aid of this interweaving of different genres we discover a unique kind of metaphorical discourse, one we have not encountered before. Viewed as a whole it is also different from the authentic Jesus parables we will encounter in the second part of this book. That is evident above all from the fact that the first three gospels, the Synoptics, contain no long uninterrupted "I-discourses" by Jesus, while the metaphorical speech in John 15:1-8 is part of such a continuous first-person discourse. The speech begins with "I am the true vine," which is soon repeated in verse 5, and in between and throughout Jesus repeatedly speaks in the first person.

Anyone who has a feeling for literary forms and genres must at some point be astonished and even disturbed at the profound differences between the ways Jesus speaks in the Synoptic Gospels and how he speaks in the Gospel of John. It appears that Jesus never spoke in the form we find in the Johannine metaphorical discourses. Still, the same observer, on closer examination and by listening with a sharper ear, will see how precisely and faithfully the Gospel of John illuminates what Jesus was—because behind the authentic Jesus parables stands, discreet and concealed, a claim beyond all grasping. That is something we will come to speak about in this book.

## 7. The Elm and the Vine (Hermas Similitudes 2.1-10)

The parable below comes from the second century CE and is found in a book written in Rome by a Christian named Hermas somewhere around 140; the book is called *The Shepherd of Hermas* (*Pastor Hermae*). It was later subdivided into part 1, "Visions" (*Visiones*), part 2, "Mandates" (*Mandata*), and part 3, "Similitudes" (or: Parables; *Similitudines*). I have chosen the second parable in part 3. The "shepherd" who speaks with Hermas here is an angel in the shape of a shepherd who appears in one part of the book as a kind of teacher and interpreter who authoritatively answers the many questions that are worrying Hermas. The "I" narrator is Hermas himself:[11]

> As I was walking in the field, and observing an elm and vine, and determining in my own mind respecting them and their fruits, the Shepherd appears to me, and says, "What is it that you are thinking about the elm and vine?" "I am considering," I reply, "that they become each other exceedingly well." "These two trees," he continues, "are intended as an example for the servants of God." "I would like to know," said I, "the example that these trees, you say, are intended to teach." "Do you see," he says, "the elm and the vine?" "I see them, sir," I replied. "This vine," he continued, "produces fruit, and the elm is an unfruitful tree; but unless the vine be trained upon the elm, it cannot bear much fruit when extended at length upon the ground; and the fruit which it does bear is rotten, because the plant is not suspended upon the elm. When, therefore, the vine is cast upon the elm, it yields fruit both from itself and from the elm. You see, moreover, that the elm also produces much fruit, not less than the vine, but even more; because," he continued, "the vine, when suspended upon the elm, yields much fruit, and good; but when thrown upon the ground, what it produces is small and rotten. This similitude, therefore, is for the servants of God—for the poor and for the rich." (Herm. *Sim.* 2.1-4)

We see immediately that the parable consists almost entirely of a dialogue between the Christian Hermas and the one who conveys revelation, appearing as a shepherd. At the beginning of the dialogue Hermas is looking at a vine growing up the trunk of an elm tree.

---

[11] Adapted from the translation by Frederick Crombie in Alexander Roberts and James Donaldson, eds., *The Ante-Nicene Library* 1, *The Apostolic Fathers* (Edinburgh: T & T Clark, 1867), 377.

We have already seen in the case of Jotham's fable that in the ancient Near East vines were often simply laid on the ground (something one may likewise often see today). For the most part they were elevated slightly on forked sticks so that the tendrils would not lie too close to the ground. But there was also another possibility, used especially in Italy: elms (or ash trees) were planted in advance to prepare for laying out a vineyard. Once they had reached the right height some of the branches would be sawed off, leaving only a few wide-spreading limbs. Then a vine would be planted; its branches could grow in a spiral around the elm's boughs or simply hang down from them. Particularly in Italy there were many vineyards with elms as "vine espaliers." The picture presented by those vineyards must have been very impressive, for the symbiosis between elm and vine appears with some frequency in Roman literature.[12] That same symbiosis even became a simile for human community, true friendship, and happy marriages.

Hermas draws on that then-current symbol to shape his parable, but he gives the communion of elm and vine a specific meaning. For him it is an image of the community of poor and rich in the Christian assembly, with the elm representing the poor and the vine standing for the rich because the vine yields sweet grapes, but when it lies on the ground it produces less fruit, and what it does bear is always in danger of rotting. On the other hand, if it is tied up to an elm, then "with the help of the elm" it will bear richer and better fruit.

That, however, means that even though the rich have their wealth they are beggars before God because their wealth will spoil, or better: it is meaningless. It only has meaning when the rich let themselves be held up and supported by the poor, concretely: when they help the poor with their riches. In the explication of the parable in verses 5-10, which I have not quoted for reasons of space, this is developed especially in terms of prayer: the poor are rich before God because their prayers are powerful. If the rich members of the community support the poor they will be aided by the petitions and thanksgivings of the poor that rise up to God and are pleasing to God. Thus both profit one another.

But here we are not so much interested in the theology the "Shepherd of Hermas" derives from the symbiosis of elm and vine. Our

---

[12] See, for example, Ovid, *Metamorphoses* 14.661–69.

interest is much more in the structure of the parable speech. The situation is that the parable speech develops within a dialogue between Hermas and the Shepherd. For the most part Hermas raises questions and the Shepherd offers explanations that get longer and longer. We have not yet seen any form comparable to this.

As in John 15:1-8, we are not offered a coherent parable; the material of the parable is named at the outset: "As I was walking in the field, and observing an elm and vine . . . ." Other metaphorical elements will be provided later, in the context of the interpretation.

In and of itself the dialogue form has some advantages. We will see that there is a lot of dialogue in Jesus' parables; dialogues make a story exciting. But in the case of Jesus the dialogues take place within the parables themselves, while in Hermas the initial parable of the elm and the vine is "discussed" in a dialogue.

Moreover, that "dialogue" is far from being so formally self-contained and profound as the interpretation in John 15:1-8. The text moves awkwardly and the interpretation in terms of community relationships seems strained. Above all, Hermas fails to say clearly from the beginning what the elm and vine represent. The fact that the elm is described as "an unfruitful tree" has led many interpreters to see the elm as the rich and the vine as the poor, but that is exactly what Hermas does *not* mean to say. For him the elms represent the poor and the vines are the rich. Hermas's language is quite awkward: he confuses readers more than he helps them.

To be honest, I chose this rather stilted and badly organized metaphorical speech from the *Shepherd of Hermas* primarily because it is such a good contrast, so that other parables may appear all the better when set over against it: Jotham's fable in Judges 9:8-15, for example; the parable of the poor man's lamb in 2 Samuel 12:1-4; the song of the vineyard in Isaiah 5:1-7; and then, in part 2 of this book, Jesus' parables. To be able to truly appreciate his parables we also need to see how frequently the ancient world produced parables that went wrong or were awkwardly told.

## 8. The King Who Gained a People (Mekhilta Exodus 20.2)

The following text will serve as a model of the extraordinarily large number of *rabbinic* parables. It appears in the Mekhilta of Rabbi Ishmael on the book of Exodus. This Mekhilta, a kind of commentary, underwent its final editing in the second half of the third century CE.

The biblical text commented here contains the Ten Commandments (Exod 20:2-17). Instead of the whole text, only the first words are quoted; readers or hearers then knew which text-complex was the subject. The interpretation is as follows:[13]

> "I am the L-rd your G-d": Why were the ten words [= commandments] not stated at the beginning of the Torah? An analogy: A man enters a province and says to them [= the inhabitants]: I will rule over you. They respond: Did you do anything [good] for us that you would rule over us? [What does he do?] He builds the [city] wall for them, provides [a water conduit] for them, wages war for them, and then says: I will rule over you—whereupon they respond: Yes! Yes! Thus [Footstool = circumlocution for the divine name] took Israel out of Egypt, split the sea for them, brought down manna for them, raised the well [= split the rock] for them, brought in quail for them, waged war with Amalek for them, and then said to them: I will rule over you—whereupon they responded: Yes! Yes! (*Mekh. Exod.* 20.2)

This example illustrates very well the structure of many rabbinic parables: the biblical text to be interpreted or (more often) the first words, standing for the whole text, are given first. Then follows a parable, beginning in the dative case. Finally, in a separate section, the parable is explained.

In this case the full text of the Ten Commandments is not commented serially; rather, this is about a special question that will prove to be of extreme importance for the theological understanding of God's commandments as a whole. That special question is introduced with great pedagogical skill. Someone asks, apparently quite naïvely: if the Ten Commandments are so fundamental for the relationship between Israel and its God, why are they not at the beginning of the whole Torah, even before the story of creation in Genesis 1?

The answer then given by means of the parable and commentary on it is: because God's commandments are challenges to Israel, and keeping them can only be a response to what God has already done for this people out of pure love for them. *Therefore, before the Ten Commandments were given, God's gracious action in God's people had to be told in the texts of the Torah.* In the text quoted here that preceding, attentive

---

[13] *Mekhilta de-Rabbi Jishma'el. Ein früher Midrasch zum Buch Exodus* (Berlin: Verlag der Weltreligionen, 2010). English LMM.

action of God is summarized in the brief statement, "I am the LORD your God," to which, of course, must be added "who brought you out of the land of Egypt, out of the house of slavery." The readers or hearers obviously know and are reminded in the commentary that after the rescue from Egypt came the passage through the Sea of Reeds, the gifts of manna and quail, the bounty of water from the rock, and rescue from the hands of the Amalekites. Only then did Israel come to Sinai, where the Ten Commandments (and with them Israel's whole social order) were given. So the commandment was preceded by multiple saving actions on God's side.

From a purely theological point of view that is presented with remarkable clarity and relevance by this parable, for the principle of grace dominates not only the New Testament but also the Old. God's endless giving, without any reason, precedes any and all commandments.

Still, if we look at the parable (and its commentary) it seems altogether to lack the stringency of Jotham's fable and the weight of the poor man's lamb. This parable is, to put it mildly, a construct— because, after all, this is not how powerful people who want to be king somewhere are liable to act. Either they think they already have a right to rule or they seize the rulership by violence. The parable is well constructed as a way to illustrate God's actions, but it seems to have little relation to reality. It is a "construct."

That, in fact, is the accusation that Christian interpreters of Jesus' parables have repeatedly thrown at the rabbinic parables. They are said to be artificial and divorced from reality, in utter contrast to the fresh, down-to-earth parables of Jesus.[14] Certainly that is related to the fact that the rabbis for the most part were interpreting a particular biblical passage, and they would force their interpretation of the text into parable form. Jesus' parables, on the other hand, were not told for the purpose of interpreting passages from the Bible; they were interpretation of the reign of God that was now coming to be.

---

[14] Cp., e.g., Adolf Jülicher, *Die Gleichnisreden Jesu*, vol. 1 (Freiburg: Mohr [Siebeck], 1886), 170–71: "Whenever rabbinic variants of gospel parables are pressed upon us the comparison is unfavorable to them; almost all of them are somehow artificial; they are indeed clear and easily comprehended but they are not true, not compelling; their power to persuade is not even close to that of Jesus' parables: either the echo of the school with its compulsion and pedantry cling to them or they are mere series of comparisons that occupy the imagination and support memory." English LMM.

This last observation is absolutely correct. Jesus did not interpret biblical texts in his parables. But we must not simply accept the accusation that the rabbinic parables are "constructs." The fact that a parable is constructed need not be something fundamentally negative. When, in a well-known fable of Aesop, a lion, a fox, and a donkey go hunting together and kill a deer, that is obviously a construct, and yet the fable turns out to be a skillfully shaped and highly intelligent text.[15] And when in Jotham's fable all the trees except the bramble refuse to be king, that is likewise a construct—but what a text it is, and what an attack on the arrogance of the powerful! And when Jesus tells of a vineyard owner who in the evening pays the last workers who have toiled only a short time the same amount as the first—is that not a construct?

We need to be cautious about accusing a text of being "constructed." It may be that precisely what is constructed will prove to be constructive. It could be that when the rabbis' students memorized and studied the parable from *Mekhilta Exodus* they were deeply irritated at the man who tried to gain a people by good deeds because they knew that there is no such person—and in the same moment they were led by their irritation to understand that, in fact, it all happened, because the text is speaking about God, and God's actions are absolutely different from those of power-seeking human beings who want to rule over others.

### 9. The Man in the Well (Friedrich Rückert)

When we talk about parables the concept of "allegory" often arises, or there is a discussion of "allegoresis." We need to be somewhat clearer about what that means. For that purpose I will use a poem by the German scholar Friedrich Rückert (1788–1866).[16] The poem's title is not "Allegory" but "Parable." Rückert was Germany's first orientalist and is supposed to have been master of some forty languages and dialects.

---

[15] See the masterful interpretation of this Aesop fable by Wolfgang Harnisch in *Die Gleichniserzählungen Jesu* (see n. 2 above), 16–20.

[16] The text of Friedrich Rückert's "parable" is taken from Reinhard Dithmar, ed., *Fabeln, Parabeln und Gleichnisse* (Munich: DTB, 1978), 213–25. English LMM.

A man went down to Syria,
leading a camel by the hand.
The beast, in a ferocious mood
suddenly began to brood
and wheeze so truly awfully
his leader then was forced to flee.
He ran, and then he saw a well
more or less along his path.
He heard the beast behind him chuff:
it must have driven him off his nut.
He crawled away into the well;
he didn't fall; he seemed to sail.
A berry bush was growing gladly
out of the shattered fountain's belly;
The man clung to it like cement
and shouted out his sad lament.
He looked above, and saw with fear
the camel's head a hand's breadth near
trying to reach and grab him back.
He looked below, into the deep
and there beheld a dragon's keep;
the dragon gaped with unblocked rage
and hoped to drag him to its cage
if he should happen to fall down.
So, trembling between the two
the poor man saw a third thing, too:
the bramble upon which he hung
was rooted in the well's cracked wall,
and there he spied a pair of mice.
One was black, the other white.
He saw them, there, both white and black
biting at the root, snick-snack.
They gnawed, they nipped, they dug, they scratched
till the dirt fountained from the crack.
And as the dirt did trickle down
the dragon gazed up from its lair
to see the bramble, its roots freed,
falling with the luscious prey.
The man, in fear and need and panic
displaced, besieged, and threatened 'round
swinging on the vine's thin rope
looked to save himself—no hope.

And as he gazed around in terror
he saw a twig of bramble nodding:
a limb with ripened berries laden!
Overwhelmed with his desire
he thought not of the camel's rage,
or of the dragon in the deep,
or even of the clever mice
while berries danced before his eyes.
He let the beast above him snort
and under him the dragon hark
and close to him the mice still gnawing,
he grabbed the berries, as was meet,
thinking they were so good to eat,
gulped them greedily one by one
and through the sweetness that he got
his fear and terror were forgot.

You ask: who is that crazy fool
who easily forgets his fear?
Know this, my friend, that man is you;
take in the meaning I give here.
The dragon in the well's great deep
is the yawning jaw of death;
and the camel's threat above
is this life's full fear and need.
You it is, 'twixt death and life
swinging on the world's green branch.
The two mice gnawing on the root,
the branches, too, on which you light
to save you from the mouth of death—
the mice: they are called day and night.
The black one gnaws in secret dark
from nightfall quietly till morning;
then, from dawn till night doth fall
the white one undermines it all.
And here, between these horrid snares
you're tempted by the berries' savor,
forget the camel's threat to life
and the dragon death below
and the mice by day and night—
nothing draws you from devouring
berries, all that you can snack,
nibbling on the well-grave's crack.

## How Parables Work

Clearly, Friedrich Rückert had a flair for poetry. People say that in his best years he wrote a poem a day. The irony that runs throughout is gorgeous, and many of the rhymes are masterful, such as "Abend" (evening) and "wurzeluntergrabend" (undermining the root). Anyone who tries to write rhymes has to work them out, but apparently they simply leapt from Rückert's pen. We can also see very clearly from this text what an allegory is: the metaphorical level is precisely parallel to the factual level and many elements of the metaphorical level correspond precisely to the facts. In this case we find the following:

| | | |
|---|---|---|
| dragon | → | death |
| camel | → | fear for one's life |
| green bush | → | world |
| white mouse | → | day |
| black mouse | → | night |
| sweet berries | → | sensual pleasures |
| well | → | grave |

An allegory, then, is a story that has to be decoded piece by piece. The model for allegory is probably our dreams, where the oddest images and events combine. Then we usually try to decode the dream. Sometimes we succeed; more often we don't.

Among the parables and parabolic speeches we have thus far discussed, the song of the vineyard in Isaiah 5 and the speech about the faithless wife in Ezekiel 16 are definitely allegories. The parable of the poor man's lamb in 2 Samuel at least contains allegorical elements, because the little lamb's eating from the poor man's table and resting in his bosom certainly represent a motif that can be decoded.

It is already more difficult in the rabbinic parable of the king who gained a people for himself. The point of comparison is in itself only the forthcoming, gracious action of a king, but for every Jewish hearer that king was naturally, from the beginning, none other than God.

Obviously there are texts that are composed as allegories from the outset, but there are also texts that are not allegorical and yet have subsequently been treated and interpreted as such. Then we speak of "allegoresis." Here, too, an example can illustrate what I mean.

The parable of the good Samaritan (Luke 10:30-35), which I will treat in detail below, was for Jesus a narrative primarily meant to show how people act in the reign of God. But Christian interpreters were not satisfied with that. They sought a deeper sense in the story beyond "Go and do likewise!" They tried to unlock every individual part of the story, and that decoding looked like this:

Jerusalem is Paradise, Jericho is the world. The man traveling from Jerusalem to Jericho is Adam and his "falling among robbers" is original sin. The Samaritan is Christ and the donkey on which he sits is Christ's earthly body. The inn to which Christ brings the fallen man is the church, the innkeeper is the apostle Paul, the oil and wine with which the wounded man is anointed point to the sacraments, the two denarii the Samaritan gives the innkeeper are the Old and New Testaments, and the promised return of the Samaritan is Christ's return. We can see that the parable thus becomes a reflection of the whole of salvation history. People treated all Jesus' parables in much the same way.

Giving Jesus' parables a deeper sense in this way and decoding every tiniest detail down to the last letter probably satisfies a certain longing to play the detective, but it is done at the expense of the parable itself, which is thus broken to bits. To salve the reputation of the ancient interpreters who took pleasure in such allegoresis we should, of course, add that this method of giving a more profound meaning to normal narrative texts was widespread in antiquity and was considered a high art.

In one thing the allegorizing theologians of the early church and the Middle Ages were certainly correct: Jesus' parables were not banal, everyday texts. They spoke of the reign of God. And as we will see, in speaking about the reign of God they also spoke of the mystery of Jesus, his mission and his saving work. But that means that with the aid of allegoresis those earlier centuries developed what was really present in Jesus' parables, though they did it in their own way. We, too, have to interpret Jesus' parables in terms of the reign of God that has come in Jesus and thus, at the same time, in terms of the one who brought it.[17]

---

[17] For the justification of an allegoresis of the Bible rightly understood and meaningfully applied, cp. Marius Reiser, *Bibelkritik und Auslegung der Heiligen Schrift. Beiträge zur Geschichte der biblischen Exegese und Hermeneutik*, WUNT 217 (Tübingen: Mohr Siebeck, 2007), 99–118, esp. 113–15.

## 10. The Perfect Swimmer (Martin Buber)

In this first section of the book we are asking about how parables function, and we will end with one more parable, this one from the book *Tales of the Hasidim* by Martin Buber (1878–1965).[18] In that well-known and treasured book Buber collected a great number of narratives from the sphere of Hasidism, and he not only collected them but gave them a coherent form.

Hasidism is a particular form of Judaism that developed in Eastern Europe in the eighteenth century. Among its fundamental ideas is that God's glory is present throughout the world and can be experienced everywhere and in all things. Hence, for example, prayer can be ecstatic joy that envelops the whole body.

That was not entirely new in Judaism, of course. People had long applied Psalm 35:10 ("All my bones shall say, 'O LORD, who is like you?'") to prayer, which is why many Jews move their upper bodies back and forth while praying, but in Eastern European Hasidism the sense was much stronger, so that leaping, dancing, and ecstatic joy were added. The following tale should be understood against that background.

> When the rabbi of Lentshno's son was a boy he once saw Rabbi Yitzhak of Vorki praying. Full of amazement he came running to his father and asked how it was possible for such a zaddik to pray quietly and simply, without giving any sign of ecstasy.
> 
> "A poor swimmer," answered his father, "has to thrash around in order to stay up in the water. The perfect swimmer rests on the tide and it carries him."

Like most of the texts Martin Buber offers in his *Tales of the Hasidim*, this story makes a statement that is at first perplexing and yet for that very reason is a persuasive insight into an important aspect of faith. In this case it is about prayer that allows itself to be borne altogether by God and rests in God.

Certainly if we drop the sphere of imagery from the brief story we will have a text that is not only short but banal. "A poor swimmer has to thrash around in order to stay up in the water. The perfect swimmer rests on the tide and it carries him." That is not even a story;

---

[18] Martin Buber, *Tales of the Hasidim*, trans. Olga Marx (New York: Schocken Books, 1947), 199.

it is a mere description of the difference between a swimmer familiar with the water and a beginner. Therefore our example shows once again[19] that any parable theory that separates every parable from its context and tries to see it as an autonomous aesthetic construction in and for itself is doomed to failure.

But is this really a parable? If so, it is only because of the narrative context. Without that we would not know that a parable was being told, nor would we understand what it means to say. It is only from their context that those two sentences lose their banality, become a parable, gain meaning, and shed light on a particular practice of prayer.

We find similar texts from Jesus: brief comparisons with situations or happenings drawn from ordinary life and familiar to everyone; they need not even be told, as a brief allusion suffices—but that, because of the circumstances in which they occur or the shape given them, have become texts about the reign of God.

In such cases we often ask ourselves: should we really regard such texts as parables? Wouldn't "metaphor" be a better definition? Think of the saying about the "speck in the eye" (Matt 7:3): "Why do you see the speck in the eye of your neighbor [in faith] but do not notice the log in your own eye?" Is that a parable? Probably, with most New Testament scholars, we would sooner call it a "metaphor" and not a "similitude," much less a "parable."[20]

But what about the "budding fig tree"? In Mark's version it reads: "From the fig tree learn its lesson: as soon as its branch becomes tender and puts forth its leaves, you know that summer is near" (Mark 13:28). Is it a parable or simply a metaphor? The boundaries are really slippery here.

---

[19] See "The Lion, the Bear, and the Snake" above.

[20] That is, however, exactly what we find in the great, useful handbook by Ruben Zimmermann, et al., eds., *Kompendium der Gleichnisse Jesu* (Gütersloh: Gütersloher Verlagshaus, 2015). There brief metaphors of this kind are treated together under the heading "Parables," along with those we would call "similitudes." The reasoning is found on pp. 17–29 of the book. Cp. also Ruben Zimmermann, "Parabeln—sonst nichts!" in idem and Gabi Kern, eds., *Hermeneutik der Gleichnisse Jesu*, WUNT 231 (Tübingen: Mohr Siebeck, 2011), 383–419, at 404–5. For "similitudes" vs. "parables," see n. 1 above.

To take a third example, consider Luke 6:39: "Can a blind person guide a blind person? Will not both fall into a pit?" Again the question: metaphor or parable? The length of a text cannot be a measure in such cases because there are very short Jesus sayings that are generally considered "parables." One example is Matthew 13:33: "The kingdom of heaven is like yeast that a woman took and mixed in with three measures of flour until all of it was leavened."

That parable is just one sentence. Do we call it a "parable" because an "event" or a "process" is depicted, rather than a fixed image? In fact, most of the forty Jesus parables to be examined in part 2 are about an "event" or "happening" that is "told" rather than being "referred to," and the minimum requirement for "telling a story" would be that at least two events happen in sequence so that the original situation is changed.[21] So if there is no "story" in this defined sense, would it not be better to call it a "metaphor"? But what, exactly, does "changing the original situation" amount to?

It would not make much sense at this point to construct a refined theory of parables in order to establish clearly-defined types. No normal person speaks in pure genres, and neither did Jesus. Pure genres are scholarly constructs that are, as such, altogether reasonable. So when, in what follows, we collect forty parables and interpret them we must expect from the outset that the list will be made up of several types as well as fluid transitions between different types, and certainly there will be some blurring of the line between these and mere metaphors.

---

[21] Cp. Detlev Dormeyer, "Gleichnisse als narrative und metaphorische Konstrukte—sprachliche und handlungsorientierte Aspekte," in Zimmermann, ed., *Hermeneutik der Gleichnisse Jesu*, 420–437, at 423.

# Part Two

## Jesus' Forty Parables

From time to time, in referring to Jesus' parables, I have used the phrase "reign of God." That was no accident. The main part of this book, beginning here, will show that Jesus' parables as a whole speak directly or indirectly about the reign (or kingdom) of God. Just as an aside: Matthew usually speaks not of the "kingdom of God" but of the "kingdom of heaven." That is the same thing. "Heaven," in Judaism, like "the Footstool," "the Almighty," "the Eternal One," or "the Name [= Ha-Shem]," is a respectful circumlocution for "God."

In what follows, certainly, I will not speak only of the "kingdom of God" but also, repeatedly, of the "reign of God" (or, in Matthew, the "realm of heaven"). The underlying Greek phrase is always the same, namely, *basileia tou theou* (Matthew: *basileia tōn ouranōn*), and both translations are correct, but "reign of God" is more accurate, because the reference is to a dynamic event: God establishes divine *reign* or *royal rule* in Israel and in the world. Often the word refers at the same time to the *sphere* in which God's reign is accomplished, so "kingdom" or, better, "realm" of God is not wrong. I will use both, since both are useful, but also to emphasize that they refer to the same thing.

If we say "God establishes his rule" that is obviously a very human way of speaking and is therefore subject to misunderstanding. The "reign of God" is something completely different from any human rule. Also, it must not necessarily come from a distance. It is already present and encompasses both creation and history. It is only "coming" in the sense that it is "announced" and "accepted," often against the resistance of habit, hardening, and human malice. Sacred Scripture is profoundly certain that there are things in the world that are opposed to God, indeed, that there is an assembled power of evil that stands against the reign of God. It uses a variety of names for that potential power, including "demons." These are the demons of society—a society in which there is much that is good and true but that is often purely self-centered, resists God, and so constantly creates potential evils—that are hostile to life.

Jesus not only spoke about such demons but opposed them. He expelled demons, and in doing so he made room for the reign of God.

He said, "If it is by the finger of God [= the power of God] that I cast out the demons, then the kingdom of God has come to you" (Luke 11:20). But Jesus can also say of the reign of God that it is still "coming." He tells his disciples to pray "your kingdom come" (Luke 11:2). That means: the reign of God is, in principle, already present in Jesus, but it still has to establish itself throughout the world, against the powers opposed to God. Thus it has both a present and a future aspect.

That connection between the coming of the reign of God and the collapse of demonic rule is important. It is the background for the first Jesus parable we will now examine.

### 1. The Successful Break-In (Luke 12:39)

The text we will first consider is found in Luke's gospel.[1] It is part of a longer discourse spoken to Jesus' disciples, beginning at Luke 12:22 and extending to 12:53. The immediate context speaks about constant readiness and faithful waiting in expectation of the returning Christ, but no one knows the day and the hour, so there is only one thing to do: be watchful and faithfully carry out the tasks of discipleship in the church. In the midst of that discourse we find the following:

> [K]now this: if the owner of the house had known at what hour the thief was coming, he would not have let his house be broken into. You also must be ready, for the Son of Man is coming at an unexpected hour. (Luke 12:39)

This probably assumes a rather large household in which one wouldn't immediately hear someone breaking in. The word for "breaking into" in the text literally means "digging one's way into." That was the current term for "breaking in," and it rests on the fact that houses often had clay walls, so there was no need to pick the lock; you simply dug a hole through the wall, "dug your way through."

---

[1] Luke 12:39 comes from the Sayings Source (Q). Its Synoptic parallel is Matt 24:43-44. The two texts are nearly identical except that Matthew has "part of the night" instead of "hour." Cp. also *Gos. Thom.* 21 and 103.

For Luke the evangelist this text (as its context shows) was about Christ's return. The "Son of Man" will come like a thief in the night. What is the point of comparison? Obviously the Son of Man is not being called a thief; he is not a crook taking someone else's property. The point of comparison, rather, is the unpredictability of that One's coming.

The early church often spoke of the "Day of the Lord" that comes like a thief in the night: see, for example, 1 Thessalonians 5:2-4; 2 Peter 3:10; Revelation 3:3; 16:15. This was a fixed and frequently used expression intended to emphasize the suddenness of the *parousia*, the impossibility of anticipating Christ's reappearance. The *Sitz im Leben* (lived situation) of the comparison was the experience that Christ's second coming, so deeply longed for, still had not happened; time was running on and abuses were arising in the church. For that very reason constant watchfulness and unbroken expectation were called for! In the "household" of the church it was above all the responsible figures who had to prove themselves reliable and watchful servants.

Clearly, then, we are in the time after Easter, but that does not necessarily apply to the individual components of the Lukan speech-composition, especially not to the core statement here. That comes from Jesus, because the image of the "thief in the night" betrays the audacity we repeatedly encounter in Jesus' parables. The early church certainly did not invent "like a thief in the night." The image is too daring. It must be traceable to a Jesus parable. But what was the original intent of the parable? Here the grammar gives us a clue.

The verb that underlies "if the owner of the house *had known* . . . he *would not have* let" is rightly translated in English versions as past-contrary-to-fact, in accordance with the Greek grammar. Thus the parable does not warn against a break-in that may happen in the future but looks back at one that has already taken place. We could also remove the sentence from its present context and thus from its "application." Then we have a fragment of a parable about a successful break-in, and that break-in would be—in line with the fundamental theme of Jesus' parables—the coming of the reign of God. In that case the sense of the text would be: The reign of God has already come, is present, has already happened.

That kind of interpretation is not gimmickry: not at all. First, we have made use of a real possibility for translation—one that is affirmed by standard English versions. Second, the application of the parable to the returning Son of Man is self-contradictory, because according to the parable the householder cannot be on guard since she or he does not know when the break-in will happen. The disciples themselves do not know when the Son of Man will return, but they are supposed to keep watch anyway. So the application does not fit the parable.

Third, there are significant parallels to the statement of the hypothetical parable. I have already mentioned one of them, namely, the saying in Luke 11:20: "[I]f it is by the finger of God that I cast out the demons, then the kingdom of God has come to you." So Jesus says "the reign of God is already here, and it has come into the world through me, through my expulsion of demons." Seen in that light, the parable that underlies Luke 12:39 might originally have read:

> With what shall I compare the reign of God? It is with the reign of God as with a break-in that could not be averted. If the householder had known the hour at which the thief would come, she or he would not have allowed the house to be broken into. But the owner did not know, and so the thief got into the house.

If that reconstruction is correct we are looking at a genuine parable, and one that reveals to us an unfathomable, almost terrifying awareness behind it: Jesus—and with him the reign of God—has broken into the spaces of the old society, the sphere in which the demons and the gods of this world hold sway, our comfort zones, the familiar places where we humans build the house of our lives. People would have resisted; they would not have let it in; they would have secured themselves and boarded up all the doors and windows. But it took them by surprise. It came like a thief in the night: sneakily, in silence, unexpectedly, such that no one could have anticipated it. With it the reign of God was suddenly there—in the midst of the old world. If we read the text that way it becomes a shout of victory!

The question, of course, is: do we dare to isolate verse 39 this way, based on a past-contrary-to-fact, and then expand it into a genuine parable? I think we may, because there is yet another reason for such a reconstruction: the next parable we will look at, the one about the strong one. It has something in common with the parable of the successful break-in and even carries it a step further.

## 2. Overpowering the "Strong Man" (Mark 3:27)

Mark 3:27 also speaks about someone breaking into a house, but it goes far beyond the statement in Luke 12:39; it talks about the householder being bound and the whole property stolen:

> [N]o one can enter a strong man's house and plunder his property without first tying up the strong man; then indeed the house can be plundered. (Mark 3:27)

First, as regards the metaphorical level: the social-historical background of this text is foreign to us; the saying presupposes a situation of explosive social tensions that led to a phenomenon relatively common in antiquity: "social banditry." It also existed in Israel at that time.[2] People who were utterly destitute banded together and attacked the estates of the rich to plunder them. First they had to overcome the resistance of the guards; then the owner would be bound or killed and all the moveable property stolen. Here again we see Jesus' audacity: he compares his own actions not only with the actions of a thief but even with those of a bandit or a whole gang of robbers.

As regards the form of our text, this is one of those cases in which it is not clear whether we should speak of a "metaphor" or a "parable." On the one hand there are enough building blocks to make up a story, even a thriller: breaking into the house, binding the owner, plundering the household. So is this a "change of circumstances," hence a "narrative," and so a parable? But there is no "telling," only a "statement" of a possible situation. Still, if we look closer it appears that this is not just any *possible* situation because the text speaks of a particular "strong man." Let us lay aside all the linguistic fine points and ask about the meaning of the whole. What is the text talking about?

In the Markan context this is the situation: scribes who have come from Jerusalem (as a kind of investigating committee?) express their opinion of Jesus' expulsions of demons. They cannot deny his powerful therapies, but they interpret them in their own way: Jesus

---

[2] See further Annette Merz, "Jesus lernt vom Räuberhauptmann (Das Wort vom Starken), Mk 3,27," in *Kompendium der Gleichnisse Jesu: Methodische Neuansätze zum Verstehen urchristlicher Parabeltexte*, ed. Ruben Zimmermann, et al., 2nd ed. (Gütersloh: Gütersloher Verlagshaus, 2015), 287–96.

himself is possessed by demons. He acts within the realm of demonic powers, and by the might of the highest of all the demons he drives others out (Mark 3:22).

Jesus responds to their scurrilous accusation as follows: if Satan were to arise against and quarrel with himself, by that very act he would lose his power (3:24-26). In reality he has lost it for a completely different reason: someone stronger[3] has broken into the strong one's house, bound him, and plundered his property (3:27).

Jesus does not merely state that as fact, however; he sets it before his audience in the form of an "argumentation" according to the following logic: *If* someone wants to seize and plunder the house of a strong person, *then* she or he must first be in a position to overpower and bind the strong one. That is, she or he must be the stronger of the two. So Jesus "argues," but his argument presupposes a fact. The historical context (that is, the objection of the scribes) makes it clear that Jesus himself has entered the "house of the strong man." It has already happened!

Here it is not only Mark or his tradition that presents the argument; in this passage we hear the voice of Jesus himself, because he does not speak with crude insistence: "I am the one who has entered the house of the strong man" or "I am the stronger one." He "addresses" the situation in which a powerful person is robbed after being bound. That kind of indirection with regard to his own person, that discreet language, is characteristic of Jesus. We will encounter such tactful reticence from him again and again.

In conclusion let me simply say a few words about the "house" that plays such an important role both in the parable of the successful break-in and in that of the overpowering of the strong man. In the parable of the successful break-in it was an ordinary house or perhaps a somewhat larger farmstead. The one about overpowering the strong man seems to imply something more. In antiquity, and above all in biblical language, "house" had many nuances. It could refer to the family or a whole dynasty. Still more: "house" could also mean the state or the government. The Egyptian "house of slavery" (Exod 20:2) was nothing other than the Egyptian nation.

---

[3] The parallel in Luke 11:21-22 speaks of a "stronger one," but this is probably an altogether correct reworking by Luke of the Markan text.

This observation is not unimportant to our text. The "Strong One," that is, the highest of all demons, is not represented in our text by a simple homeowner or head of a household. This is the one who holds power over all "national entities," that is, the master of an entire empire with multifaceted resources in terms of powers and capabilities for violence. Jesus has come against those powers. He has driven them out by the power of God (Luke 11:20). He has broken into their realm, into the utterly unconquerable forces and unfreedoms of society; he has helped people to become free and thus made space for the reign of God. Hence the parable in Mark 3:27 sheds light on the shout of victory in Luke 12:39: "if the owner of the house had known at what hour the thief was coming, he would not have let his house be broken into."

### 3. The Treasure in the Field and the Pearl (Matthew 13:44-46)

The parables of the successful break-in and the overpowering of the strong man speak of the inbreaking of the reign of God into a world ruled by powers and evil forces. Where did Jesus get the strength to encounter those powers? And where will his disciples get them? Will heroic efforts be needed? Anyone who wants to know whether the reign of God demands only heroic action and utmost effort from human beings needs to listen to the parables of the treasure in the field and the pearl of great price:[4]

> The kingdom of heaven is like a treasure hidden in a field, which someone found and hid; then in his joy he goes and sells all that he has and buys that field.
> Again, the kingdom of heaven is like a merchant in search of fine pearls; on finding one pearl of great value, he went and sold all that he had and bought it. (Matt 13:44-46)

We see immediately that this is a double parable. We have a number of similarly structured double texts from Jesus—compare especially Luke 11:31-32 about the queen of the South and the Ninevites.[5]

---

[4] This double parable survives only in Matt 13:44-46.
[5] See further on such double structures Marius Reiser, *Jesus and Judgment*, trans. Linda M. Maloney (Minneapolis: Fortress Press, 1997), 209–10.

Evidently such two-part, parallel-structured compositions did not originate in post-Easter catechesis. Jesus himself must have loved repeating the same point in different metaphors, thus shedding light on it from different angles. Besides, by this method he was better able to fix the material in his hearers' minds.

In this text the parallel structure is especially striking. Two people each come upon something extremely valuable and precious, and they give up everything they have to acquire it. But the two actors are very different: first there is a day-laborer or wage worker who has to work in a field that is not his own (he will subsequently buy it). The other is a wholesale merchant with business connections everywhere (the corresponding Greek word, *emporos*, never refers to a small retailer). Still another difference is readily apparent: the day-laborer stumbles over the treasure purely by chance while the wholesaler has long been in search of costly pearls.

Apparently Jesus means to say by this contrast that the reign of God is open to everyone, the rich and the poor, and it can be found in a variety of ways: suddenly, unexpectedly, by accident, or it may be that someone has always longed for and looked for it and then, one day, comes upon it at last.

There is still another point to be noted: both parables are extraordinarily brief and could not be briefer. We have to ask ourselves: did Jesus really tell such short stories? What is more thrilling than stories about hidden treasure? Given two such stories that are so exciting by their very nature, why did he not spin them out and tell them in such a way as to heighten the tension throughout? Why, for example, didn't he tell about how poor the worker really is, how he starts to plow the ground, then hits something hard with the plowshare, digs out a clay pot and sees that it is full of silver coins, looks around furtively and quickly shoves the earth back over the find—and then how he buys the field, digs up the treasure, rushes home, and dances for joy with his wife and children? What a wealth of story material!

Otherwise, why didn't he tell how the wholesaler was in a city market somewhere abroad and discovered a pearl on a merchant's table mixed in with every kind of bric-a-brac and immediately realized that one of his wealthy customers would give him a fortune for it? He puts on a poker face and starts bargaining. The shrewd seller immediately realizes that he can make a deal here, and the pearl gets more and more expensive, but the wholesaler goes all out. He offers everything he has and makes the deal of his life. Why did Jesus let such narrative stuff slip away?

The answer could be that of course Jesus told his parables at much greater length and in more exciting fashion; it was only the teachers and theologians of the early communities who had to put them into a brief form and shape them to fit a more manageable pattern so they could be handed down more easily. That could be true.

Still, it might have been very different. It could be that, at the end of a long speech about the reign of God, Jesus told a brief parable the audience could remember. Its function would have been to form a conclusion to the sermon and send the audience away with something to think about.[6] Then everything superfluous would have to be dropped and the essentials clearly stated. Or Jesus could also have inserted a short, tautly-shaped parable into the flow of his speech or at the beginning of a speech. We have to reckon with a number of possibilities.

In any case Jesus must have been a storyteller who knew when to speak at length and when to keep it short and compact. He knew how to play the instrument of language. I am constantly in awe of the frugality and brilliance of this double parable, and the more I reflect on it the more confident I am that it could not have been told as fully and at length as, for example, the one about the lost son (Luke 15:11-32).

Just two more remarks on the metaphorical aspect of the parable of the treasure in the field. It assumes as obvious something that is no longer true today: the concealment of treasure. Then it was the order of the day: at that time—for the poor, at any rate—there was

---

[6] Klaus Berger points out that, according to the rules of ancient rhetoric, "imagery, as an impressive, dramatic element, belongs at the end, in the *peroratio* [peroration, the intense conclusion of the speech]." See his *Formen und Gattungen im Neuen Testament*, UTB 2532 (Tübingen and Basel: Francke, 2005), 110. Marius Reiser (*Sprache und literarische Formen des Neuen Testaments. Eine Einführung*, UTB 2197 [Paderborn: Schöningh, 2001], 145) points to a text from Jerome (*In Matt.* 18.23, at MPL 26, 137 B): "It is customary in Syria, and even more so in Palestine, to join parables to all of one's words. In this way, by comparisons and examples, hearers can grasp what cannot be grasped by simple commands." (Translation by Thomas P. Scheck in Jerome, *Commentary on Matthew*, Fathers of the Church Patristic Series [Washington, DC: CUA Press, 2008], 213.) See also Martin Hengel and Anna Maria Schwemer, *Jesus und das Judentum. Geschichte des frühen Christentums* I (Tübingen: Mohr Siebeck, 2007), 398.

no such thing as a bank, and normally not even a house that was not vulnerable to break-ins. On the other hand there were constant wars, robberies, burglaries, and fires. Consequently, money and valuable objects were buried, and it could easily happen that, as a result of wartime events and upheavals, buried treasures were not retrieved and lay forgotten. It certainly happened that someone came across a treasure buried in a field. There were even people who specialized in searching for old treasures; among Jews they were known as "moles," "woodpeckers," or "termites."[7]

There is something else that needs discussion with regard to the imagery of the parable of the treasure in the field. Why does the man buy the field? Why not just go there at night and dig up the treasure? According to the story he safeguards his find by buying the field. Of course New Testament scholars have discussed the judicial treatment of found items at the time, but it is not easy to determine. The precise legal situation was complicated, and Jesus does not go into it, probably for that very reason. His story presupposes that the finder buys the field in order to be absolutely sure the treasure will not be taken from him. Of course, in order to do so he has to sell everything he has: his miserable hut, his donkey, his tools. He may also have to borrow money. The hearers can imagine all that for themselves; Jesus doesn't say it. He knows that in a good parable you have to leave out a lot.

What about the imagery in the second parable? We have already seen that it plays itself out in a different milieu. It does not take place in the country but in the city, perhaps in the course of a mercantile journey and probably even in a foreign country. We cannot altogether exclude the idea that the wholesaler deals directly with the pearl merchant. There are a lot of possibilities here, but they are not described. All that is important to the storyteller is that the wholesaler understands something about pearls and is constantly searching for them. In antiquity, pearls were highly desirable; they were in that time what big diamonds are to us. Immense sums were paid for high-quality examples.

---

[7] See H. L. Strack and Paul Billerbeck, *Das Evangelium nach Matthäus. Erläutert aus Talmud und Midrasch* (Munich: Beck, [1922]; 3rd ed. 1961), 971–72. Finding no German equivalents for the Aramaic terms, Billerbeck invented some: "Erdaufwühler" (excavators), "Wandabklopfer" (wall-tappers), "Balkenaufbrecher" (beam-disembowelers). I think the people in Jesus' time would have been more imaginative.—LMM.

Well, what do the two parables want to say? In each case the introduction is key. It does *not* say, for example, "The reign of God is like a hidden treasure" or even "it *is* a hidden treasure." We have to add to it: "It is with the reign of God as with the whole story in which a poor worker finds a treasure. And it is with the reign of God as with the whole story of how a wholesale merchant finds his fortune by acquiring a precious pearl." More precisely: It is *with entry into* the reign of God as with the two stories that are told here.

The whole event is equated each time with the reign of God: from the lucky find through the selling of the property to the huge deals the day-laborer and the wholesaler make in the end. Here many, if not most, interpretations prove to be too narrow and one-sided as they try to find the key point or the precise meaning of the two parables in a single part.

For example, it has been said that the point aimed at in both parables is the gigantic value of what is found. The reign of God is as precious as the treasure and the shimmering pearl.

Another position says: no, the infinite value of the reign of God is not what is crucial here. This is rather about how, because of the unimaginable value of the reign of God, one must sacrifice everything else. It is about giving, about renunciation of possessions, about unlimited willingness to sacrifice. Certainly for Matthew "selling everything" was the key point of the double parable (cp. Matt 13:22)—but was that so for Jesus?

No, other interpreters say: that was not the key point for Jesus either. The day-laborer was faced with a unique opportunity that would never come again in his impoverished life. Likewise the merchant: never in his life would he behold another pearl like that. So the parables' audience should recognize the unique situation in which they are placed. Now, at this hour, God is offering them salvation, and now, in this hour, it must be seized.

A fourth position says: no, you can't really understand the parable of the treasure in the field that way. The day-laborer acquires his discovery dishonestly, not to say by fraud. He leaves the owner of the field in the dark about what he has found. Moreover, the wholesaler must not let the seller know what price he will demand from his own customer. Both of them, the day-laborer and the merchant, thus belong among the "immoral heroes" in Jesus' parables, and what Jesus really wanted to put before the eyes of his audience here was that what is at stake is decisive action, total dedication that is so goal-oriented and uncompromising that it risks everything on one roll of the dice. The reign of God needs people who act like that.

Another, fifth position interprets the double parable this way: The whole point is the overflowing joy with which the two finders sell everything. The accent lies there, and only there, and it is precisely from there that the whole parable has to be interpreted.

To think that two relatively brief, simple parables can create so much controversy! We have to criticize the five types of interpretation I have so briefly sketched here because they do not really do justice to the narrative structure of parables. Despite all brevity and conciseness, there is a real "story" being told here, and it is in the nature of stories that one is carried along by them and then may possibly see the world and oneself in a new light—or, in the case of Jesus' parables—that one senses for the first time what the reign of God might really be about. But that means that we must not apply Aristotelian logic to focus the story on a single element, a clearly distinguishable point of comparison. While the story always has an internal sense of direction that is by no means arbitrary, in order to grasp it one needs, in both instances, to surrender oneself to the whole story, follow it step by step, continually discover new things in it.

Obviously the treasure and the pearl are of incomparable value. Clearly the opportunity is unique. It will never come again. Obviously one must act decisively in such a situation, risk everything and go all out. Clearly one must give away everything to attain the reign of God. "Those who lose their life for my sake will find it" (Matt 10:39). That terrifying paradox appears in our double parable also, just as it arises again and again throughout Jesus' preaching.

Nevertheless, all that is embedded in and must be read in light of the overwhelming joy with which the two treasure-finders act. "In his joy he goes" cannot be overlooked. To that extent the fifth position is correct. The wholesaler's fascination with the find is so great that it determines the whole event. The day-laborer does not hesitate for a second, any more than the merchant does. Both of them are enraptured: by the brilliance of the treasure and the shimmer of the pearl. They have been seized by a joy beyond all measure. The fact that—as we see in the action of the day-laborer—they still act wisely is by no means out of the picture.

Here Jesus utters a crucial truth, and what is so delightful is that he does not formulate it in theory but tells a story. To be moved by

God's cause so that one gives everything for it is ultimately not something done out of simple consciousness of duty, "you should!" or even "you must!"

Evidently it is only possible for a human being to freely will what God wills when she or he concretely beholds the beauty of God's cause and so is seized by joy, by desire for what God wants to do in the world, so that the "desire for God and God's cause"[8] is greater than the sum of human self-focusing.

The merchant holds the pearl he has finally found to the light, and the day-laborer digs both hands into the pot of silver coins. For Jesus the reign of God is tangible and visible. It does not exist only within human beings and is not hidden somewhere beyond history. It can already be seen, touched, acquired, and dealt with, and for that very reason it fascinates people and makes them willing to change their whole lives for the sake of this new thing—and all without losing their freedom. The beauty and joy of the reign of God are ultimately the force that moves Jesus' disciples and causes God's grace to prevail in the world, again and again.

It seems to me that this double parable is a key with which we can unlock a deeper understanding of Jesus himself. Every really good text someone speaks or writes is in some sense autobiographical, and that is true of this pair of parables. Here Jesus is telling us something out of his own story and the fundamental choice he made for his life. Maybe he did so quite unconsciously, or maybe it was a conscious act, but if the latter it was done reticently and with the greatest degree of tact.

Jesus himself, after all, had given everything for the sake of the reign of God. He gave up the security and comfort of a family and a spouse. He did without a house or property or any other form of security. Still more serious: he avoided putting himself at the center of everything and thus exercising religious power—the kind of power that is surely the most sublime and dangerous kind of power there is.

Jesus lives not for himself, his own person, but surrendering utterly and solely to God's cause, or more precisely to the reign of God that is now coming. But what is decisive is that this fundamental choice for the sake of God did not make him a crushed and tortured person

---

[8] This is the title of a book by Ludwig Weimer: *Die Lust an Gott und seiner Sache—oder lassen sich Gnade und Freiheit, Glaube und Vernunft, Erlösung und Befreiung vereinbaren?* (Freiburg: Herder, 1981).

breathing forth fear of having fallen short, or a person who turns the self-denial he has not really learned to cope with into aggression against others.

Jesus possesses unheard-of freedom. He is not a model of one who is tormented, grim, dissatisfied, or who has fallen short of his goal. He is no fanatic, utterly convinced that he must force others to adopt his own position. Nor is he the type of the hero, tragic or otherwise. He remains to the end a free person, despite the radicality with which he goes his way. He remains to the end a man full of generosity and humanity.

The double parable of the treasure and the pearl gives the hearer or reader the key to that inner freedom and unbrokenness that Jesus had: indeed, Jesus gave up everything and goes on giving everything to the end; in the end he has to die. But he does it all like the day-laborer and the wholesaler, who did not waste a second on regret over the loss of their former property but acted, both of them, in unspeakable joy and fascination. Everything else pales before the splendor of the "find."

Evidently what Jesus speaks of in the parable of the treasure and the pearl is something he himself had experienced: he was seized and overcome by the joy of the reign of God—and not a reign of God that will come sometime but the one already beginning, the one that can be attained now, the one that anybody can barter and exchange today.

The reign of God is already happening here, in this world—today. It is reality wherever people believe the Gospel, accept the reign of God, let their lives be changed by its fascination—when they turn from their own life projects to the new one that God wants to create. The double parable of the treasure and the pearl speaks about this earth, about now, about today. And in doing so it speaks as clearly as can be about the presence of the reign of God.

## 4. The Budding Fig Tree (Mark 13:28-29)

The parable of the budding fig tree fits well here. Again we are looking at a very short text, similar in its brevity to a simple metaphor.

> From the fig tree learn its lesson:[9] as soon as its branch becomes tender and puts forth its leaves, you know that summer is near. So also, when

---

[9] Literally: "from the fig tree learn the parable."

you see these things taking place, you know that he is near, at the very gates. (Mark 13:28-29)

We find this text in Mark, Matthew, and Luke, shortly before Jesus' passion, as part of the great eschatological discourse. In Mark and Matthew it is absolutely clear that the one at the very gates is the "Son of Man."[10] After all, just before this all three Synoptic Gospels have spoken of the coming of the "Son of Man" on the clouds of heaven (Matt 24:30; Mark 13:26; Luke 21:27).

The question, however, is: did Jesus himself use the parable of the budding fig tree to speak of the coming of the Son of Man?

To find the answer we have to begin with the expression "when you see these things taking place." This is a reference to events previously spoken of in the eschatological discourse, where it was said that the coming of the Son of Man in clouds would be preceded by particular "signs" pointing to the end of the world and the *parousia* of the Son of Man: false prophets, wars, earthquakes, famines, persecutions, disintegration of families, and the desecration of the temple (Mark 13:5-23). When all that happens—so our parable summarizes—the end is near and the Son of Man is "at the very gates."

Did the historical Jesus speak of such apocalyptic "signs" before the end of the world? We cannot know for certain, but we do know that he spoke of "signs" by which to recognize the coming of the *reign of God*: "the blind receive their sight, the lame walk, the lepers are cleansed, the deaf hear, the dead are raised, the poor have good news brought to them" (Luke 7:22).

We also know for certain that he absolutely rejected apocalyptic "portents" *at least for the reign of God* (Luke 17:20-21). Why? Because the reign of God is not something far off; it is already pressing forward. It is coming; it is already present. "If it is by the finger of God that I cast out the demons, then the kingdom of God has come to you" (Luke 11:20).

Consider this as well: the greening of the fig tree is in itself a positive image. Just as spring arouses in us images of hope, not associations with decline, hunger, sickness, and war, so it was in Israel as well. We need only to think of texts from the Song of Songs: the following passage, for example—

---

[10] Luke alone speaks here (21:23) of the "kingdom of God" rather than of the "Son of Man," but that probably stems from Lukan redaction and does not rest on an older tradition.

> for now the winter is past,
> > the rain is over and gone.
> 
> The flowers appear on the earth;
> > the time of singing has come,
> > and the voice of the turtledove
> > is heard in our land.
> 
> The fig tree puts forth its figs,
> > and the vines are in blossom;
> > they give forth fragrance. (2:11-13)

Such texts positively compel us to think of what we can learn from the budding of the fig tree: not apocalyptic "portents" of the end, but "signs of recognition" for the nearness, the appearance on the horizon, of the reign of God. The parable could have read:

> From the fig tree learn the parable: as soon as its branches become tender and put forth their leaves, you know that summer is near. So also, when you see these things taking place [namely: the healings of the sick and the possessed], know that the reign of God is near.

The fig tree was especially well suited to be a "sign of recognition" in this sense. In southern lands, and of course in Israel also, nearly all the trees—the olive, the oak, and the locust, for example—develop their new leaves among the old ones still on the tree. Only the fig tree (and the grapevine) are different: the fig is almost the only tree that sheds all its leaves in winter (or in the rainy season). Hence the buds of the new leaves are especially obvious, and the fig tree became a symbol of spring, or better—since in Israel spring is only a very brief transitional period—a symbol of the approach of summer.

Evidently Jesus refers to the buds on the bare fig tree, highly visible as they are, to point to what is now happening: God's new world, the time of salvation, the reign of God. God's reign is coming as surely and as rapidly as summer follows the swelling and budding of the fig tree's branches. More even than that: in reality the striking changes in the fig tree not only predict the arrival of summer; when those buds appear summer has already come.

## 5. The Mustard Seed (Mark 4:30-32)

All the parables treated thus far speak about the reign of God—its surprising arrival, its breaking into the world—and about the fascination the reign of God can set loose. We must, of course, assume that the profound assurance, the very confidence of victory with which Jesus proclaimed the reign of God did not meet with approval everywhere.

Jesus' proclamation of the now-inbreaking reign of God encountered opposition. People must have objected: "Where is the change in the world you are talking about? Nothing is changing in this country. The Romans are still plundering us. Those who work with them get richer and richer; the poor are more and more exposed to them. Look, to this point everything has remained just as it was before. And are you telling us that this helpless little group wandering with you through Galilee is the beginning of the true, eschatological Israel? When God finally intervenes, won't his act look completely different—powerful, fitting for a ruler, irresistible—and won't it change everything in an instant?"

A lot of contemptuous or worried objections would have been voiced in those or similar words at the time. Jesus answered such protests with parables like the mustard seed (Mark 4:30-32), the yeast (Luke 13:20-21), the seed growing secretly (Mark 4:26-29), and the abundant harvest (Mark 4:3-9). These are parts of a whole group of parables on related themes. I will begin with the parable of the mustard seed.[11]

This parable is also brief. It can be brief because it compares the reign of God to something familiar to Jesus' listeners, something that happens before their eyes every year. Jesus compares the reign of God with what happens when mustard seeds are scattered:

> With what can we compare the kingdom of God, or what parable will we use for it? It is [with it as with] a mustard seed, which, when sown upon the ground, is the smallest of all the seeds on earth;[12] yet when it is sown it grows up and becomes the greatest of all shrubs, and puts

---

[11] We have received the parable of the mustard seed in two versions: from Mark and Q, the Sayings Source. Luke took his version (Luke 13:18-19) almost word for word from Q, but Matthew shaped a combined text from Mark and Q (Matt 13:31-32). It seems to me that Mark offers the more original version because he speaks appropriately of the mustard plant as a *lachanon*, "garden shrub," and not as a "tree." In Mark the birds nest on the ground in the shade of the mustard bush, as one can often observe in reality, while in Q they build their nests in the bush (or: tree) itself. Q also lacks the contrast between "small" and "great," which is essential to the parable.

[12] The NRSV translation "smallest of all the seeds on earth" is literal.

forth large branches, so that the birds of the air can make nests in its shade. (Mark 4:30-32)

To speak briefly of the botanical facts: this is most probably about black mustard (*brassica nigra*), whose seeds are unusually small. One of them weighs about a milligram and measures some 0.9 to 1.6 millimeters across. But it very quickly grows into an annual bush with treelike limbs. Its average height is about a meter and a half (roughly four and a half to five feet). On the Sea of Galilee it may even grow as tall as nine or ten feet. The minuteness of the seed was proverbial in Israel (cp. Luke 17:6).

But what is this parable about? The text is explicit: Jesus is speaking of the reign of God. Certainly he does not compare the reign of God directly with the mustard seed. God's rule does not simply correspond either to the mustard seed or to the mature bush; rather, it is represented by the whole process in which a seed the size of a pinhead becomes a great shrub. So it is clear that our parable does not speak of the reign of God in static terms but rather of its coming: more precisely, this is about the dynamics of the reign of God.

At present the reign of God is still tiny, unimpressive, easily overlooked, apparently ineffectual. But it is unfolding, growing, spreading, gaining more and more strength, and—another image—the birds of the air nest in its shade.[13]

Every modern reader of the parable must be struck by the fact that at the end it speaks not simply of "birds" but "birds of the air [= heavens]." Why? The answer seems clear. In the first place, this is simply an extremely common biblical expression. When Jesus prayed the psalms or recited other biblical texts (the method of meditation in his time) he would have encountered the expression "birds of the air/heavens" again and again (cp., for example, Pss 8:8; 79:2; 104:12; Gen 1:28, 30; 2:19; 6:7; Jer 7:33; Ezek 31:6).

If we pursue this expression further, however, we encounter an image in the prophetic books reflecting the power of Near Eastern

---

[13] Many interpreters consider the "nesting of the birds" as a post-Easter expansion of the parable. Why? because there is an allusion here to Ezek 31:3-6 and/or Dan 4:7-9. But that argument is not at all convincing. Why shouldn't Jesus, who knew his Sacred Scripture to an astonishing degree, make a play on it? Besides, without the impressive reference to the "nesting birds" and the associated background the parable would lack any real conclusion.

kings. They themselves, together with their kingdoms and empires, are depicted as a giant cedar in whose shade many living things dwell, including the birds of the air. Here is an example from Ezekiel 31:3-6 (but see also Ezek 17:22-24 or Dan 4:7-9):

> Consider Assyria, a cedar of Lebanon,
> with fair branches and forest shade,
>> and of great height,
>> its top among the clouds.
> The waters nourished it,
>> the deep made it grow tall
> . . .
> its boughs grew large
>> and its branches long,
>> from abundant water in its shoots.
> All the birds of the air
>> made their nests in its boughs;
> under its branches all the animals of the field
>> gave birth to their young;
> and in its shade
>> all great nations lived.

This is an impressive example of how one might speak of a king in the ancient Near East (although here the depiction of the tree's magnificence is preparation for the description of its demise: cp. Ezek 31:10-13). Obviously these highly symbolic texts did not envision the king as purely an individual; he represents his whole empire and the society that lives through him, as is clear from the listing of all the living things that are integral to the picture of this tree: the birds of the air that nest in its branches, the animals of the field who give birth to their young beneath it, the many nations that live in its shade (that is, under its protective shield). The king is depicted, together with his kingdom, as a cosmic "world tree"—a highly sophisticated but also extremely dangerous imperial ideology of rulership that showed its dreadful reverse side again and again in the history of the ancient Near East.

What does it mean that, at the end of the parable, Jesus evokes the ancient symbol of the world tree in his miniature narrative? It shows, in the first place, that the reign of God needs a people. That is evident from the multitude of living things that dwell in the shade of this world tree. In biblical theology the reign of God always requires a concrete people, a society that God has created especially for this: to make visible God's merciful rule.

But the symbol of the world tree also indicates that this is not just about Israel: the whole world is involved. "In its shade all great nations lived," says Ezekiel 31:6. We also have to keep that universal dimension of the world tree in mind when we read the parable of the mustard seed. It appears, in a small way, only at the end. But it is there.

In that case, however, our parable culminates in the statement: it may be that now, in this hour, the reign of God is as insignificant as a mustard seed and the true people of God but a tiny flock (cp. Luke 12:32), but from this obscure beginning the new thing, the utterly different thing, is already growing: an all-encompassing realm, a new world community. Indeed, all that is as *certain* to come about as that from a tiny mustard seed a giant shrub arises.

What the parable does not say, but was obvious to Jesus, was that the reign of God has nothing at all to do with the imperial claims of the rulers of his age that were associated with the image of the world tree and many others representing Near Eastern and Hellenist royal ideology. What applies here is what Jesus told his disciples on another occasion: "The kings of the Gentiles lord it over them; and those in authority over them are called benefactors. But not so with you" (Luke 22:25-26).

Obviously the parable of the mustard seed is not simply about the world tree. That symbol appears only at the end, and very subtly, in the birds' nests. The parable itself is first situated in the real, down-to-earth world of fields and their borders or, more precisely, in a vegetable garden. A parable could not possibly begin in a more ordinary way. Jesus compares the reign of God to the cultivation of cabbages and other vegetables. Certainly it would have been more impressive to begin with the proud "world tree," but Jesus spoke unpretentiously—and therefore all the more effectively—about a garden plot.

Clearly that was no accident. Jesus was very deliberate in his choice of images. The unique character of the images corresponds to the uniqueness of the thing at issue. The reign of God takes place in the midst of the ordinary, everyday world familiar to his audience. It is not far away, nor does it wait in "some time or other." It most certainly does not appear with apocalyptic, world-shaking thunderstorms, but just the way a mustard seed grows into something great. It is already happening among his hearers. Those who see what is happening here through and around Jesus and view it in faith are already seeing the reign of God. "Blessed the eyes that see what you see!" (Luke 10:23).

## 6. The Leaven (Luke 13:20-21)

In the parable of the leaven we are presented with the same everyday environment as in that of the mustard seed. It comes from Q,[14] and—except for the introduction—it has almost the same wording in Matthew and Luke. It follows immediately after the parable of the mustard seed. I will use Luke's version:

> To what should I compare the kingdom of God? It is like yeast that a woman took and mixed [Gk: "hid"] in with three measures [*sata*] of flour until all of it was leavened. (Luke 13:20-21)

The action of the parable consists of a single sentence; again we have one of those very brief Jesus parables. In terms of its language it is also striking that the woman "hides" the leaven in the flour. Is that meant to say that the reign of God is now still hidden, so that at present no one can see it? That seems very improbable. All it means is simply that the leaven is "mixed into" the flour.[15] Then it is no longer visible, but the woman's intent is not to "hide" it. Besides, for Jesus the reign of God is anything but hidden. Anybody can see Jesus' own deeds of power (Luke 11:20). They are hidden only from unbelief. Even so, such an accent (hiddenness from the nonbelieving, visibility to believers) would not fit this miniature narrative at all.

Likewise, there is nothing suspicious about the fact that the long and tedious process of kneading the dough is not described in our parable, though some interpreters have questioned it. They overlook the fact that here we are dealing with an extremely brief parable that

---

[14] The Sayings Source Q must have been a collection of Jesus' sayings used as a source by the authors of the gospels of Matthew and Luke; indeed, it can only be reconstructed by comparing those two gospels.

[15] Thus the NRSV. For the translation of ἐγκρύπτειν (*egkryptein*), "put into, hide," see Michael Wolter, *Das Lukasevangelium*, HNT 5 (Tübingen: Mohr Siebeck, 2008), 487. But this may also represent a problem of translation from Hebrew or Aramaic.

focuses only on essentials. Likewise omitted are the water, the salt, and the "rising" of the dough.

*Sata* is the plural of *saton*, the Greek word for a Hebrew measure. Three *sata* of flour are about 320 cups, which means that a huge amount of bread is being baked, far more than a normal household could use. In those days the flat loaves of bread were not stored but were baked fresh every day.

A number of exegetes think that here Jesus is inflating the story unrealistically, exorbitantly, overexpanding it as he habitually does. But we have to question whether that is really true of his parables in general. In any case there is nothing unrealistic here. Obviously a normal household doesn't need that much bread, but if there is a feast with invited guests—a wedding, for example—things are different. The parable omits any details about the situation; it simply assumes that bread has to be baked and because, as in the case of the mustard seed, Jesus is intent on the contrast he chooses a situation in which a lot of bread is needed. He can assume such a situation; there is no need to name it, much less describe it.

At any rate, by mentioning the huge quantity of flour Jesus assures himself of the audience's curiosity. His parables often present little surprises and provocations that draw the hearers out of their usual lethargy. The leaven in our parable also aims at such an effect. In Judaism leaven had a somewhat negative connotation (Matt 16:6; Mark 8:15; Gal 5:9). Nobody would talk about leaven in a parable explaining God's intentions.

As to its structure, our parable is closely related to the one about the mustard seed; the two may even constitute a double parable. In any case what is at issue here is no longer only contrasting quantities—the (relatively) small amount of leaven on the one hand and the large quantity of flour on the other. This is primarily about quality: the yeast alone leavens the flour mixture and makes the bread edible.

With this parable Jesus intends to say: no matter how tiny and inconspicuous the reign of God now appears to be, it will transform the world and give it zest. To put it more drastically: the human history of sin has made the world dull and tasteless. The reign of God will make it palatable again, restore creation, and return it to its whole abundance and tastiness. To that extent the parable of the leaven goes even further than the one about the mustard seed.

### 7. The Seed Growing by Itself (Mark 4:26-29)

The group of parables we are dealing with at present—often called "parables of growth"—also includes the parable of the seed growing by itself (Mark 4:26-29). It is one of Jesus' loveliest parables: brief, concise, positively functional in its unadorned goal-directedness—and yet filled with a marvelous kind of hope.

> The kingdom of God is as if someone would scatter seed on the ground, and would sleep and rise night and day, and the seed would sprout and grow, he does not know how. The earth produces of itself, first the stalk, then the head, then the full grain in the head. But when the grain is ripe, at once he goes in with his sickle, because the harvest has come. (Mark 4:26-29)

This parable tells of the coming of the reign of God in the image of a field that receives seed that grows, unstoppably, until harvest: "the earth produces of itself." The accent is not on the sowing; that is only the introduction to the parable. But there is likewise no heavy emphasis on the harvest, as important as it is in the end. The point here lies in the description of how the grain grows, without human effort. The parable's structure shows that the point of the statement must lie in the central part, because here the telling slows.[16]

All that seems quite strange to us today. As biologically enlightened people of our time we know how seed grows and why it grows and what agronomy can do to make it grow faster or slower, taller or shorter. The work of today's farmers is by no means finished when the seed is sown. Before the stalks are very tall there is all the spraying to be done: herbicides, fungicides, pesticides, and growth regulators to prevent the stalks from growing too tall and being flattened by heavy thunderstorms.

The approach in Galilee at that time was still very different. The parable describes the impossibility of interfering in the growth of the seed. The farmer has to wait. He "sleeps and rises night and day"—this language invokes a long series of days and nights. Then the

---

[16] A series of commentators sees the "drawing out" of v. 28 as a secondary addition from the post-Easter tradition or by Mark himself, but that misses the literary structure of the parable. Its vitality lies precisely in that retardation, formulated in terms of both the farmer's rhythm of life and the growth of the seed.

perspective shifts from the farmer to the grain; now time stretches out again: first the stalks, then the heads, then the grain in the heads. In between comes a remark: "the earth produces of itself." That "of itself" jumps out of the text at us. Here humans can do nothing. They cannot grasp or influence the miracle of growth. They only know that God's creative power is at work, the power that in the end will provide the harvest.

Commentators on this parable have often spoken of the farmer's "inactivity" and have even seen it as the *crux* of the parable.[17] That was not completely wrong. The farmer *is* inactive, as far as the grain is concerned. When the owner of land in that era had sown seed, the rest was up to the land itself. He should no longer plow or harrow the land (Isa 28:23-25). Still, we must see that the function of the careful formulation "sleep and rise night and day" is not really to portray the farmer's inactivity or laziness. The intent is instead to depict *the progress of time*. The farmer's days and nights correspond to the opening, growing, and ripening of the grain. Both—the farmer's rhythm of life and the ripening of the grain—stand in parallel and are meant to show that the process of growth is beyond the reach of any human interference. Only God is at work here, and no one can prevent God from working. Hence it is best not to speak of the "inactivity" of the farmer but of his "lack of participation."

Like the parable of the mustard seed, this text ends with an allusion to Scripture—in this case Joel 3:13, where we read "put in the sickle,[18] for the harvest is ripe." That allusion to the book of the prophet Joel puts an exclamation point on the end of the parable and names its purpose: at the end comes the harvest, the emergence of the reign of God *in its fullness and perfection*. There is not the least excuse for denying this allusion to Jesus: he knew his Scripture. It was always present to him. Why should he not have been able to allude to Scripture? In this case it may not be a *thematic* allusion but simply the use of biblical language. At this point the coming of the "judgment on the nations" (as for Joel) or even the eschatological coming of the Son of Man as world judge were not in view. But we cannot be absolutely sure. It is possible that here, as elsewhere, Jesus is indirectly alluding to his own mission.

---

[17] I myself have fallen into that temptation in the past.

[18] Probably Joel means "Send the harvesters with their sickles [into the field]."

Conclusion: our parable, from beginning to end, is about the coming of the reign of God, but it does not mean that the reign of God will come only if it is first sown. It is most certainly not about its coming gradually, as the grain slowly ripens. The point here is, first of all, that human beings cannot bring about the arrival of the reign of God; they cannot force it into existence—most certainly not by violence, as the Zealots thought. Human beings can only wait. God's reign will be brought about by God, and God alone—and God will surely bring it.

But above all the parable reveals God's creative power and command over history. No one will prevent God from working and bringing salvation. The human response to that knowledge about God can only be a profound trust that relies on God.

Certainly all that is only one side of the coin. To talk about the reign of God we are forced to speak in mighty "arcs of tension." That is why, in anticipation of the reign of God, Jesus calls his hearers to ultimate decision and the application of all their strength. Simply compare the parables of the assassin (*Gos. Thom.* 98), the money given in trust (Matt 25:14-30), and the crooked manager (Luke 16:1-7). But we will treat that group of parables later.

## 8. The Abundant Harvest (Mark 4:3-9)

As we have seen, the reign of God, at first encountered only in modest guise and unnoticed by many, will in the end have transformed everything. No one can prevent God from bringing about this new world; Jesus is absolutely confident of that.

But can we trust such assurance? Does Jesus see the world as it really is—its misery, its darkening, its refusals, the massive character of its enmity toward God? In the end isn't his confidence unworldly? The fact that no one can rightly accuse Jesus of that is clear from another text from among the "parables of growth":

> A sower went out [to the field] to sow. And as he sowed, some seed fell on the path, and the birds came and ate it up. [Other seed fell on rocky ground, and when the sun rose, it was scorched since it had no roots.][19] Other seed fell among thorns, and the thorns grew up and

---

[19] This part of the parable in Mark is awkward and overburdened. There must have existed an older version that was shorter and more incisive. I am making an exception

choked it, and it yielded no grain. Other seed fell into good soil and brought forth grain—[some yielded thirty[20] and some sixty and some a hundred].

Differently from the parables of the mustard seed, the leaven, and the seed growing secretly, this one does not immediately tell a story of success. On the contrary! Three-quarters of the parable depicts opponents who threaten the growth of the grain and destroy some of the seed. Only the last quarter of the parable speaks of success.

However, we would completely miss the sense of the parable if we were to see it as a kind of statistic, a final accounting of God's success in the world, concluding that three-fourths of God's efforts go for naught and only a quarter are successful. That is to say, the parable of the sower is in no way a parable about "four kinds of soil," "many fields," "different kinds of fields," certainly not "various kinds of soil." That kind of labeling misses the point of what the parable means to say, because it tells a *story*—even if it uses shorthand—and it is a dynamic story with a goal, one that clearly steers toward a climax.

We recognize that dynamic of the parable when we notice what the seed's enemies do in the several cases: first we hear about birds who peck up part of the strewn seed, the part that has fallen on a hard-packed path. In that case the kernels never germinate at all. They immediately become prey for the birds.

Another share of the seed has better chances: it germinates and sprouts. But then the sun quickly dries it up because the layer of surface soil on the underlying limestone is too thin.

---

here by attempting to reconstruct the older version by analogy to the other parts of the parable. Certainly this reconstruction has no meaning for the interpretation of the parable; it is only meant to show the high probability that this parable, too, was succinct and consistent.

[20] Modern translations (including the NRSV and NABRE) show a rare unanimity in translating Mark 4:8 "thirty[fold]" and "sixty[fold]" and "a hundredfold." That is clearly a distortion of the Greek text and, at least as far as German is concerned, is probably owing to the powerful influence of Martin Luther's translation. The Greek *hen* can never transform successive cardinal numbers into numeric adverbs. Matthew and the Vulgate show how the Greek text is to be understood. The fact that a Hebrew or Aramaic model might have contained a numeric adverb does not change the fact that this is a wrong translation.

The part of the seed that falls among the thorn bushes comes closer to succeeding: it germinates, sprouts, and grows, but it cannot set new seed because it is choked by the thorns that have grown up with it.

Thus the length of the seed's life increases; the story could culminate in success. On the other hand, the destruction of the seed would be all the more depressing. Suspense among Jesus' audience must have been increasing at every step. How will it all turn out? Will there be a fourth stage like the others in which the fully ripe grain will be destroyed—maybe by a heavy storm just before the harvest or by a wildfire (Isa 5:24)? Or will the parable turn out well after all? Where is Jesus going with this parable? His audience are already used to surprises from him, and at that time people who listened to parables were familiar with the fact that parable-tellers frequently followed the 3 + 1 formula, which meant that something completely new and different could be expected in the fourth part.

At this point the majority of Jesus' listeners were certainly not in the dark. A lot of them were small farmers, tenants, day-laborers, all of them familiar with farming. They probably found Jesus' description completely realistic.[21] It is only a multitude of New Testament scholars who are puzzled. A hundredfold yield? That is completely out of the question, they say.

Those interpreters could have noticed, after all, that the text says nothing at all about a hundredfold yield of *the whole sowing*, but paths once broken dig deep ruts out of which the exegetical carriage is not easily lifted. No, we read over and over again that even the best soil does not produce a hundredfold harvest. This goes against every normal experience. Jesus is deliberately exaggerating again. He does not simply want to depict the farmers' reality in his time. He has increased the yield of the fields to a fantastic size because he wants to say that the reign of God and its abundance explodes all human experience.

I will take the liberty of quoting a few expressions from the commentaries: "does not fit with reality," "obvious exaggeration," "here the interpretation clearly affects the image," "turning away from

---

[21] The act of sowing on the path was part of the realism. It assumes that sowing preceded plowing, a sequence not unfamiliar even to the improved techniques of Roman agriculture that were then dominant. Cp. Columella, *De re rustica* 2.10.

reality," "unimaginable," "narrative exaggerations," "success that explodes the real dimensions," "far surpassing reality," "elevated to the miraculous," "a wondrous surplus that nature does not normally produce," "the yield of the grain completely surpasses real conditions."

I myself believed that kind of New Testament exegetical logic for some time. But it is not conclusive by itself because the "thirty," "sixty," "hundred" simply does not represent the relationship between the quantity of seed sown and the overall yield. It is only about the yield of seeds that fall on good soil. Of course, that still leaves the question: can a single seed, or a particular quantity of seed, yield a hundred seeds? That seems impossible.

And yet it was precisely on that point that a farmer gave me a better idea. After a lecture I had given in a rural congregation near Tübingen he said to me (in good Swabian, of course): "Those big quantities Jesus talks about are completely normal, because some of the seeds 'tiller' themselves: that is, they split into several stalks."

I had never heard the word "tillering"[22] and I immediately tried to trace it. To my astonishment I came across a whole series of earlier authors who had pointed out the phenomenon of "tillering" in this connection, but no one paid any attention to them any more.[23] Further research brought me the following results:[24]

1. The sprouting seed only produces a single shoot at the outset, but at a very early stage the bottommost node (the so-called "tillering node"), lying far below the surface of the soil, puts out side-shoots; these, still beneath the earth, cause a branching of the principal stem. So it is that from a single seed there often comes a whole lateral nest of "tillers" that may even be very different from each other.

---

[22] Or: "stocking."

[23] Gustaf Dalman, for example, describes the phenomenon of stocking (counting an average of "up to 20 stems from a single root; near Nain I once counted 44 stems"). He was not aware of the technical term "tillering," however. Cp. Gustaf Dalman, *Arbeit und Sitte in Palästina*, vol. 2: *Der Ackerbau* (Gütersloh: Bertelsmann, 1928–39; repr. Hildesheim: Olms, 1964), 243–44.

[24] For more detail see Gerhard Lohfink, "Das Gleichnis vom Sämann (Mk 4,3-9)," *BZ* 30 (1986): 36–69; repr. idem, *Studien zum Neuen Testament*, SBA.NT 5 (Stuttgart: Katholisches Bibelwerk, 1989), 91–130.

2. It seems that, as far as the number of stems from the "tiller" is concerned, Jesus is keeping within a realistic average. Because he has to work schematically in the story, he uses a maximum of three stems, and he estimates a yield of thirty grains per stem.

3. Experiments at the Faculty of Agricultural Sciences at the University of Hohenheim in Germany have produced the following statistical average yields from grain sown in open fields:[25] wheat in the field (that is, not in a single-plant culture), under the usual conditions, produced an *average* tillering of 1.6 stems. That small number of stems is striking at first glance, because in a normal field one can count a great many more stems on the "wheat stalks." However, 1.6 stems is an average. Many of the grains that were sown have perished. A further result was that the *average* number of grains in each ear was thirty-one. Thus a summary of two notable values from that Institute!

4. We may conclude from this: it appears that in our parable Jesus presumes the phenomenon of tillering. He must have been familiar with it. Above all, that he gave thirty as an average grain yield per stem is amazing. Either everybody knew about that in those days or Jesus had counted the grains at some time or other. Sixty grains would then come from two stems and a hundred from three stems per stalk. The fact that Jesus speaks of only three stems is even more astonishing, because as I have already said, most grain stalks have many more stems. But Jesus is working schematically and he wants to build a "sequence" that is clear to the audience, starting with the realistic number thirty.

5. Obviously we have to ask whether one may simply apply current experiments to grain production back then. We may. The Roman author L. Junius Moderatus Columella wrote a twelve-volume work on agriculture, *De re rustica*, in the first century CE. He was familiar not only with the phenomenon of "tillering" (*fruticatio, fruticare*) but even advises that at an early stage the seeds should be heaped up so

---

[25] The following botanical results are drawn primarily from information given me by Professor Dr. W. Aufhammer, former director of the Institute for Plant Cultivation at the University of Hohenheim. I want to express my gratitude here for his willingness to help.

they will "tiller" more.[26] As far as the number of grains produced, we are in the happy position of having unearthed heads of grain engraved in gold that were placed in ancient graves as gifts. When we count the grains we again arrive at an average number of thirty.

So it seems to me we have clearly demonstrated the background of Mark 4:8 as regards the science of agriculture: part of the seed that is sown falls on good ground, and from some of that part come thirty grains per seed sown (that is, there was no "tillering" in that part). Another group of seeds yields sixty grains per seed sown (here there was a "tillering" with two stems). Yet another group of seeds produces ninety to a hundred grains per seed sown (from a "tillering" with three stems).

Hence the odd sequence of thirty, sixty, ninety (one hundred) is immediately plausible. There is no question of expanding on reality: quite the contrary! Jesus was a very sober observer who permitted no fantasizing in an area with which his audience was familiar. Instead, he lovingly described it in detail and was altogether in a position to state average quantities.

It is also clear that here again the story is about the work of God. The parable depicts how the reign of God comes into the world. As with the other "parables of watching" we would miss the progression of the narrative if we were to say that only the rich final harvest is the reign of God. No, the parable depicts the coming of the reign of God from the first line on. Its coming includes the sowing, the adversaries who do it the utmost damage, and then finally the abundant harvest that stands on the stalk in the end, despite all those who oppose it.

And what part does Jesus himself play in the parable? Is it only about God? That is hard to imagine. Obviously it speaks first and last and in every sentence about what God is doing now in Israel and beyond Israel in the world, and yet Jesus also speaks indirectly and with reticence about himself. He is the sower who sows the word of proclamation. He is also the one who sows people (Mark 4:16, 18, 20; cp. Jer 31:27). He has to bear the attacks of his opponents. He experiences how his adversaries frighten people who really want to follow

---

[26] Columella, *De re rustica* 2.9.11.

him and try to destroy his mission. And he sees how his seed grows in spite of it all. But Jesus doesn't say any of that explicitly. It is his way often to leave unspoken what applies to himself or only to hint at it tactfully.

In that light, of course, the battle provoked by Adolf Jülicher (1857–1938) in his two-volume *Die Gleichnisreden Jesu*[27] misses the point altogether. Jülicher made it his goal to weed out every last allegorical remnant from Jesus' parables and focus everything on a single point of comparison. The effort had become necessary in order to put an end to a number of abstruse allegorizings from previous centuries. But in so doing Jülicher was unable to do justice to the multilayered character of parables, and above all the multidimensionality of Jesus' parables. If he had read his Old Testament more carefully he would have seen there that even Old Testament parables contained allegorical elements: for example, the famous parable of the vineyard in Isaiah 5:1-7 or the striking parable of the poor man's lamb in 2 Samuel 12:1-4.

Now for a look back! Mark 4:3-8 is like all seed parables: the wheat (or barley) is sown, the mustard seed has fallen into the ground, the leaven has been kneaded into the flour. God's cause is already ripening, no matter how great the destructive power of its opponents. Naïve otherworldliness or starry-eyed faith in progress this is not. Jesus himself was assuredly aware of the "impossibility" of God's cause in the world. That is why, in the group of parables we have just considered, he describes not only the unstoppable growth of the reign of God but also the terrifying minuteness of its beginnings. More than that: he portrays the frightening superiority of its opponents, who threaten the work of God from beginning to end.

In all this Jesus deliberately avoids the path opened by Jewish apocalyptic in the first century CE. It too was deeply affected by the miserable situation of the people of God and the earthly power of God's enemies. But the apocalypticists of that time drew a different conclusion from those events than Jesus did. For them it was no longer

---

[27] Adolf Jülicher, *Die Gleichnisreden Jesu*, 2 vols. (Freiburg: Mohr [Siebeck], 1886).

conceivable that God could still succeed in a world so depraved and dying. Therefore they said that God's promises can no longer be fulfilled in "this world," "this age."[28] God must intervene violently in history to destroy the old world with fire and create a new world, a "new age." Only there can God's promises be made real.

Jesus is no apocalypticist. He can make use of apocalyptic imagery, but he does not teach an apocalyptic system. Above all, he never succumbs to the dualism of apocalypticism. That is already clear from the material of his parables of growth.

After all, we have seen that this is everyday stuff. Jesus doesn't just speak about the world tree; first of all he talks about a banal mustard bush. He takes his pictorial material from the vegetable garden. He talks about what a married woman in Israel did every day: grind flour, make dough, knead in yeast, and bake flat loaves of bread. He talks about the scrubby fields belonging to the little people in the Palestinian hill country, where the soil layer on top of the chalk cliffs was often very thin, where there were no fixed, fenced-off roads but only footpaths, and where thorns and thistles were really hard to root out.

With the aid of a world that lay before his hearers' eyes every day he pictures the coming of the reign of God and so makes it clear that God's new world will not come only when the previous world has collapsed; it is coming already, now, in the middle of the everyday life of the old one.

In his seed parables Jesus pictures a silent revolution—God's revolution—and he tells us that this overturning of all conditions will succeed: now, in this creation, in this history, and not only in the apocalypticists' "beyond." That is exactly why he uses creation motifs for his argument within the group of parables of growth, above all the growth of grain. He argues in terms of the world his hearers know.

And he tells us that God is not powerless; despite all enemies, God will succeed—not by using force but instead through human freedom. God pursues every individual and, respecting each one's freedom, seeks to win her or him for God's cause. This "pursuit of the individual" is marked by profound mercy and infinite kindness. That is the subject of the next group of parables.

---

[28] Especially impressive is 2 Esdras 4:26-32; 7:30-36.

## 9. The Two Debtors (Luke 7:41-42)

The parable of the two debtors is found only in Luke's gospel, and there within a narrative that had a rather long and varied history of tradition behind it even before Luke got hold of it (cp. the divergent versions in Mark 14:3-9; Luke 7:36-50; John 12:1-8). In Luke's version Jesus has been invited to dinner by a Pharisee named Simon, and during the meal a public sinner comes in, throws herself at Jesus' feet, kisses them, and anoints them with an expensive scented oil: that is, with the perfume of the period. This incident leads to a conversation between Jesus and the Pharisee. The latter had been offended by the scene. As part of the conversation Jesus tells the following parable:

> A certain creditor had two debtors; one owed five hundred denarii, and the other fifty. When they could not pay, he canceled the debts for both of them. Now which of them will love him more? (Luke 7:41-42)

As we can see, the parable is an extremely brief story. The material itself could have offered more. We have papyrus notes from antiquity bearing the names of the lender and the debtor, the amount of money owed, the monthly interest, the term of the loan, and the punishment for nonpayment—all down to the last detail. Information of that kind would have made the parable less bland. But all elaborations and decorations are omitted here, and for good reason. The parable is an argument used as part of a dialogue; hence it must be as brief as possible.

Still, there seems to be one thing missing, and we ask ourselves why it is not part of the narrative: why, exactly, were the debts canceled? It is precisely at this point that one would like to know more, since that kind of generosity is not really normal among professional lenders; quite the contrary! There has to be a reason why they were both forgiven everything; in fact, such a reason is given in another of Jesus' parables (cp. Matt 18:27). Why is no ground for the action given in this one?

Here, as in a whole series of Jesus' parables, we are confronted with an unusual, even rash "extravagance," something Jesus permits himself quite often in his parables. In the world of that time, just as in ours, moneylenders were neither heroes nor beloved characters. There was always something shady about them. The lender in this parable, too, must at first have seemed to the listeners to embody that kind of negative role—but only at the outset. The audience would very quickly have guessed that this could be about God because, as the fifth petition of the Our Father in Matthew's version shows, biblical language could use the same word to describe monetary obligations and the debt of sin: "Forgive us our debts as we also have forgiven our debtors!" (Matt 6:12).

Moreover, in the Our Father and other biblical texts that appeal to God's mercy there is nothing held back: the *whole* debt is forgiven unconditionally. Given the context—the story of the sinful woman or, more broadly, the historical context of Jesus' treatment of sinners—it had to dawn on the hearers: he is talking about God! Above all, that had to happen when Jesus added the question: "Which of them will love him more?"

Do any of us love moneylenders, even if they forgive our debts? No! We are surprised, uncertain, confused, shamed, moved, or grateful. But love the moneylenders? No way! The word "love" creates a different set of associations, above all our love for God. After all, Jesus' audience spoke the "Hear, O Israel" from Deuteronomy 6 every day: "You shall love the LORD your God with all your heart, and with all your soul, and with all your might."

With the appearance of the word "love" the levels in the parable have definitively shifted. Now it had to be clear to everyone that the shady moneylender was really God, who—as Jesus' dealings with sinners demonstrated—forgives all guilt, all debts. Just as the moneylender is suddenly no longer a moneylender, so before God human debts, human sins, are no longer debts, no longer sins. For those who come to Jesus and believe the Gospel, all debt is forgiven.

Should we agree with a whole group of interpreters that this Jesus parable is not authentic? Was it just invented to provide a powerful, though seemingly artificial, argument for the dispute with the Pharisee in the story of the sinful woman? I prefer to assume the contrary. The parable reveals something of the skill of Jesus the teller of parables, and it is a precise fit with the reign of God, which overturns everything—the reign of God that Jesus not only proclaimed, but lived.

## 10. The Lost Sheep (Matthew 18:12-14)

We receive this parable both in Luke 15:4-7 and in Matthew 18:12-14, but in different contexts. In Matthew it is about attentive common life in the Christian community, which as a whole is an assembly of "little ones,"[29] that is, of weak and corruptible people (cp. Matt 18:6-10). In Luke's gospel, by contrast, Jesus is justifying his attitude toward sinners before Pharisees and scribes (cp. Luke 15:1-2). It is usually assumed that the parable existed in Q, but there is dispute over whether Matthew or Luke has the more original version. The two evangelists certainly have a basic text in common, but there are differences. It is possible that Luke accommodated his story to the one about the lost coin (15:8-10) to create a double parable, but that is not certain. I will use Matthew's version:

> What do you think? If someone has a hundred sheep, and one of them has gone astray, does he not leave the ninety-nine on the mountains and go in search of the one that went astray? And if he finds it, truly I tell you, he rejoices over it more than over the ninety-nine that never went astray. So it is not the will [before][30] your Father in heaven that one of these little ones should be lost. (Matt 18:12-14)

Again we are confronted with a parable whose "narrative" is as concise as can be. Every superfluous detail has been consistently eliminated. Obviously that happens because the whole thing begins with a question. While the question-structure is not maintained throughout the whole parable, it could easily have been continued more or less this way: "And if he finds it, does he not rejoice over that *one* more than over the ninety-nine that never went astray?" Parables couched in such a style, one that seeks agreement, simply have to be brief (cp., e.g., Luke 14:28-30, 31-32).

---

[29] That is one interpretation of Matthew 18. It is also possible to read it as saying that within the community there are "little ones," that is, members who can be led astray and therefore must be shielded against temptation.

[30] The literal translation "will before your Father in heaven" is incomprehensible to us today. It refers to the visually imagined scene in heaven. God is in the heavenly throne room, surrounded by angels like a staff of assistants, and makes known the divine ruler's will: in our case, profound joy. God's will, we might say, "stands in the room." It is no accident that Luke's parallel parable of the lost coin speaks at this point of the "angels of God" (15:10). Cp. also Matt 18:10 ("in heaven their angels continually see the face of my Father in heaven").

Think how much has been left out here! Is the "someone"[31] in the story the owner of the sheep or a hired shepherd? Does he return home with the sheep in the evening to a sheepfold near the house, or does he travel with them through the hills for a week or more at a time, moving wherever they can find something to eat? But above all: what happens to the sheep left behind when the shepherd goes in search of the one? How are they protected? *Are* they protected? Does the shepherd leave the sheep untended and run a huge risk for the sake of that one sheep?

None of that is part of the story; if it were, the parable would lose its incisiveness. The hearers can picture it for themselves, but their minds have to work fast because the parable-teller is already making the crucial statement toward which everything is aimed, the one thing that matters: the enormous joy of the shepherd who finally finds the sheep. How and where it is discovered—in a good piece of pasture the sheep has found, or caught in a thorn bush, or having slipped down into a hard-to-reach gully—all that is omitted. The narrator is completely concentrated on the joy of the finder.

The application ("So it is not the will before your Father in heaven that one of these little ones should be lost") comes from Matthew; it is his way of adjusting the parable to the context of a discourse on community life (Matt 18:1-35). Hence this final verse cannot help us in determining the *original* placement of our parable.

Thus the question remains: what was the situation in which Jesus spoke this parable? and what did he want to say with it? Here Luke is probably closer to the original. He introduces the parable of the lost sheep (and the two parables that follow it) as follows:

> Now all the tax collectors and sinners were coming near to listen to him. And the Pharisees and the scribes were grumbling and saying, "This fellow welcomes sinners and eats with them." So he told them this parable. (Luke 15:1-3)

With this introduction Luke seems to have hit pretty precisely on the situation in which the parable was originally located, because it appears to be directed to people in Israel who were unhappy about Jesus' association with toll collectors and sinners; they found it objectionable (cp. Mark 2:13-17). With the parable of the lost sheep Jesus

---

[31] Greek: τινι ἀνθρώπῳ; not "a shepherd" (NRSV); also not "a man" (NABRE), as *anthrōpos* means "human being."

justifies his own behavior—but not only that; he tries to win over his opponents.

How does he try to win them over? What kind of argument does he use? Does he speak first and primarily of his own joy? Not at all: he emphasizes God's joy. That is less evident in Matthew's version (18:14) than in Luke's, where the emphasis is much stronger (15:7).

Still, even if it remains unspoken by Matthew and Luke it would have been clear to everyone listening to the parable at the time that this is about God. From the very beginning the text moves within a "field of imagery" made up of fixed metaphors familiar to every devout person in Israel from Scripture and the synagogue liturgy: God is Israel's shepherd (Isa 40:11; Ps 80:2); God is the shepherd of every person in Israel (Gen 48:15; Ps 23:1); God gathers the scattered sheep of Israel and leads them back to the land (Jer 31:10; Ezek 34:13, 16; Mic 2:12); God rescues God's sheep when the appointed shepherds fail them (Jer 23:1; Ezek 34:1-16); God pastures these sheep "on the mountains of Israel" (Ezek 34:13).

Thus the Old Testament contains a dense network of image-statements according to which it is *God* who is the true shepherd of God's people and who gathers them again and again as one flock. In light of this semantic net every listener at that time had to assume that when Jesus spoke positively about a shepherd in a parable he was in all probability talking about God—and yet Jesus spoke this parable in a situation in which he was justifying himself. He justifies *his own* attitude by speaking about *God's* attitude.

So we find ourselves again face to face with the phenomenon that can be called the "christological inclusion." Jesus speaks about God and by doing so he speaks about himself. We will encounter this inclusion again and again. The parable of the lost sheep is "a veiled assertion of authority: Jesus makes the claim for himself that he is acting in God's stead."[32]

## 11. The Lost Coin (Luke 15:8-10)

The parable of the lost coin (lit.: "lost drachma") is found only in Luke's gospel, where it forms a double parable with that of the lost

---

[32] Joachim Jeremias, *The Parables of Jesus*, rev. ed., trans. S. H. Hooke (New York: Charles Scribner's Sons, 1962), 132.

sheep. As we have already seen in the case of the treasure in the field and the pearl, the coupling of two parables establishes a contrast: first the poor day-laborer, then the rich wholesaler; first the accidental finding of a treasure, and in contrast the long search for precious pearls.

There is a similar contrast in Luke 15:3-10: first the shepherd (who in Israel could only be male because he was outdoors and in motion all day), and then a woman who—except during the harvest—was more closely tied to the house. Thus we have before us a composition in which a man and a woman are placed alongside one another as "agents" of equal importance—something that was anything but taken for granted in those times! Since that juxtaposition of a man and a woman is found elsewhere in Jesus' speech as well—compare the double saying about the queen of the South and the Ninevites in Luke 11:31-32—there is some reason to think that this was a double parable from the outset: one about a lost sheep and one about a lost coin. Still, that is a question we can leave open! The parable of the lost coin reads:

> Or what woman having ten silver coins [= drachmas], if she loses one of them, does not light a lamp, sweep the house, and search carefully until she finds it? When she has found it, she calls together her friends and neighbors, saying, "Rejoice with me, for I have found the coin that I had lost." Just so, I tell you, there is joy[33] in the presence of the angels of God over one sinner who repents.

As with the lost sheep, the parable begins as a question, and as before the climax of the text is joy—joy at what has been found after such a laborious search. That is so obvious in the text that nothing more needs to be said—and yet some information about the social background of the parable can shed more light on the reason for the rejoicing.

The fact is, this woman is destitute. Her house does not even have windows; light comes only through the door. She has to light a tiny oil lamp in order to see anything, and since that is not enough she has to sweep the earthen floor and poke into the corners so that, just maybe, she will hear the coin clink against the rocky ground.

---

[33] The Greek text has the future tense here, but the reference is not to the final judgment: it is about every sinner who now (in the hour of Jesus' preaching) repents. Whenever a sinner repents, joy will rule in heaven.

Above all: what was the value of the lost coin? Still today women in some places wear gold or silver coins as adornment for their hair or as necklaces. Those are wedding gifts or were acquired as capital for use in time of need. What the woman in the parable has lost and what is so precious to her is a drachma: a silver coin worth approximately one denarius. That is not a small thing, but it is not much. A sheep was worth eight drachmas; a lamb could be had for four.[34] For this poor woman, at any rate, that one drachma was extraordinarily precious. The ten drachmas were apparently her security against evil days. Only in light of that situation can we understand her joy over the painfully sought and finally recovered coin.

When Jesus has related this seeking and finding—or, better, when he has sketched it, for here again he keeps it very brief because he has no need to describe the situation—once the sketch is finished he orchestrates it somewhat more fully. He ends the parable with a real Near Eastern scene: the woman runs to her neighbors. The story has to be told and dramatically described. Her listeners join with her in rejoicing—though the story does not tell of their shared joy since everyone can imagine it.

Instead of a scene of rejoicing there is an even fuller orchestration: The scene widens to reveal the joy in heaven, where the angels rejoice just as the woman does. According to a gorgeous statement by Karl Barth the angels play before God on their instruments nothing other than Johann Sebastian Bach (only in private do they play Mozart). So the broader scene shows the whole heavenly court, with God enthroned at its center. There—and that also means, naturally, in the heart of God—great joy reigns, just as with the woman, because the woman's joy and that of her friends has become an image of the joy in heaven over every sinner who is found or, from the sinner's point of view, every sinner who allows herself to be found.

## 12. The Lost Son (Luke 15:11-32)

Indescribable joy abounds in heaven over every individual sinner who allows himself to be found: that is, who repents. So says the "application" of the parable of the lost coin. How such repentance can look, concretely, is illustrated by the parable of the lost son, which Luke adds next:

---

[34] Cp. Marius Reiser, "Numismatik und Neues Testament," *Bib* 81 (2000): 457–88.

There was a man who had two sons. The younger of them said to his father, "Father, give me the share of the property that will belong to me." So he divided his property between them.[35] A few days later the younger son gathered all he had and traveled to a distant country, and there he squandered his property in dissolute living. When he had spent everything, a severe famine took place throughout that country, and he began to be in need. So he went and hired himself out to one of the citizens of that country, who sent him to his fields to feed the pigs. He would gladly have filled himself with the pods that the pigs were eating; and no one gave him anything.[36] But when he came to himself he said, "How many of my father's hired hands have bread enough and to spare, but here I am dying of hunger! I will get up and go to my father, and I will say to him, 'Father, I have sinned against heaven and before you; I am no longer worthy to be called your son; treat me like one of your hired hands.'" So he set off and went to his father. But while he was still far off, his father saw him and was filled with compassion;[37] he ran and put his arms around him and kissed him. Then the son said to him, "Father, I have sinned against heaven and before you; I am no longer worthy to be called your son." But the father said to his slaves, "Quickly, bring out a robe—the best one—and put it on him; put a ring on his finger and sandals on his feet. And get the fatted calf and kill it, and let us eat and celebrate; for this son of mine was dead and is alive again; he was lost and is found!" And they began to celebrate.

Now his elder son was in the field; and when he came and approached the house, he heard music and dancing. He called one of the slaves and asked what was going on. He replied, "Your brother has come, and your father has killed the fatted calf, because he has got him

---

[35] The juridical implication of this statement is that probably the younger son receives a significant lump sum and in return renounces his right to inherit, while the older son receives the full right of inheritance. At any rate, that interpretation fits v. 31: "all that is mine is yours."

[36] That is how this sentence is presented in nearly every translation, but it does not make sense. Who could prevent a swineherd from simply taking part of the pigs' food? He's not being watched every minute. Might it originally have read: "for no one gave him anything to eat"? We have to leave the question open; in any case the import of the statement is clear: the man is in great distress.

[37] Some translations (e.g., the German *Einheitsübersetzung*) read something like "he felt pity [or: compassion] for him." That is too weak. From the Greek text it should at least read "He was seized with compassion." This is about more than "pity." The compassion (= suffering with) pictured here is σπλάγχνον, an emotional response that shakes the person at depth, in the gut (or, as frequently in Scripture, in the *womb*).

back safe and sound." Then he became angry and refused to go in. His father came out and began to plead with him. But he answered his father, "Listen! For all these years I have been working like a slave for you, and I have never disobeyed your command; yet you have never given me even a young goat so that I might celebrate with my friends. But when this son of yours came back, who has devoured your property with prostitutes, you killed the fatted calf for him!" Then the father said to him, "Son, you are always with me, and all that is mine is yours. But we had to celebrate and rejoice, because this brother of yours was dead and has come to life; he was lost and has been found."

The artistry of the narrative itself commands our admiration here. Obviously the narration comes not only from Jesus but also from Luke, who was himself a competent storyteller. It is no accident that many famous pictures in the great museums of the Western world are based on stories by the evangelist Luke. When, in the middle and at the end of the parable, the father says "[he][38] was dead and [is alive again];[39] he was lost and has been found" (Luke 15:24, cp. v. 32) the formulation comes from Luke; we know that because the keyword "found" links the parable of the lost son to those about the lost sheep and the lost coin (cp. Luke 15:5-6, 9). This linking of the three parables had to be done by Luke, who most certainly worked over the text of our parable. Still, on the whole it is a text that comes from Jesus. Perhaps we could say that the genius of the master left traces on the work of his successors as well.

But now, finally, let us turn to the parable itself! I will begin with the less important matter, though it is really not unimportant at all. With this parable as with others, despite its length, a lot has been left out. For example, the mother of the lost son is completely invisible. She never appears. Why? Introducing her would have made the narrative thread more complicated. It is in the nature of good parables to show an utterly simple plotline. Hence the number of characters is always limited, and therefore a lot that needs explanation is left to the imagination of the listeners—and to their knowledge as well! They didn't need to have it explained because it was all part of their everyday world. For us, on the other hand, explanation is required.

---

[38] Verse 24 "this son of mine"; v. 32 "this brother of yours."

[39] So v. 24; in v. 32 the NRSV reads "has come to life." The Greek wording is nearly identical in the two verses.

Thus everyone at that time understood the symbolic quality of the father's gestures and actions when he sees his returning son. The first is that he runs to meet him. That must have made a profound impression on Jesus' hearers, because no Near Eastern man "runs" in such a situation, most certainly not the head of the family. He would stand in front of his house, awaiting the new arrival with dignity and at the most taking a symbolic step in his direction. But not only that: this father has already embraced and kissed his son before the latter can utter a single syllable. Still more: he interrupts the son's confession of guilt and orders that a festal garment, a ring, and shoes be brought for him, and he orders the slaughter of the fatted calf.

The meaning of these actions would have been clear to the audience: by embracing his son the father prevents him from falling on his knees and kissing his feet. The father's kiss honors his son and receives him back into the family. The ring bears a seal, and the robe is the best and most beautiful garment reserved for feasts. Still more: the killing of the fatted calf signifies that a feast is to be celebrated, a real Near Eastern festival with good food and with singing and dancing that will go on late into the night.

We have an idea of what a "fatted calf" is, but not a precise picture. In detail, it was this way: in biblical times calves were fed green fodder. Only the calves chosen (by wealthy people) to be fattened for a feast were given grain as well. Evidently in the context of our parable there is only one fatted calf, which makes it clear what this father is willing to offer for this feast.

Another detail in the story is rather foreign to us: we hear that the younger son, when he got into trouble in foreign parts, got work on an estate where he took care of the pigs. For Jesus' audience that made it crystal clear: this young man was absolutely finished. He had not only squandered the portion of the estate allotted to him; he had also lost his faith. That is obvious because he turned to a Gentile for help (no Jew would be raising pigs), and no Jew in the employ of a Gentile could live his faith. Among the Gentiles there was no kosher food, no Sabbath, no way of keeping the law. So Jesus' hearers understood that this man no longer had any respect for the law or for God. He is at an end in every respect. His whole misery is exposed when verse 15 says: "He would gladly have filled himself with the pods that the pigs were eating; and no one gave him [anything]." Here, too, every hearer knew what was going on. The "pods" are those of the carob tree, whose outer hulls are leathery and hard to digest. They were primarily fed to animals, but poor people also ate them in times of need when there was nothing else. The younger son is really finished.

So much for certain realities in the text! More important are observations about the way the narrative thread runs in the parable. I have already referred to the entire erasure of the mother. That allows for the father alone to run to meet his son, and what is important here is how the encounter between father and son is staged.

Before this encounter the lost son has pictured his miserable situation in an "inner monologue." He has already rehearsed what he will say to his father on his return. When he finally stands before his father he repeats in detail what he had planned—but with a crucial difference: his father does not let him recite his speech to the end. He interrupts him by telling the servants to give him new clothes.

Those orders to the servants are themselves an important narrative detail, not only because they avoid a dialogue with the son that would have retarded the narrative instead of advancing it. The father's orders to the servants whereby he interrupts his son's confession of guilt are a much better demonstration of the father's attitude than any dialogue could have produced. He acts out of unspeakable joy. Nothing at all is said about the son's guilt; it is no longer part of the story.

The fact that the narrator does not permit a dialogue between father and son at this point does even more. It creates space for something different and more important to the narrative: throughout the whole parable the father is the only one who acts. By interrupting his son's speech he seizes the initiative, as he had already done before: he ran to meet his son. In fact, the father's initiative began even earlier: the text says "while he was still far off, his father saw him."

Here depth psychology, for once, has its place. Why does the father see the son when he is still far off? It could be accidental, but at the same time it shows that this father was expecting his son; he yearned for him; his very yearning had drawn the son back. Misery and hunger were not the only reasons why the son returned home.

We should also notice that the father not only goes to meet his *younger son*. He does the same for his *elder son*: he leaves the feast and goes out to him. He does not summon him into the house. Here, too, the father keeps the initiative.

Consider also that the narrator constructs a fairly long dialogue between the father and the elder son, the only dialogue in the whole parable. That, of course, is no accident. The narrator devotes so much time to that dialogue because the elder son's words and attitude precisely embody those of Jesus' opponents among the Pharisees. All of it is so carefully attuned and so artfully told that no one but Jesus can be the narrator.

However, there are a number of other fine points in this parable. For example, the older son disrespectfully interrupts his father's pleading with him, and he speaks not of his "brother" but instead of "this son of yours." The father corrects that condescending expression and says "this brother of yours." We could collect a whole series of such observations: for example, what the servant tells the older brother and what he omits. This parable is both a literary and a theological work of art. We should notice how the father tries to justify his actions to his older son. He says: "we had to celebrate and rejoice, because this brother of yours was dead and has come to life; he was lost and has been found."

It may be that these words most profoundly characterize the father: after all, what he states is not really a justification. It is a helpless attempt to make his joy comprehensible to the elder son, who is full of bitterness and outrage. "We had to celebrate and rejoice." This almost touching defenselessness shows more than all the rest: this father is a lover, one who is moved to the depths of his heart. After all, love always includes defenselessness, the sister to self-surrender. It often makes true love look like foolishness.

All that being said, one should not get the impression that this parable is only about the father's initiative; there is also an initiative on the part of the son. It was he who had to look his real situation in the face. It was he who had to grasp that he was guilty of leading a dissolute life. It was he who had to repent. It was he who had to take the road back to his father. And it was he who made a confession of guilt. We dare not minimize or set aside any of that; it is also theologically significant. The younger son really turns back, even in the literal sense. He regrets what he has done and pleads for forgiveness—in fact, he begs God for forgiveness ("I have sinned against heaven")—and at the same time he entreats his father for forgiveness. We must never reduce Jesus' longer parable stories to a single point, a single *tertium comparationis*. These are stories, after all, narratives with all the complexity that belongs to a good story.

In spite of what I have just written, I still contend that it is the father who takes the initiative, and the parable is dominated by the father's actions. The father is the real actor, the agent in the story, and it would be more proper to name the parable not for the lost son but for the father. Only the father appears in all five scenes in the story.

In addition we need to take another look at the two parables that precede this one: the man who has a hundred sheep and loses one arises and goes after the lost sheep till he finds it. Who takes the initiative: the sheep or the shepherd? It is just the same with the woman who has ten drachmas and loses one; she goes in search of the lost drachma until she finds the coin that is so precious to her.

Thus again, in the linked series Luke has created, the parable of the lost son is primarily and above all about the father's initiative. The parable itself affirms it; the father says, "My son was lost and is found." The three parables are tightly linked; ultimately their intent is to say the same thing.

Certainly we have to ask ourselves: is this just Luke's theology, or is there an internal connection among the three parables beyond that of Lukan redaction? If so, is it a connection that already existed for Jesus? It would have to have been carried out in Jesus' real practice.

Certainly there was such a real practice in the life of Jesus! The three parables reflect precisely what Jesus did. He went after the lost and the sinners (Luke 19:1-10). He ate with sinners and the despised (Mark 2:15). He defended them against their accusers and those who looked down on them (Mark 2:17). The three parables in Luke 15 reveal a strong link to Jesus' own way of life. That, too, binds them together.

Here another question arises: who is the father in the parable, Jesus or God? Obviously the father in our text represents God. The parable of the lost son intends to say: this is how God is. God looks with love even on those burdened with guilt, those who are lost. God is overcome with joy when one who is lost returns. God forgives unconditionally and without asking for reparation. God forgives even when human beings can no longer do so. The father in the parable mirrors God.

Still, that is not saying enough, because at the same time the father represents Jesus. In these three parables Jesus is defending his attitude and actions toward sinners against the charges of his opponents. He justifies his own practice. More precisely: he justifies his actions by pointing to God. What Jesus does is completely transparent toward *God*. We simply cannot separate Jesus' actions from those of God.

So Jesus justifies his own actions against his opponents by telling about how God acts. What, more precisely, were his opponents' objections? As we have seen, Luke formulated the charge this way at the beginning of the three parables of the lost: "This fellow welcomes sinners and eats with them" (Luke 15:2).

We should not dismiss such a claim too rapidly. When the Pharisees and scribes kept their distance from public sinners they were trying to live according to Psalm 1, which is placed as an epigraph at the beginning of the whole Psalter:

> Happy are those
> > who do not follow the advice of the wicked,
> > or take the path that sinners tread,
> > > or sit in the seat of scoffers;
> > but their delight is in the law of the LORD,
> > and on his law they meditate day and night. (Ps 1:1-2)

This speaks of sinners from whom one should distance oneself, and the men and women with whom Jesus sat and ate were just such sinners. It would be wrong to make light of their lives or romanticize them. Jesus did not do that, either. But still: he ate with them. "Eating with them" is by no means a way of making contact for pastoral purposes. It means more than that, namely, God's acceptance of them. It means: "God is turning to *you*. God's whole love belongs to *you*."

We have to see precisely where Jesus' opponents took offense. What they saw as scandal was not that God can forgive even serious sin. People in Israel had always believed that. What embitters the Pharisees and scribes here is that salvation is being promised to people who have not changed their ways at all. In the eyes of Jesus' opponents, repentance is something different. It is hard work on oneself, unconditional return to Torah and complete restitution. Only then could one hope to receive God's mercy.

The elder son reflects that position to the last detail. He thinks in the categories of a fixed and unrelenting order of law. The one who owes must pay. The one who has caused damage must make restitution. Someone who has lived a life like that of his brother must not have it too easy. Such a person must first demonstrate that he or she has really changed. A few years as a wage worker with the hope of eventually receiving full pardon would be just the thing for him. But to receive him back into the family immediately—and not only that, making a feast for him—seems utterly unheard-of. Wouldn't that be to declare his own reliability and correctness meaningless?

So in the end the question remains: will the elder son (and those he embodies) remain outside, trapped in bitterness, or will he realize that his father is acting on a level that far surpasses the usual reflexes and morality (that is, that the sinner must first demonstrate his or her repentance)? Will he perhaps even take note that the Psalter contains not only Psalm 1 but also Psalm 103, where it is said of God:

> He does not deal with us according to our sins,
>     nor repay us according to our iniquities.
> For as the heavens are high above the earth,
>     so great is his steadfast love toward those who fear him;
> as far as the east is from the west,
>     so far he removes our transgressions from us. (Ps 103:10-12)

How will the elder son behave? Will he remain bitter toward his father, or in the end will he, after all, join in the feast that has already begun? Some interpreters say that with his sharp reproaches to his father the elder son has spoken his definitive "no." He has denied himself the festal joy and he will remain fixed in his denial.

But does that interpretation fit the story? After all, the father is fighting for his elder son. He does not condemn him. He does not shut him out. He pleads for understanding. Above all, he does not punish him for staying away. That in itself favors an open-ended parable. But more than that: if everything were already settled here, why didn't Jesus say so? He could have ended the parable with the statement, "But he turned away and did not join in the feast." As the text stands, the ending remains open, and in that way it becomes Jesus' wooing of his opponents. It is, in fact, an entreaty in the form of a story, a plea that they might understand his actions toward sinners and thus the action of God.

In closing our look at this longest of Jesus' parables, let me say this: I emphasized with regard to the group of parables of growth that Jesus remains within the realm of reality and permits himself no fantasizing; otherwise he could not have convinced his audience. But in light of the parable of the lost son the question arises once again: is this parable also true to reality, or does it somehow rupture it?

We shouldn't make things too easy for ourselves. The misery into which the younger son fell when he was in foreign parts is quite dramatic, but it does not seem in any way artificial. That is how it may turn out when a young woman or man leaves the family and goes abroad. It happened often in Israel in those days because the land was impoverished and the better opportunities for a good life in the Diaspora were tempting. The elder son's reaction is also well within the realm of the possible. He represents a world in which achievement and good behavior are fundamental, and with them the unrelenting connection between deeds and consequences.

But the father's attitude positively turns this world upside down. Isn't it true that here, in the person of the father, the new world of the reign of God breaks through in the midst of the story world? Does that violate the plane of the imagery and its reality? At this point does the parable demand that its hearers accept unreality?

On the other hand: if Jesus were arguing here in extravagant terms, even unrealistically, could he hope to convince his hearers, and above all his opponents? It is true that the father's behavior is unusual, disquieting, almost frightening in its defiance of the norm. But isn't that what happens everywhere in the world, at least *in nuce*, when real love happens—self-surrendering and self-forgetting love? Is there no such thing as love like that? Would those listening to the parable necessarily have found the father's love unreal and inappropriate?

We must, of course, reckon with the fact that parables do not remain within the world of their imagery with mathematical exactness. We have to expect that they do not always comply with the formal rules constructed by biblical scholars. Certainly in the poor man's lamb (2 Sam 12) the prophet does not attempt to formulate a parable true to its genre in every detail. We already saw that in that case the "pure" genre of the parable was shattered. The lamb drinks from the poor man's cup at mealtime and lies in his bosom (2 Sam 12:3). That is, here the imagery is utterly transparent to the subject: the marriage of Uriah and Bathsheba. The case is similar with the song of the vineyard (Isa 5:1-7). So we have to reckon with the possibility that the world of God may breach the imagery in some of Jesus' parables also. If that happens, it must be pointed out in each case.

For the present I would like to leave the whole of this very difficult but also extremely revealing question open. I expect we will find Jesus parables in which reality is not in any way disturbed, but there may also be Jesus parables in which that very thing happens. The whole question will arise again in the very next parable. There, too, the story is about the profound disturbance, indeed, the disruption, that happens when God's new world breaks into ours and calls into question the rituals and models we have so laboriously constructed.

## 13. The Laborers in the Vineyard (Matthew 20:1-16)

The great parable of the laborers in the vineyard is found only in Matthew's gospel. We do not know where he got it; it is certainly not from Q. Thus it appears that there were Jesus texts in circulation and being carefully handed down even outside Mark and Q. The last sentence of the parable, about the "first" who will be "last," was very probably added to the parable as a "commentary" in an early stage of transmission. It would have been a freely-circulating saying of Jesus (cp. Mark 10:31; Luke 13:30) that does not really fit the parable. The introduction, "for the kingdom of heaven is like," probably comes from Matthew.

> For the kingdom of heaven is like a landowner who went out early in the morning to hire laborers for his vineyard. After agreeing with the laborers for the usual daily wage, he sent them into his vineyard. When he went out at about nine o'clock [the third hour], he saw others standing idle in the marketplace; and he said to them, "You also go into the vineyard, and I will pay you whatever is right." So they went. When he went out again about noon and about three o'clock [around the sixth and the ninth hour], he did the same. And about five o'clock [around the eleventh hour] he went out and found others standing around; and he said to them, "Why are you standing here idle all day?" They said to him, "Because no one has hired us." He said to them, "You also go into the vineyard." When evening came, the owner of the vineyard said to his manager, "Call the laborers and give them their pay, beginning with the last and then going to the first." When those hired about five o'clock came, each of them received the usual daily wage [a denarius]. Now when the first came, they thought they would receive more; but each of them also received the usual daily wage [a denarius]. And when they received it, they grumbled against the landowner, saying, "These last worked only one hour, and you have made them equal to us who have borne the burden of the day and the scorching heat." But he replied to one of them, "Friend, I am doing you no wrong; did you not agree with me for the usual daily wage [a denarius]? Take what belongs to you and go; I choose to give to this last the same as I give to you. Am I not allowed to do what I

choose with what belongs to me? Or are you envious because I am generous?" So the last will be first, and the first will be last.

The parable probably takes place at the time of the harvest, the "crush." The grapes are ripe and must be gathered as swiftly as possible. Every hour counts. Of course it is odd, and it sounds unrealistic, that the landowner repeatedly goes to the marketplace, but it is not altogether distant from reality because in the case of a very large vineyard it often becomes apparent, as the work goes on, that a good many laborers will still be needed; those already engaged will not suffice.[40]

Probably, after all, we shouldn't even ask such questions, since the parable-teller evidently wasn't concerned with them. So we have to restrain ourselves from wanting to fill in some of the gaps in the course of the action. The thread of the narrative is as taut as it can be and has no room for imaginative additions.

Thus, for example, the parable has nothing to say about the discussions between the individual laborers and the landowner. In reality he would surely have given his manager the task of paying the workers. How is it, then, that he suddenly reappears in the action? Did a delegation of workers descend on him? Or was he present from the outset when they were paid off? It is futile to speculate about these things. The parable is not interested in such details; they would only distract us and are best set aside.

The mood that pervades the whole parable is another matter; it needs consideration because in this parable we cannot find the least hint of the joy that marked the days of the grape harvest in ancient Israel. There is nothing of the happy shouting that rang out over the vineyards, none of the blessings shouted at the harvesters by passersby (Ps 129:7-8). The parable presumes a grey, matter-of-fact environment in which work is nothing but toil.

The reason is pretty clear: Jesus' parables offer us an astonishingly accurate picture of the social conditions in Palestine in the first century CE. The times when free farmers in Israel joyfully harvested their own vineyards lay in the past. Most of them had long since lost

---

[40] This is an important point noted by Wolfgang Harnisch, *Die Gleichniserzählungen Jesu. Eine hermeneutische Einführung*, UTB 1343 (Göttingen: Vandenhoeck & Ruprecht, 1985), 179.

their land to wealthy estate owners. The Romans and the minor officials subject to them demanded such high taxes and fees that every operation had to be extremely profitable and so was forced to streamline production. Effectively, then, agricultural enterprises had to be large, and they needed a cheap workforce: either slaves or underpaid day-laborers. Family farms were scarcely able to make ends meet any longer, and many of the former owners of such farms worked by the day. They were hired in the morning at the market and were paid off in the evening. Work went on from sunrise to sunset, from daybreak to full dark.

In such a workday a laborer earned just about enough to feed the family for another day. If such a worker was not hired in the morning, the children in that family would go hungry the next day. The parable reflects those conditions; it was a joyless work world, and to that extent Jesus is being completely realistic.

Therefore we have no reason to look down on the laborers hired at the first hour when they demand a fair wage system. From their point of view they are altogether in the right. It is true that a denarius was not a bad wage for a day's work and probably more than the norm. But for the last hired, who had worked only an hour in the cool of the late afternoon, to be paid just as much as those who had suffered the day's heat over long hours was not only unjust but inhuman. That is how the "first" thought. Weren't they right?

Every society, even the basest slave-state, survives only because some degree of justice is preserved. Without that the society will break apart. In that light we can understand the angry protest of the worker who evidently becomes a spokesperson for the others. And in that light the end of the parable is, at first glance, "impossible."

In the case of this parable we really have to ask: doesn't it rupture the plane of realistic imagery and construct something unreal? We could put it this way: the parable that began so realistically now suddenly reveals its subtlety; in an instant, in the middle of the everyday grayness, something new explodes into history—something totally unusual that not only upsets the characters in the parable but startles the listeners as well.

Obviously we could argue that even such a benefactor as the landowner in the parable is not completely impossible. He could exist. But it seems that Jesus here permits himself a narrative that deliberately rolls over into the surreal. And it is no accident that he does it precisely *here*. He did not allow it in his parables of growth, where he spoke of natural processes that had to be described with precision and in detail. This parable, on the other hand (and the same is true for the lost son), is about people—human beings with their cryptic natures, their limitations, their "evil eyes," but also their unfathomable generosity—and it is precisely in this area that Jesus can afford a story that leaps into things unusual, even startling or upsetting. This is the only way he can express the outrageousness he is about.

Only when we are clear about all that can we gain access to the real meaning of the story, for in it two worlds—or we could say two different forms of society—are in collision.

On the one hand the parable soberly and realistically describes the old society that always gets the upper hand, even in the place where Jesus wants to assemble the people of God anew. In that society it's every man or woman for him- or herself and everyone struggles for her or his own existence. In it there is envy when one has more. It is the endless conflict between those "on top" and those "on the bottom." And rivalry exists also—perhaps even more—between those who belong to the same social class. Their constant comparing of themselves with others leads to ongoing mistrust and enduring power struggles.

To keep such struggles at least somewhat in check there is law, one of the most valuable of all human achievements. It is quite right that workers in that kind of society fight for their rights. In a world built on rivalries they have no other choice.

The mastery of the parable consists precisely in the fact that, with the greatest economy of means, it shows how God's new world suddenly erupts into the old society, because the story turns out quite differently from what the listeners expected. They had supposed that the last, who were idle almost all day, would receive only a few copper coins. That they received just as much as the first must have been a shock to Jesus' listeners. The bottom dropped out from under them. All familiar standards were snatched away. But if they open themselves to the parable they fall—not into the abyss; rather, their feet then rest on the land where God reigns, God's new society.

In the reign of God, different rules apply. Certainly work goes on from morning till evening here as well. God's world is no Lotusland. But here work has dignity, and no one need go home in the evening full of care and anxiety. No one is alone any longer. But above all: it is possible to live without rivalries, and that is because there is something here that is greater and more expansive than all private desires: work for God's cause. It is precisely this common cause, desired by all, that creates a solidarity making it possible to share in others' suffering and rejoice in the joys of others.

In the parable, certainly, that new society has not yet come to be; it is only visible in a preliminary way in the landowner, who—contrary to all experiences in the old society—is "good" (Matt 20:15). The Greek text has ἀγαθός for "good," and generally it is translated "generous" in this passage: "are you envious because I am generous?" That, at any rate, is how the NRSV has the landowner speak to one of the agitated laborers.

A literal translation of the Greek text, however, reads "is your eye evil because I am good?"[41] That is not exactly the same, because the basic meaning of *agathos* is "good" in the sense of "useful," "suitable," "excellent," "proper." When the landowner pays the last as much as the first he is acting "properly," rationally, and therefore well. Certainly he is not acting "rationally" according to the rules of a society shaped by battles over distribution; his actions are rational by the rules of the reign of God. Jesus was the first to fully grasp the rationality of the reign of God. That is reflected, for example, in the demands of the Sermon on the Mount, in the theme of "nonviolence" (Matt 5:38-42). That is the only way to create real peace. In principle Jesus rejected any kind of violence or force in the reign of God and so initiated an unforeseeable future history. Thus he is the suitable, the excellent human being.

Once again, at the moment when Jesus told the parable the new thing had not yet spread; it was visible, but provisionally: only in himself, the one most suitable for the reign of God. But it would soon become visible also in his disciples and sympathizers, namely, in the rare moments in which they abandoned their own rivalries and aided one another in solidarity.

All that probably makes it clear that we are missing the point of the parable if we see its theme as nothing more than the overabundant beneficence of God. Certainly its ultimate statement is about God's limitless and undeserved kindness, but if that were the only message

---

[41] See NRSV *ad loc.*, note c.

of the parable it would remain completely nonbinding. Everyone who believes in God talks about God's goodness. Such talk costs nothing and changes nothing. If Jesus had only talked about God's generosity he would not have been nailed to the cross.

The grumbling of the laborers from the first hour reflects that of those among Jesus' contemporaries who were outraged at the new thing he was beginning with his disciples: a common life growing out of continual forgiveness and solidarity and in which, as a consequence, latecomers and sinners who had absolutely no merits to offer could also find a place.

Thus Matthew 20:1-16 is not about an abstract attribute of God. Jesus talks about God's limitless generosity solely from the point of view that this generosity has become reality since his own appearance and exists in the form of a new society that is beginning to grow around and through him.

The parable talks about how this new reality is breaking into the weariness and hopelessness of the people of God. It is a stupendous event. It puts the lowest on top, awakens hidden fears, evokes outrage. But it also allows hope to flower and bestows profound joy.

In the parable of the laborers in the vineyard Jesus depicts what is happening now, in this hour: the coming of the reign of God. He interprets, he shows what is already happening before the eyes of his hearers—its impetus still hidden and yet becoming visible. Therefore the parable does not offer timeless teaching. It uncovers things that are already happening, and in doing so it sets them free. A new way of living comes to light.

The listeners can engage with the thing the parable is talking about. They can enter into the story told in the parable and allow Jesus' words to put new ground under their feet. They can ask Jesus to accept them into his circle of disciples where the new thing is already starting to grow, or they can become sympathizers of the Jesus movement and so give support to the new world that is beginning there.

Thus Jesus' words are effective; they create reality, but not only in words. Jesus heals the sick, he drives out the demons in society. He begins to live a new society, together with his disciples.

In telling the parable of the laborers in the vineyard that so precisely describes the gloomy social circumstances of his time Jesus was certainly thinking also that the harvest season in Israel must finally become what, from God's point of view, it had always needed to be: a time of jubilation and cries of joy. He also thought that now, with the Good News of the reign of God, must finally be fulfilled what Israel's Torah had always sought: sisterhood and brotherhood, equality and freedom.[42]

## 14. The Judge and the Widow (Luke 18:1-8)

The parable of the judge and the widow comes to us only from Luke. It is significantly shorter than the one about the laborers in the vineyard. There we saw that a narrator can work with "gaps" and need not develop and ground everything in detail. That frugality in narration is all the more evident in the parable of the judge and the widow.

> In a certain city there was a judge who neither feared God nor had respect for people. In that city there was a widow who kept coming to him and saying, "Grant me justice against my opponent [in court]." For a while he refused; but later he said to himself, "Though I have no fear of God and no respect for anyone, yet because this widow keeps bothering me, I will grant her justice, so that she may not wear me out by continually coming [lit.: come and give me a black eye]." (Luke 18:2-5)

Is that the end of the story? If so there were probably a lot of listeners who were irritated and asked, "Is that really all there is? Of course it is clear that the widow gets her rights, but it would be nice to hear all about it, and to have more details about the case at issue."

But the listeners' expectations are disappointed. The story goes no further, and it does not need to because it has already said everything; all that remains is for it to be interpreted. So this is not a straightforward narrative. There is an "introduction," then a presentation of the two "actors," and then nothing but an "internal monologue" on the part of the judge—and within that monologue comes the crucial part of the story. Jesus' narrative technique is highly refined.

To begin with let us look at the first part of the parable. Two people appear: a judge and a widow. The judge has no fear of God and cares nothing about the negative judgment of other people. Probably that

---

[42] Cp. Gerhard Lohfink, *Im Ringen um die Vernunft: Reden über Israel, die Kirche und die europäische Aufklärung* (Freiburg: Herder, 2016), 15–22.

means he is willing to accept bribes and has a bad reputation on that account. But he cares nothing about his reputation.

Then the widow enters the picture. No one at that time needed an explanation about the status of widows: demographically speaking, there were far more widows then than there are now because women were significantly younger than their husbands when they married. Correspondingly, from a purely statistical point of view, they died later than their husbands. Wives rejected by their husbands were also counted as "widows." And since it was very difficult in antiquity for women to establish an independent existence, widows were often powerless and fell into the hands of others. They were especially vulnerable in the courts of law, particularly since they were not permitted to appear in person.

It is no accident, then, that Jesus chooses a woman, not a man, as a contrast to the powerful figure of the judge, and not just any woman, but a widow. Thus it was clear to his hearers that this woman was helpless before the judge.

Given the presentation of the judge and the widow at the beginning of the parable, the ending already seems fairly clear. Won't the widow be defeated, as so many widows were in those days? We ourselves need only to open the Bible (Job 24:3; Ps 94:6; Sir 35:15-26; Isa 1:23; 10:1-2; Ezek 22:7, and so on). The people listening back then knew all about it without recourse to the Bible.

So how will the story end: Negatively for the widow? But could it be that God will intervene? Will something bad happen to the judge? Or will he repent and finally return to dispensing justice in the sense of Exodus 22:21-23? At the beginning of the parable there are still a lot of possibilities. The listeners are on tenterhooks and hope for an exciting story.

No such luck: they don't get to hear a story—or, more precisely, they hear a narrative, but it is packaged in the judge's internal monologue. That is the ingenuity of this parable. The judge's monologue shows that the woman is getting on the man's nerves. She is annoying because she keeps coming back and making trouble, and therefore he will finally give her justice so there won't be a public scene. The judge's monologue makes it clear—and this is the only thing that matters in this parable—that *this judge remains godless and without a conscience*. He will help the widow, but only because he can't take any more of her constant pleading and begging. He has simply had enough.

Thus the narrative is artfully structured, and its art consists above all in what it omits. Its language is interesting as well. Just to take one tiny detail: the Greek word for "hit in the face" (lit.: "smack under the eye") comes from the vocabulary of boxing. The judge is really afraid that it could come to a very ugly public scene that could result in his getting a black eye, with dreadful consequences for his reputation. So the parable gets a comic twist. The audience would most certainly have roared with laughter at this picture of the judge.

And what does Jesus mean to say with this parable? More precisely, what does the story have to do with the reign of God? Let me begin by repeating the observation that nothing really happens in the parable. The judge's internal monologue is central, and it characterizes him as a man who never changes. He is and remains without a conscience. He gives in only because the woman gets on his nerves. Thereby, of course, the scene presents us with a clear antithesis to God. The text of Sirach 35:15-19, for example, depicts God quite differently:

> for the Lord is the judge,
> and with him there is no partiality.
> He will not show partiality to the poor;
> but he will listen to the prayer of one who is wronged.
> He will not ignore the supplication of the orphan,
> or the widow when she pours out her complaint.
> Do not the tears of the widow run down her cheek
> as she cries out against the one who causes them to fall?

This text from Jesus ben Sirach, which can be read as a contrasting background to our parable, shows with crystal clarity that God is absolutely different from the judge in the parable. God listens to people and respects them, and when the oppressed cry to God for help they receive their rights from God.

The key point of the parable is couched in the kind of conclusion that was especially popular in Jewish parables: "from the lesser to the greater." If a judge who treads justice underfoot finally helps the widow, simply because he has had more than enough of her insistence, how much more will God help God's own when they cry for help. God will immediately give them justice. A "commentary" appended to the parable expresses precisely this crucial point:

> Listen to what the unjust judge says. And will not God grant justice to his chosen ones who cry to him day and night? Will he delay long in helping them? I tell you, he will quickly grant justice to them. (Luke 18:6-8)

The question, of course, is: *who* is saying that? In the gospel text Jesus says it as an application of and conclusion to the parable, but such commentaries were often added to Jesus' parables after the fact, as we already saw in the case of the laborers in the vineyard. These commentaries were designed to interpret the particular parable and apply it to the present. We can see the same thing here, but in this case the interpretation is so fitting that it could easily have come from Jesus himself. (Contrast the delay of the case on the part of the judge with God's acting "quickly.") Besides, the parable needs a conclusion. It is hard to imagine that Jesus did not interpret the story. Could it be, then, that the application in Luke 18:6-8 contains something[43] that belonged to the original parable discourse? We can leave that question open!

And now once again the question: what does all that say about the reign of God? That realm is a world-changing power. When God establishes sovereignty the world will be put in order, and God will show what was creation's intent. God will establish divine law and thus, at last, create justice for those who have no rights, the rejected and the raped. And they won't have to wait for it. The God who creates justice is already at work. The reign of God is breaking in, is already present. Human beings only have to open themselves to it, to ask for it. In the Our Father, Jesus even has his disciples explicitly pray for the coming of God's kingdom (Luke 11:2). Here, then, we are at the heart of Jesus' proclamation of the reign of God.

The context (Luke 18:1) shows that it was the evangelist Luke who made this parable about the reign of God into one about the need to pray without ceasing. In doing so, Luke accented and expanded an aspect that was already present in Jesus' parable. That he certainly could do. But originally the parable of the judge and the widow was directly about the reign of God.

---

[43] We are not dealing with v. 8c: "And yet, when the Son of Man comes, will he find faith on earth?" That part was most certainly added by Luke.

## 15. The Importunate Friend (Luke 11:5-8)

Closely related to the parable of the judge and the widow is the one about the importunate friend, again given only by Luke (and in *Gos. Thom.*). What relates the two parables so closely is especially the common theme of "asking," but not in the same form: the two are completely different in that respect. As we have seen, the parable of the judge and the widow centers on an "internal monologue" by the judge. In contrast, the first and longest part of the parable of the importunate friend consists of a single question:

> Suppose one of you has a friend, and you go to him at midnight and say to him, "Friend, lend me three loaves of bread; for a friend of mine has arrived, and I have nothing to set before him." And he answers from within, "Do not bother me; the door has already been locked, and my children are with me in bed; I cannot get up and give you anything." I tell you, even though he will not get up and give him anything because he is his friend, at least because of his persistence he will get up and give him whatever he needs. (Luke 11:5-8)

The interrogative in the first part of the parable is so long that at least *readers* might forget that it is still a question. Then in the second part the text expands the unimaginable condition even further! For someone to have to resort to a circumlocution of this sort in order to make the course of the argument clear goes against our modern sense of style. We would probably write something like this:

> Suppose that one of you had a friend and you would go to him around midnight and say to him: "Friend, lend me three loaves of bread—because a friend of mine is just passing through, and I have nothing to offer him." Can you imagine that he would answer from within: "Don't bother me! The door is long since locked, the children and I have gone to bed; I can't get up and give you [anything]"—is that even conceivable? No, that would be impossible!
>
> But even if, for once, we accept the unimaginable—namely, that the man does not get up and help because this is his friend—because of the noisy intrusion he would certainly get up and give whatever is needed.

The parable presumes the conditions in a closely-built village. There is no marketplace where one could buy something even late in the evening. So the case here postulated takes place in the country where every morning the village wives bake loaves for the day to come and where everyone knows who has something in her or his house; people know their neighbors. The house belonging to the friend who is being asked for help is, like nearly all the houses in the village, small and humble. It contains only one room that doesn't even have windows and is also the bedroom. The door is fastened with a beam passed through two large iron rings. The people who live here are extremely poor. The man who has been surprised by visitors has no food on hand. Here people literally live "from hand to mouth."

To understand the parable we also need to know something about the social significance of Near Eastern hospitality. A guest is entitled to more than just a place to sleep. It was then, and is now, a matter of course that any guest must be served, given the best that one has, and afforded whatever aid is necessary. The same is true not only for the host but for all the host's connections. Anyone who does not give aid to a guest or support someone who needs help because of a guest suffers a loss of honor. That one's reputation is besmirched forever.

Therefore it is impossible for the man who had long since gone to sleep, together with his family, not to help his friend. But Jesus even exaggerates the case by saying that even if the man would not get up because of the iron law of hospitality he would certainly do so because of the scene that would result from all the knocking and shouting in the middle of the night. It would be all over the village by morning.

This background in itself shows that the narrator could have presented the scene in much more colorful detail. For example, the late arrival of the guest who is passing through: nothing is said about the person's arrival at the point in the story where it belongs; it gets only passing mention in the host's plea. Likewise the wife of the disturbed sleeper does not appear, but only the children do. So the whole story is extremely compressed. It is condensed so that everything fits into the one question, one whose answer is obvious: no one would act that way. Everyone would get up and help.

Here, then, the argument is presented as indisputably obvious. And behind that argument—exactly as in the parable of the widow and the judge—lies a conclusion from the lesser to the greater: if, because of the law of hospitality, people can count on the help of others, how much more may Israel and every individual in it count on God. God will help those who belong to God when they are in need.

Obviously trust in God's help was a matter of course on the basis of the Old Testament; Jesus does not need to emphasize it. How often the psalms beg for divine help—and how often they speak of reliance on being heard! How often they speak of trusting in being heard *immediately*! Psalm 66:17 says: "I cried aloud to him, and he was extolled with my tongue [for having heard my plea]."

To repeat: trust in God's help was a thing taken for granted in light of the Old Testament. Jesus did not need to tell a parable about that. Therefore we need to read this parable in light of the reign of God, which Jesus proclaimed. The inbreaking reign of God radically intensifies what was already true in Israel: the intimacy of trust between human beings and God. All are now empowered to rely on God's action with unlimited trust, even with an urgent immediacy.

Luke focuses the whole story on prayer again: he places this parable immediately after the Our Father (11:2-4) and adds images of praying with childlike trust (11:9-13).

## 16. The Banquet (Luke 14:16-24)

With the parable of the banquet I am beginning a new series.[44] What they all have in common is a juxtaposition—either of two persons, as in the parable of the Pharisee and the tax collector (Luke 18:9-14); or within a whole group of people, as in the parable of the ten bridesmaids (Matt 25:1-13); or a polar opposition, as in the parable of the fishnet in which there are good and bad fish (Matt 13:47-48). There is always a contrast and almost always a separation.[45]

What I mean by contrast will be especially clear in the parable of the banquet. Here it is the difference between the wealthy invitees

---

[44] The parables of the lost son (Luke 15:11-32) and the judge and the widow (Luke 18:1-8) could also be included in this group, but in this volume, because of their theology, they are located elsewhere.

[45] Literary criticism, or more precisely parables theory, here speaks of a "dramatic triangle" consisting of the "sovereign actor" who dominates the whole parable and the opposing figures, presented as antithetical twins. In the parable of the banquet the householder is the sovereign actor and the people from the streets make up the second part of the twinned pair, contrasting with those first invited.

who do not come because they are busy with their own affairs and the poor and social outcasts who ultimately fill the banqueting hall:

> Someone gave a great dinner and invited many. At the time for the dinner he sent his slave to say to those who had been invited, "Come; for everything is ready now." But they all alike began to make excuses. The first said to him, "I have bought a piece of land, and I must go out and see it; please accept my regrets." Another said, "I have bought five yoke of oxen, and I am going to try them out; please accept my regrets." Another said, "I have just been married, and therefore I cannot come." So the slave returned and reported this to his master. Then the owner of the house became angry and said to his slave, "Go out at once into the streets and lanes of the town and bring in the poor, the crippled, the blind, and the lame." [Soon afterward] the slave said, "Sir, what you ordered has been done, and there is still room." Then the master said to the slave, "Go out into the roads and lanes, and compel [those you find] to come in, so that my house may be filled. For I tell you, none of those who were invited will taste my dinner." (Luke 14:16-24)

In the early church this was seen as one of the most important of Jesus' parables, but over the centuries it suffered, at least in part, from a horrifying course of interpretation. This parable especially, together with other gospel texts, was misused to prove that God had rejected Israel for all time. The last sentence in particular was interpreted in that sense, namely: "none of those who were *first* invited will taste my dinner."

This parable also appears in Matthew 22:1-10, but in a much-expanded and altered version. There the evening banquet has been transformed into a wedding feast prepared by a king for his son. Likewise, the nonappearance of those invited is described differently: they don't apologize; they are altogether indifferent to the invitation. Even when invited a second time they do not come. One goes to his farm, another to his business, still others—paradoxically—assault the servants sent with the invitation and kill them. That rouses the king to anger; he sends his army to lay the murderers' city in ashes. Only after that bloody intermezzo does the wedding feast take place; the servants go into the streets and bring everyone they can find into the banquet hall: "good and bad."

After that comes the part that always angers congregations who hear the parable in Matthew's version: one of those brought in to the feast is not wearing a wedding garment. At the king's command he is bound and cast into "the outer darkness," which the hearers or readers can only equate with eternal damnation. Hence the indignant question from today's churchgoers: "How can someone hauled in from the street (and from a burning city at that) own a wedding garment?"

It is quite clear that this expanded version of the parable is not from Jesus. The version we find in Matthew 22 was certainly worked over by pre-Matthean redactors and then by Matthew himself. He is looking back at the history of recent decades, from Jesus' appearance to his death and the persecution of the first messengers of the Gospel and then to the destruction of Jerusalem. Still more: he is reflecting on the problems of the Gentile church in which many who have undeservingly acquired entry into the people of God are living without their wedding garments—that is, without repentance and sanctification. Thus the elaborate description of the ejection of the unworthy guest.[46] In its Matthean version the parable condemns the high priests and elders, the Sadducees and Pharisees (cp. Matt 21:23, 45-46), but equally or even more sharply criticizes moral lassitude in the Gentile Christian communities. Obviously I hold to Luke's version in the context of this book. What does Luke tell us?

The parable begins in the world of the "best people," who are so wealthy that they can afford to put on a festive banquet with a relatively lengthy guest list. It is true that only three are mentioned, but they are representative for the others. We are already familiar with this "rule of three" in popular storytelling from the parable of the bramble (Judg 9:8-15) and the one about the abundant harvest (Mark 4:3-9).

The three invitees chosen from among the others are also wealthy types who fit within the host's social circle: the first has bought a field, and it is most certainly not a little garden plot. The second has acquired five yolk of oxen—that is, ten oxen yoked in pairs—a very lavish outlay. The third, finally, has taken a wife. At this point it is clear that we are dealing with an escalation: first the field, then ten oxen, then the wife who, if she is lovely and clever, has necessitated the payment of a high bride-price and many other expenses. So these invited guests are well-placed people.

---

[46] Here Matthew is adapting a parable that originated in another context: cp. no. 28 below.

Now the storyteller allows himself another "extravagance" such as I have spoken of before: those invited do not come—not a single one. They all make excuses. The parable began so realistically: that after the initial invitation the guests would be invited (or, better, "fetched") a second time, immediately before the banquet, was the general rule in urban circles (cp. Esth 6:14). And yet after this realistic introduction the parable seems suddenly to tip over into unreality. Could it happen that all those invited to a banquet would refuse? The parable-teller at this point intensifies matters.

Obviously everyone today who tries to understand the parable asks: why didn't the invitees say right away, after the first invitation, that they would be prevented from keeping the engagement? Let me try to answer that.

It is possible, regarding the sale of the field, that it had been paid for but from a legal standpoint only became the buyer's possession by his or her act of walking its boundaries. If that was supposed to take place in the presence of witnesses, the date for carrying it out would not have been known at the time of the invitation. We can speculate that something similar could be the case with the purchase of the oxen. Was it a requirement for completing the sale that the beasts had to be yoked and their performance tested in the presence of the buyer? Then, too, there could have been time conflicts. The Roman author Columella, at any rate, in his handbook on agriculture, describes at length what patience and effort were required to teach two animals to move steadily and at the same pace under the yoke. Hence the purchase of such a span would necessarily have been preceded by a demonstration of "moving under the yoke" (Columella, *De re rustica* 6.2). The seriousness of the excuse in the case of a marriage is altogether clear. It would not need to be about the wedding night itself; a Near Eastern wedding involved a multitude of unforeseeable preparations and negotiations.

All of these considerations show us, at best, that the refusals were not necessarily capricious. If they are accurate, the people declining the invitation were not just making lazy excuses. We owe them some consideration: the invitees acted within the routines with which we are all familiar and under the force of necessities that fall on all of us.

Despite all this their actions are rightly portrayed as wrong and reprehensible. They are showing contempt for a feast that really ought to have commanded their whole consideration and feelings. Their refusal is described as a catastrophe that evokes great wrath from the householder. That wrath then produces the contrasting event of which I spoke at the beginning: now the host invites the polar opposites of those "fine folks" to whom the invitation was initially given, namely, the poor and socially stigmatized people of the city.

Next comes an escalation that is lacking in Matthew: because there is still room, even the bedraggled folk from the roads and ditches *outside the city* are dragged into the banqueting hall. We can leave open the question whether this heightening was already part of the original Jesus-parable or not. I am more inclined to see it as an expansion of the original parable in light of the later mission to the Gentiles, but independently of this added quirk in the narrative the parable already contains enough problems.

How can we solve the puzzle of this peculiar story? We can do so only by answering the question: given the nature of this story, whose extravagance and boldness show that it must have come from Jesus, how did the original listeners react to it?

Did they suspect from the beginning that the story of a "festive meal" must be describing God's joyous banquet about which Scripture had already spoken (Isa 25:6-8)? The notion of an eschatological banquet must have been widely known even in contemporary Jewish society. At any rate, in the "introduction" to this parable Luke speaks about "eating bread in the kingdom of God" (14:15) as if it were a matter of course. Certainly that introduction in all probability comes from Luke, but for at least some among the listeners didn't the key words "great dinner" or "banquet" offer at least a clue that this would be about God's own eschatological banquet to come?

Or were the listeners shocked by the outrageous idea that *all* those invited had declined? Did they notice at that point that this could not be about a normal dinner party? Or was it only when the poor and despised were brought in that they realized that Jesus was speaking of his own way of acting, his going out to the shunned and rejected?

If they didn't get it by that point, still they must have been brought by the completely unrealistic closing words of the householder (none of those invited would taste of the dinner) to realize at last that this was about God and the terrible danger that Israel was spurning God's invitation now being issued through Jesus. That, at any rate, is the subject of our parable, and the audience's understanding would have come about at different times and at different points in the course of the parable.

One thing, at any rate, seems certain to me: a parable theory that does not account for several different metaphorical ignition points is inadequate—and that is true for almost all of Jesus' parables. This one contains a whole series of moments at which the image-level shifts, or could shift, to the "case" of the reign of God, and at which the listeners could therefore notice without any interpretation that this was about something other than the crazy story of a man who wanted more than anything else to have his banquet-hall full.

It is about much more than that. Hence the so startling unanimous refusal of the respectable; hence the partygiver's wrath; hence the invitation to the derelicts and then, at the end, the threat addressed no longer to the servant but to those hearing the parable: "I tell you, none of those who were invited will taste my dinner!"

As we look back over European history with its unbelievable persecutions of Jews by baptized Christians, we owe this parable in particular a closing remark. The narrative of the banquet in no way excludes Israel from salvation—not even in Matthew's version, which alongside its appeal to the Gentile Christians directs itself only to Jesus' *opponents* in Israel. The larger context in which Matthew has embedded it (Matt 21:23–23:39) is absolutely clear in showing that this is about Jesus' opponents and not the people as a whole.

We should also notice that the original parable is a moving and urgent appeal by Jesus to those in Israel who reject his message to repent and receive the Gospel. The parable is meant to shock and frighten; it is meant to warn, to reveal blindness, to lead to repentance. And still it utters no eschatological judgment. But above all: today the parable speaks to *us*, to us Christians, who find a thousand reasons to ignore the banquet offered to us.

## 17. The Fishnet (Matthew 13:47-50)

The parable of the fishnet is found in the canonical gospels only in Matthew,[47] where it concludes the first major parables composition

---

[47] Outside the canonical gospels the parable of the fishnet is also found in *Gos. Thom.* 8, there as a parable of a great fish that is preferred to all the smaller fish. That alteration of the material could point to a gnosticizing reshaping of the parable of the fishnet.

in that gospel, following those of the treasure in the field and the pearl (13:1-53).

> Again, the kingdom of heaven is like a net that was thrown into the sea and caught fish of every kind; when it was full, they drew it ashore, sat down, and put the good fish into baskets but threw out the bad. So it will be at the end of the age. The angels will come out and separate the evil from the righteous and throw them into the furnace of fire, where there will be weeping and gnashing of teeth. (Matt 13:47-50)

For the moment we have to ignore the interpretation Matthew gives this parable (vv. 49-50), because Matthew is here introducing a topic that is central for him: the judgment of the world (cp. Matt 8:12; 13:41-42; 22:13; 25:30, 41). We will have to see whether the subject of "world judgment" (or "last judgment") is simply equivalent to the theme of this Jesus parable. But first we should address the level of the imagery!

The "sea" is, of course, the Sea of Galilee (cp. Matt 4:18). The small fishing enterprises around the lake sometimes used casting nets but were primarily dependent on the much larger seines. A seine (or dragnet) had an upper rim that was kept on or near the surface by floats while the lower rim was loaded with stones or lead to make it sink. Then the whole net would be dragged by two boats in ever-narrowing circles toward the beach. Not all the marine creatures in the Sea of Galilee were regarded as edible. Small marine animals and every kind of fish that lacked fins or scales were regarded by Leviticus 11:9-12 as detestable and unclean; they therefore could not be eaten or sold.

Thus there are no difficulties on the image level. What Jesus describes, or rather tells here in the most succinct form possible, was familiar to every person in Galilee. If Jesus was on the beach when he spoke, it might be that those near him could watch fisherfolk at work while they were listening to him.

Jesus spoke clearly of the "gathering" of Israel. He said: "Whoever is not with me is against me, and whoever does not gather with me scatters" (Matt 12:30 // Luke 11:23). And as his situation grew more grave he said: "Jerusalem, Jerusalem . . . how often have I desired to gather your children together as a hen gathers her brood under her wings, and you were not willing!" (Matt 23:37 // Luke 13:34).

Moreover, in the prayer he taught his disciples he had them pray at the outset, in the very first petition, for the gathering and healing of the people of God, because the Our Father begins with an allusion to Ezekiel 36:22-28.

These words matched Jesus' actions: he accepted invitations from Pharisees (Luke 14:1), he debated with the Sadducees (Mark 12:18), he ate with tax collectors and sinners (Mark 2:15), he held up a Samaritan as a model (Luke 10:30-35), he accepted a Zealot into his closest circle of disciples (Luke 6:15), and above all he created the Twelve as a sign of his will to bring about the eschatological gathering of Israel, the people of the twelve tribes (Mark 3:13-19). Everything Jesus ever did must be understood as a signal of his unconditional will to call the people of God together, bringing it from brokenness to unity, and to gather it for the reign of God.

In the event, what took place was not only a gathering of Israel but a separation as well. What happened is nowhere more accurately formulated than in the words of Simeon in Luke 2:34: "This child is destined for the falling and the rising of many in Israel, and to be a sign that will be opposed." Especially in the leading circles of Jerusalem, but not only there, Jesus encountered bitter opposition that emerged more and more clearly.

Jesus' intent was not to divide but to unite. But where he encountered unbelief he created division, so that he himself was forced to say: "I came to bring fire to the earth, and how I wish it were already kindled!" (Luke 12:49). That "incendiary" statement is followed by a commentary: "Do you think that I have come to bring peace to the earth? No, I tell you, but rather division!" (Luke 12:51). Jesus was forced to experience division even within his own family (Mark 3:20-21).

It was a peculiar paradox: the one who desired to gather Israel, and did so, simultaneously divided it. There is much in favor of the idea that in the parable of the fishnet Jesus is describing exactly this paradox of gathering and dividing and is trying to make it comprehensible to his audience, because in the parable both things happen: first the gathering of the many fish in a single net—and then immediately the selection, and so the division.

It is better not to read the sorting out of the useless fish immediately and exclusively on a moral plane. First of all, we have here a perfectly simple description of the process of sorting: first the gathering and then, necessarily, the division. It seems that in this everyday aspect of the lives of fisherfolk Jesus has illustrated for himself and his audience a terrifying side of the reign of God. The presence of that reign that he proclaims—it gathers and creates community, but it inevitably leads also to definitive separations.

Matthew, in interpreting this division brought about in Israel by Jesus, speaks altogether and exclusively on the moral level, referring to the "evil" who will be thrown into the fiery oven (Matt 13:50). Obviously the division Jesus brings about in Israel traces ultimately to evil, to human enmity toward God. In that Matthew is quite right. But what Jesus has in mind is much more. It is not only the enemies of God who oppose God's reign. Also part of the picture is the broad front of sluggishness, inertia, lack of understanding, looking away, or complete indifference. Those who are characterized by those things are likewise "useless" for the reign of God and contribute to the fatal division. Besides all that, Matthew demands a complete and utter division at the final judgment, but that again is only a part of the reality. For Jesus the gathering and dividing of Israel are taking place already, in the hour of his appearance. The end-time event is happening in the world of today.

One final observation: in the Old Testament the one who scatters and gathers, brings together and divides, is God (Deut 20:3; Jer 31:10; Ezek 20:34-38, and frequently elsewhere). It is no different with Jesus, as the first petition of the Our Father shows—and yet Jesus, in his own person, gathers and divides, as if he stood in the place of God. We should pay attention to that background, too, in reading this parable. Here, as elsewhere, Jesus not only speaks about God's action but identifies it with his own.

## 18. The Weeds in the Wheat (Matthew 13:24-30)

As in the previous parable good and bad fish are contrasted, so the next one contrasts wheat and weeds. The parable of the weeds in the wheat is part of Matthew's special material. There is a parallel in the Gospel of Thomas (*Gos. Thom.* 57), but it is only a brief summary of the parable in Matthew 13:24-30. Matthew's text reads:

> The kingdom of heaven may be compared to someone who sowed good seed in his field; but while everybody was asleep, an enemy came

and sowed weeds [darnel] among the wheat, and then went away. So when the plants came up and bore grain,[48] then the weeds appeared as well. And the slaves of the householder came and said to him, "Master, did you not sow good seed in your field? Where, then, did these weeds come from?" He answered, "An enemy has done this." The slaves said to him, "Then do you want us to go and [pull up the weeds and] gather them?" But he replied, "No; for in gathering the weeds you would uproot the wheat along with them. Let both of them grow together until the harvest; and at harvest time I will tell the reapers, Collect the weeds first and bind them in bundles to be burned, but gather the wheat into my barn."

A lot of New Testament scholars have trouble with this parable. Some of the relevant books on parables do not even touch it. A whole group of interpreters find it unrealistic. They ask: who would ever get the idea of sowing darnel? One scholar even asks where the enemy would have gotten such a large amount of darnel seed.[49] That sort of consideration leads to suggestions that the parable should be shortened to make it easier to understand. The result is usually that the enemy who sows the darnel disappears along with the sowing of it. Quite a few interpreters go even further and deny that Jesus ever used this parable.

The main reason for this wrestling with the parable of the weeds, however, is that soon after, at 13:36-43, Matthew offers an extended interpretation of our parable that is a classic allegoresis. Readers are

---

[48] Literally "began to bear fruit" (ingressive aorist).

[49] Thus Ulrich Luz, *Matthew 8–20*, trans. James E. Crouch, Hermeneia (Minneapolis: Augsburg Fortress, 2000), 255 and n. 29. In regard to this objection, permit me a personal recollection. During World War II, because of the bombing raids on Frankfurt, I lived in the country, in the Rhön valley, where I helped a farmer every day on his little farm. In those days the grain was still scythed by the men, the women bound it into sheaves, and later it was threshed with flails on the threshing floor. My job was to sift the layer of grain that remained on the floor, using a big sieve I had to shake back and forth. The large grains remained in the sieve while the much smaller weed seeds fell through. In the end there was a pretty big heap of those seeds, which of course were burned or fed to the chickens and doves. The fields in those days (before herbicides) produced not only grain but a lot of weeds. How does Ulrich Luz know that it was not much the same in Israel's agriculture at that time—namely, that there was not only threshing and shoveling but sifting as well? For the subject of "sieves" and "sifting" see Gustav Dalman, *Arbeit und Sitte in Palästina*, vol. 3 (Hildesheim: Olms, 1964), 139–48.

presented with a long list of decoded words that are to be applied when reading, like this:

| | | |
|---|---|---|
| the householder | → | the Son of Man |
| the field | → | the world |
| the good seed | → | the children of the kingdom |
| the darnel | → | the children of the Evil One |
| the enemy | → | the devil |
| the harvest | → | the end of the world |
| the harvesters | → | the angels |

No wonder such allegorization became less and less acceptable in the wake of the European Enlightenment. The crucial step was taken, as we have said, by Adolf Jülicher. His two-volume book on parables, published in 1866 and 1899, sowed a profound resistance to any kind of allegorizing in the field of exegesis. In his time that was very much needed. But Jülicher tried to apply his radical cure to extirpate even the tiniest rootlets of allegory from Jesus' parables, and there he went wrong because he made Jesus' parables unapproachable. They resisted understanding and declined to the level of moral platitudes. Still: Matthew's excessive allegorization, especially in the case of the parable of the weeds, shares responsibility for the simplifications Jülicher applied.

But back to the text! The allegorization in Matthew 13:36-43 has shifted far too much emphasis to the harvest, which is broadly pictured as the end of the world and the final judgment. It is this point in particular that very probably has contributed to the reservations about the parable of the weeds that I described above. But the parable itself does not contain that heavy emphasis on the end of the world. Here the weight is not so much on the harvest as on the growth of wheat and weeds together *until the harvest*—and that interim period is entirely absent from Matthew's allegorizing interpretation. That means we must interpret the parable without any regard for its allegorization.

I have already indicated that quite a few interpreters have problems with the enemy who sows weeds during the night. Isn't that kind of treacherous act really bizarre? And yet there are other parables in which Jesus talked about things going on in the night—for example, the parable of the successful break-in (Matt 24:43) or the one about the importunate friend (Luke 11:5-8).

Moreover, is it really as unlikely as some commentators assert that one who hates a neighbor would pollute the neighbor's wheat field with weeds? Here, finally, we have to say something about darnel (*Lolium temulentum*). It was very common in the countries around the Mediterranean (and previously in Europe as well), and it was feared because it somewhat resembled wheat and was often infected with a mold that was poisonous to the nervous system. Sowing darnel could do severe damage to one's enemy; it was a kind of chemical attack. Certainly the sowing of darnel was no more bizarre than the assertion by Jesus' opponents that "by the ruler of the demons he casts out demons" (Mark 3:22). That was their way of poisoning what Jesus was doing for the sick and the handicapped.

I am still baffled by one commentator's[50] remark about the supposedly peculiar words of the householder at the end of the parable. As we have seen, the verse reads:

> [A]t harvest time I will tell the reapers, Collect the weeds first and bind them in bundles to be burned, but gather the wheat into my barn.

Here it is said to be odd that we learn nothing more about the process of reaping; it is simply assumed. Moreover, that assumption produces a "speech within the speech." What is so remarkable about that? Doesn't it, on the contrary, reveal the artistry of the parable-teller? He dispenses with the continuing narrative of events and instead puts what still needs to be said on the lips of the householder. With this artistic narrative touch, in fact, the weight is taken off the harvest itself and more stress is laid on the interim period when the wheat and darnel grow together. Jesus does something similar, as we have seen, in the parable of the judge and the widow (Luke 18:1-8). There, too, nothing is said about the outcome of the story. The judge's inner monologue makes it clear how the tale will end.

So let us suppose that what we have here, at least in its basic form, is an authentic Jesus parable, one whose artistry fits exceptionally well with Jesus' talent for storytelling. In this parable a weed called

---

[50] Cp. Luz, *Matthew 8–20*, 252.

darnel plays a significant role. It was an effective means for grabbing the attention of an audience in that era. But what is this hotly-debated parable really all about?

The crucial point in the parable is the waiting, the doing nothing. The weeds are permitted to grow along with the wheat. Now, in this interim period, they cannot be removed without destroying the whole sowing. Parables scholars have long since pointed out that this addresses the subject of the "pure community," and that is true. The discoveries at Qumran have acquainted us, through the "Community Rule" (1QS) and other writings, with a Jewish community of that period that set itself apart, regarding itself as a holy eschatological community that expelled all sinners or imposed severe punishments on them. We can see something similar in the Pharisees' lay study groups (*chaburot*), though their discipline was by no means so rigorous.

Jesus' preaching and practice did not correspond to that model of a holy, self-separating community. Certainly he, too, wanted to gather and sanctify the eschatological people of God; that is why he created the Twelve as a sign and growth center for the Israel that was to be gathered. A larger group of disciples, female and male, gathered around that center, and beyond them, in a more extended group, were all those who did not travel with Jesus but remained in their houses and dwellings, where they received the disciples who were on the road. There were friends,[51] supporters,[52] people who rendered occasional assistance,[53] the curious,[54] and even beneficiaries.[55] Above all, the Jesus movement was made up of despised people, social outcasts, and sinners. So Jesus gathered, but he did not segregate.

It is not easy to imagine, and it cannot be demonstrated, that during his public activity Jesus was attacked for his openness to people on the margins and those who had incurred blame (cp. Mark 2:16). In that case he could have defended himself against such outside attacks with this parable. God alone can draw the line between those who are truly evil and those who are good. Jesus would certainly not have equated the sinners with whom he associated with poisonous

---

[51] John 11:1-3.
[52] Luke 8:1-3.
[53] Mark 9:41.
[54] John 3:1-13.
[55] Mark 9:38-39.

weeds. The point of comparison would have been the *association* of holy and unholy, good and evil. Now, *at this hour*, a clear and clean distinction cannot be drawn. In fact, Jesus said elsewhere, we have to suppose that the real wickedness does not lurk among the sinners but is at home with those who elevate themselves above the outcasts and the sinful. In the next chapter I will treat the parable of the Pharisee and the tax collector, in which the tax collector, despite his guilt, goes home justified while the Pharisee does not (Luke 18:14).

If what I have said is correct, the question immediately arises whether the parable of the weeds in the wheat does not contradict the one about the fishnet insofar as it pleads for patient waiting. After all, the latter said that *now* is the time for decision; *now* the separation is being made. I don't see a problem here. Jesus' preaching cannot be reduced to a single line of "truths" and most certainly cannot be brought together in an ironed-out system. There are definite tensions in it:[56] for example, between "already" and "not yet," between judgment and mercy, between Israel and the nations, between the reign of God that comes "by itself"[57] and yet must be sought for with one's whole strength.[58] And Jesus said not only "whoever is not with me is against me"[59] but also "whoever is not against us is for us."[60]

It always depends on the situation in which a pointed word or a disturbing parable was once spoken. Often it takes a lot of effort for us to reconstruct the situation, or it is simply impossible. For that very reason it is appropriate to suppose that even the weeds in the wheat is an authentic Jesus parable—and even in this parable there would not have been only a single point at which the image level and the subject coincide, namely, *the waiting*. Instead, the figure of the householder would already have been transparent to God, or Jesus.

## 19. The Pharisee and the Tax Collector (Luke 18:10-14)

This parable, too, depends on contrast—this time between two persons. It comes to us in Luke's gospel and appears immediately after the parable of the judge and the widow.

---

[56] For the tensions in Jesus' proclamation cp. Gerhard Lohfink, *Das Geheimnis des Galiläers. Ein Nachtgespräch über Jesus von Nazaret* (Freiburg: Herder, 2019), 123–212.
[57] Mark 4:26-29.
[58] Matt 25:14-30; Luke 16:1-8; *Gos. Thom.* 98.
[59] Luke 11:23.
[60] Mark 9:40.

> Two men went up to the temple to pray, one a Pharisee and the other a tax collector. The Pharisee, standing by himself, was praying thus, "God, I thank you that I am not like other people: thieves, rogues, adulterers, or even like this tax collector. I fast twice a week; I give a tenth of all my income." But the tax collector, standing far off, would not even look up to heaven, but was beating his breast and saying, "God, be merciful to me, a sinner!" I tell you, this man went down [from the Temple Mount] to his home justified rather than the other. (Luke 18:10-14)

Unlike the parable of the weeds in the wheat, this one is a great favorite. It is continually being interpreted and celebrated. It seems to appeal to us, and it appears to be as clear as the situations in fairy tales, where there is nothing but good and bad. Hansel and Gretel are good, and the witch is bad. Cinderella is good, and her two stepsisters are figures of the worst kind. Isn't it similar here? The tax collector is good, and the Pharisee is bad. For centuries Christians have identified with the tax collector, despising the Pharisee and with him "all those hypocritical Pharisees." And at that very moment, without noticing it, they are standing beside the Pharisee, despising others.

Obviously these preliminary remarks are not intended to question the message of the parable, which stands athwart everything we think and do. I only want to issue a warning not to take this parable too lightly.

Let us, then, turn a closer eye on it! We recall that the parable of the judge and the widow does not begin at the beginning of the story; that is preempted by the judge's "internal monologue." This parable likewise offers no continuous narrative; it consists almost entirely of the introduction and characterization of the two actors. The crucial event is related outside the parable and there in a single statement by Jesus himself: "this man went down to his home justified rather than the other."

What we find here, then, is not a unilinear narrative in the strict sense, and yet the hearer is drawn into a theologically controversial situation. Looking at the very different forms in which Jesus structured his parables, one can only say: he must have been a storytelling genius. In this case he tells the story simply by presenting two persons and their prayers.

If we look more closely we are struck by the fact that the prayers of the two actors are of very different length. The tax collector's prayer is only a single sentence while that of the Pharisee is much longer. Those listening to the parable would have followed the Pharisee's prayer with great interest and most probably with reverence, because he was part of a group that enjoyed respect and honor in Israel. When he says that he fasts twice a week the listeners know what that means: eating and drinking nothing before sunset—a hard thing in the hot and oppressive climate of Palestine.

Moreover, they would have heard that he tithes his whole income. Of course they are also aware of what that means. In Israel 10 percent of what one earned was owed to the Levites, that is, to the temple. Torah said so (Num 18:21; Deut 14:22-27), and everyone in Israel was bound by it. But the Pharisees told themselves: when I buy something from someone, it could be that she or he has not tithed, and so I will tithe even what I purchase so that I will not share in that person's sin. That was a work of supererogation meant to fulfill the Torah as completely as possible. At any rate that seems to be the most likely explanation for "I give a tenth of all my income." This practice of "overpayment" was a mark of the profound Torah piety of the Pharisees.

The listeners knew all that. When they heard the Pharisee's prayer they were reminded of still other Scripture texts such as Psalm 119, which calls blessed those who let their whole lives be determined by the Torah, who live the precepts of Torah, loving it and sheltering within it. The one praying Psalm 119 says and prays it all in the first person, just like the Pharisee here. Wouldn't anyone feel profound respect for this man?

But then Jesus produces a tax collector: a hateful negative figure in the eyes of his audience. It was common opinion that tax collectors were people who enriched themselves at the expense of the already overburdened people in Israel. They had entered the service of the landlords and the occupation forces and were therefore objects of suspicion from the start. They were regarded as traitors and exploiters. Mustn't the parable end with Jesus' condemnation of the tax collector?

Not so fast: those who listen attentively or already know Jesus better will have long since suspected that things will turn out differently because, while the Pharisee has thanked God, his thanks were about his being unlike other people, unlike the godless. That would still have been all right, except that it turns his prayer of thanksgiving into sublime self-commendation and shows that he stands before God as a proper partner. *God* gave the commandments and he keeps them to the letter—indeed, he goes far beyond them. He knows nothing of human lostness and entanglement. Above all, he is fully unaware of his own misery. He sees the hopeless situation of the people of God only in the person of the tax collector. He despises him because, in his eyes, the tax collector does not keep the commandments, makes himself constantly unclean, exploits others—and above all, he will not change his life. As a tax collector he is altogether yoked to the system of exploitation applied by the minor royalty and the Roman occupying power.

The thoughtful element in Jesus' audience might have suspected as early as the Pharisee's prayer that this parable was not going to turn out as expected, and their suspicion would have been heightened when the tax collector was introduced, because he has exactly what the Pharisee lacks: he remains standing apart because he knows that he is far from God. He sees his lostness. He offers God his inability and his hopelessness. He does not simply ask God to forgive his sins; his cry for help is much more profound: he begs that his life may be saved—and for that very reason he is not far from the reign of God because it enters into human lostness and brings liberation.

So this parable, like the others, is about the reign of God. It cannot come to the Pharisee; it does come to the tax collector. But Jesus does not say it that way. His closing words are much more concrete and much more provocative. He says: "this man went down to his home justified rather than the other." What does that mean?

"Justified" is the same thing as "declared righteous." The Greek form here is passive, a form widely used in the Bible to speak of a divine action. The word "God" is avoided, out of reverence; hence the passive construction that does not mention the subject. Saying "the tax collector is declared righteous" thus means "the tax collector is declared righteous by God; he has been judged by God and set free." That in turn means that God has forgiven his guilt. The Pharisee, however, is not justified.

What gave Jesus the right to talk like that? Isn't he speaking in this parable as if he were acting in God's place? He judges and absolves. He himself utters divine judgment. That is just as unfathomable as the fact that the tax collector, with his way of life that is completely wrong, is absolved by God.

This parable also calls for a closing comment: was Jesus caricaturing the Pharisee here? No, obviously not! He says nothing at all about "the Pharisees." He tells of one particular Pharisee. Is he supposed to be representative of them all? We must refuse at all costs to fall into the trap of generalization. We can no more say "That's how all Pharisees were back then" than we can say "All the tax collectors at that time were just as honorable and humble before God."

Jesus is not trying to expose the whole community of Pharisees; he wants to use one particular Pharisee to illustrate the danger to which strict adherence to the law can lead: self-righteousness! We all have an element of that in us. Jesus is talking about all of us. Which of us has not thought secretly "I'm so glad I'm not like that other person!" Or maybe much worse and more dangerously "We: the good people; others: the reprobates!" That is just how every nationalistic agitation has begun, and so it is beginning again. The trap of false interpretation would snap firmly shut if the Pharisee in the parable were seen as not just a caricature of all Pharisees but of all Jews. Then we would not only have missed the meaning of this parable altogether; we would be slapping Jesus in the face.

### 20. The Merciful Samaritan (Luke 10:30-35)[61]

Like the parable of the Pharisee and the tax collector, the one about the merciful Samaritan is part of Luke's special material. It is incorporated in a dialogue between Jesus and a teacher of the law (10:25-30, 36-37). I will leave the dialogue out of the picture because it is not necessary in order to understand the original parable. In all probability it was constructed around the parable at a later date; it seems to function as a secondary "interpretation" of the parable.

> A man was going down from Jerusalem to Jericho, and fell into the hands of robbers, who stripped him, beat him, and went away, leaving him half dead. Now by chance a priest was going down that road; and when he saw him, he passed by on the other side. So likewise a Levite, when he came to the place and saw him, passed by on the other side. But a Samaritan while traveling came near him; and when he saw him, he was moved with pity. He went to him and bandaged his wounds,

---

[61] Popularly called "The Good Samaritan."

having poured oil and wine on them. Then he put him on his own animal, brought him to an inn, and took care of him. The next day he took out two denarii, gave them to the innkeeper, and said, "Take care of him; and when I come back, I will repay you whatever more you spend." (Luke 10:30-35)

Here again, Jesus contrasts people: previously it was the Pharisee and the tax collector, here a Samaritan over against a priest and a Levite. The contrast could not be sharper. The priest and the Levite come from Jerusalem because they are "going down" in the direction of Jericho, possibly through the Wadi Qelt, which even now is a route of descent from Jerusalem to Jericho. Anyone who does so can get an impression of how narrow and winding the route is, how well suited to muggings.

More important, of course, is that the priest and the Levite are returning from their service in the temple and are heading home. Many priests lived in Jericho at the time; the situation was immediately clear to those listening to the parable, and they would also have known what the path was like.

Contrasted to the priest and the Levite, then, is the figure of the Samaritan. Jews despised Samaritans, regarding them as a mixed race that no longer lived the true faith of Israel. This resulted from the fact that when the Assyrians conquered the Northern Kingdom in the eighth century BCE they deported part of the population and in their place settled groups of people from Babylon and Syria (2 Kgs 17:5-6, 24; Ezra 4:10). Hence Samaritans were seen by Jews as disreputable.

The Samaritans, in turn, responded with enmity and hatred. During Jesus' lifetime a group of Samaritans succeeded in scattering human bones throughout the columned halls and other parts of the temple during a Passover feast in order to make the holy place "unclean."[62] We need to know that background in order to get an idea of how the audience at that time would have reacted to the aid given by the Samaritan: were they surprised? amazed? unbelieving? angered? shocked?

Consider the form of this parable as well! Like many of Jesus' parables it has the briefest possible beginning. What a storyteller could

---

[62] Josephus, *Antiquities* 18.2.2 (§30).

have made of the mugging! What an exciting picture could have been painted! But Jesus knows where he needs to put the emphasis and where not. He simply says:

> A man was going down from Jerusalem to Jericho, and fell into the hands of robbers, who stripped him, beat him, and went away, leaving him half dead.

No shorter and more succinct a description of an attack would be possible. Then come the priest and the Levite. Now the narrative gets even stingier; only the essentials are told. Twice we read the brief statement: "when he saw him he passed by." "He saw him" appears a third time, now describing what the Samaritan did: he too "saw"—and then everything changes. *He* does not pass by. Here it is not only the story that takes a turn; the narrative style changes as well. Now the storyteller suddenly takes his time; the story begins to be filled out, going into detail: the Samaritan has compassion. He goes to the half-dead man. He cleans his wounds with oil and wine and binds them. He puts him on his own mount. To tell a sequence of events so briefly at the beginning and then suddenly to transition to "slow motion"—that is high narrative art in the briefest space.

Probably Jesus had learned a lot from the Old Testament. We can see the same narrative technique in the story of the binding of Isaac in Genesis 22: first there is a brief narrative, omitting everything that is nonessential. But as soon as Abraham arrives with his son Isaac at the place of sacrifice the story slows down and almost stops (cp. Gen 22:9-10).[63]

What did Jesus want to say in this parable? It cannot be accidental that we find here something that is normally absent from Jesus' parables, namely, a particular location for the action.[64] It takes place precisely between Jerusalem and Jericho. Jesus could easily have placed the action somewhere else, and he did not necessarily have to choose temple officials as those who refuse to help.

---

[63] This follows the masterful interpretation of Genesis 22 by Gerhard von Rad in his commentary on Genesis. Cp. Gerhard von Rad, *Genesis: A Commentary*, trans. John H. Marks, OTL (Philadelphia: Westminster Press, 1972), 240–41.

[64] It appears elsewhere only in the parable of the Pharisee and the tax collector (Luke 18:9-14), which takes place in the temple, and in that of the fishnet (Matt 13:47-48), located at the Sea of Galilee.

It cannot be accidental that Jericho as a priestly city and Jerusalem with its temple, as well as a priest and a Levite, are all part of the picture. Everyone familiar with Scripture would have to think of prophetic texts in which the temple sacrifices were judged and condemned as an abomination before God when not accompanied by mercy and love of neighbor. "I desire steadfast love and not sacrifice, the knowledge of God rather than burnt offerings," says Hosea (6:6). The priest and the Levite are coming directly from carrying out their sacrificial duties in the temple, and yet they make a wide circle around the man lying on the ground. Are they concerned with incurring uncleanness because of their cultic duties?[65] Our parable cannot mean to say that; it would level the contrast between the priest and the Levite on the one hand and the Samaritan on the other and thus neutralize itself since in that case each side would be equally following some part of Torah.

We have to take our starting point from Jesus' preaching. He evidently means to say: "Now that the reign of God is beginning, there must at last be fulfilled in Israel what the prophets repeatedly demanded. Now, at the latest, must the unity of worship and love of neighbor become reality."

Nothing of that unity can be seen in the conduct of the priest and the Levite, but it is different with the Samaritan, even though he worships on Mount Gerizim. That seems to me the real point of the parable: Jesus wants to prepare and gather all Israel—and to do so for the sake of what is now approaching: the reign of God. For him, apparently, the despised Samaritans are part of the people of God.[66] Jesus refuses to accept the existing separation and hatred between the two groups (cp. Luke 9:54-55). He wants to overcome divisions in Israel, and he does so not with resounding appeals but by telling a story—a story in which a Samaritan shows mercy to a Jew, a mercy that a Jewish priest and a Jewish Levite did not extend.

---

[65] Lev 5:3; 21:1-6; Ezek 44:25-27.

[66] From that point of view Eta Linnemann does not reflect Jesus' intention when she writes: "Why does Jesus mention a Samaritan here and not a Jewish layman—as his listeners were certainly expecting after a priest and a Levite? The only thing the Samaritan had in common with the Jews in the eyes of the listeners was that he too was human. If it is he who shows mercy, this mercy is something that man [sic] as such shows to man." *Parables of Jesus: Introduction and Exposition*, trans. John Sturdy (London: SPCK, 1966), 54.

How would Jesus' hearers have reacted to this story? How did they feel when Jesus chose to tell of neighborly love shown not by a pious Jew but by one of those hated Samaritans? We do not know.

It is not uncommon to find, in commentaries on this parable, phrases like "hour of humanity," "universal human sympathy, "universal love of humanity," "universal ethic of helpfulness"—or it may be said that here all "particular boundaries" of love of neighbor are demolished. Such interpretations by no means do justice to the parable.[67] Here—and in the Bible as a whole—the first point is that mutual solidarity such as is called for in Leviticus 19:18, 34 or Exodus 23:4-5 and depicted in exemplary fashion in 2 Chronicles 28:15 must ultimately be realized in the people of God.[68] If it were lived in Israel it could likewise be lived in the world.

### 21. The Two Different Sons (Matthew 21:28-31)

The following parable[69] again works with the stylistic medium of contrast: two brothers are placed over against each other as they react to an order from their father in opposite ways. The parable comes from Matthew's special material. Here again I am setting aside the context in which the parable now stands, where various pieces of text have been secondarily combined. We will consider the parable apart from its current context:

---

[67] Luise Schottroff, *The Parables of Jesus*, trans. Linda M. Maloney (Minneapolis: Fortress Press, 2004), rightly opposes such an interpretation (p. 134).

[68] In 2 Chr 28:15 we find the keywords "clothed," "provided with food and drink," "anointed," "carrying . . . them on donkeys," and "Jericho." On the often skewed treatment of the subject of love of neighbor in the Bible see, for more detail, Gerhard Lohfink, "What Does the Love Commandment Mean?," in *No Irrelevant Jesus: On Jesus and the Church Today*, trans. Linda M. Maloney (Collegeville, MN: Liturgical Press, 2014), 64–74.

[69] There is a text-critical problem in Matt 21:28-32. Leaving aside a third altogether improbable variant, there are two competing versions with a roughly equal number of textual witnesses. In version A, the text I favor, the first son originally refuses but then goes; the second son assents but does not go. In version B the reverse is true: the one who says "yes" but does not go comes first and the one who says "no" and yet goes comes second. Since at a later time the one who says "yes" but does not go was interpreted as the Jews and the one who originally says "no" as the Gentiles, it is possible that the sequence was reversed: the Jews come first, then the Gentiles. Hence my preference for version A.

> A man had two sons; he went to the first and said, "Son, go and work in the vineyard today." He answered, "I will not"; but later he changed his mind and went. The father went to the second and said the same; and he answered, "I go, sir"; but he did not go. Which of the two did the will of his father?

This parable is characterized even more than others by its extreme brevity and incisiveness. It is shaped by a carefully constructed and consistent parallelism that can be represented as follows:

$A^1$ Introduction
    $B^1$ The father's order to the first son
    $B^2$ Response of the first son
    $B^3$ Action of the first son
    $C^1$ The father's order to the second son
    $C^2$ Response of the second son
    $C^3$ Action of the second son
$A^2$ Question by the storyteller

Of course, others among the Jesus parables we have already discussed had a consistent structure of similar type, but it is good to illustrate the strict structuring of Jesus' parables at greater length in terms of a single example. Then one can see why texts of this type could be retold without difficulty.

The case is similar with jokes. How is it that many people (though not all!) can retell jokes without much trouble? It is simply because jokes are clearly structured, made up of short sentences, and aim toward a point. For example:

> Little Jonah's godfather telephones and Jonah picks up. "Jonah, let me speak to your Dad!" Jonah whispers softly, somewhat agitated: "I can't."
> "Why not?" "He's busy."
> "Then get your Mom for me!" Jonah, still whispering: "I can't do that either." "Why can't you?" Jonah says very softly: "She is busy too. The police are here."
> The godfather, increasingly worried, asks: "What is going on there? Then put one of the police officers on the phone!" "I can't." "Why?" "They are busy, too, and the firefighters are here."

The godfather is really agitated now: "For heaven's sake what are they all so busy about?" Jonah: "Shh, not so loud. I'm hiding under the sofa with the telephone and they are all looking for me."

The fact that I remember the joke and have told it several times is connected with its stereotypical structure and the many repetitions, including "busy" repeated four times. The scheme of 3 + 1 also helps us grasp the story quickly and repeat it exactly; it steers us toward the point in the fourth part. We already saw this pattern in the Jotham fable (Judg 9:8-15) and in Jesus' parable of the abundant harvest (Mark 4:3-9), and we will meet it again in the parable of the violent farmworkers (Mark 12:1-12).

Also important for the joke is the role of direct discourse and dialogue. We find both quite often in Jesus' parables and in popular narrative forms in general. Likewise characteristic of popular narration, however, is the following observation: a good joke can't sustain a long exposition; it has to get to the point quickly. Everything that can be omitted is left out in order to keep the narrative framework taut. As we have seen over and over again, Jesus makes masterful use of this technique of omission.

Finally, there is this as well: in the joke about little Jonah the ominous tension steadily increases. The father is busy; it turns out that the mother is also busy. That may be all right—but it goes on: the police are there, and they, too, are busy, and finally the fire department gets into the act. What could they all be so busy about? Every listener naturally thinks: the house is on fire! But it turns out to be something else.

Jesus, too, makes use of "heightening" quite as a matter of course: in the parable of the abundant harvest (Mark 4:3-9) the opponents' destruction of the seed gets more and more efficient, just as the tenants in the parable in Mark 12:1-12 are increasingly violent. And the fact that in the parable of the great banquet (Luke 14:16-24) not only the first person invited makes excuses but then the second and even the third all goes to show how the technique of heightening or escalation works.

This parable about the two different sons is thus tightly constructed. It has been thought through in detail, and it is even rather witty: that is, besides its strict form it has a startling point: the first son gives a negative response but acts positively, while the second responds positively but acts negatively. This produces a chiasm, a cruciform structure:

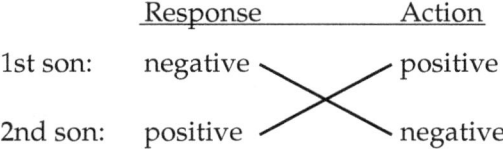

|  | Response | Action |
|---|---|---|
| 1st son: | negative | positive |
| 2nd son: | positive | negative |

Moreover, there is a still further refinement in this parable: the difference in the three addresses. The father speaks lovingly, almost tenderly, to both his sons. The first son answers his father rudely, even insolently. The second son, in contrast, addresses his father politely, respectfully, almost devoutly. All this sharpens and focuses the story: the rude son does his father's will and the obsequious one does not. These minor linguistic twists acutely demonstrate the contrast between the two sons. Taken all together, this shows that the parable simply cannot be expanded, and probably it never was.

Now, as to the content: we have seen over and over again that Jesus' parables speak of the reign of God, but is that true here as well? In studying the commentaries on our parable we encounter a certain cluelessness on the part of the exegetes. What is Jesus really trying to say in this parable? Is it simply about obedience to God, maybe even keeping the commandments? Is there any relationship between the parable and Jesus' activity? Does it have anything at all to do with his proclamation of the reign of God or is it simply a timeless model for one's attitude toward God?

It seems to me that this perplexity is unnecessary. If we look closer we can immediately find a clue in the vineyard motif. In the Old Testament "vineyard" is often an image for Israel, that is, for what is close to God's heart, what God is doing in the world.[70] Also, in the Bible God's "will" can be more than simply the Torah to be followed. The "will of God" is often what God is now setting in motion: God's intention, God's cause, God's plan.[71]

Seen from that point of view, this parable is about cooperation in God's cause, dedication to the reign of God. Here are the nay-sayers

---

[70] Cp. especially Ps 80:8-16 and Isa 5:1-7.
[71] Wis 9:13-18; Matt 18:14; Acts 22:14-15; Eph 1:3-14.

who at the start are not even slightly engaged, who have very different things in mind and yet come to realize what the hour demands. And there are the yea-sayers who speak beautiful words before God but in no way surrender themselves to the real will of God.

Since the accent of a parable usually comes at the end, this one about the different sons is an urgent warning not to miss the signs of the times but to surrender oneself to the onrushing reign of God and the demands of the hour. It is thus both a frightening and a reassuring parable. It is terrifying for those who only "talk big" before God and it's comforting for all who, when they hear God's call, are initially bewildered, put it aside, but then respond to it after all.

"A man had two sons." That is everyone's story, but perhaps it was also the story of those in Israel who lived a life far from God but then came to follow Jesus—and also the story of those who prayed to God every day but rejected Jesus.

## 22. The Rich Man and the Poor Man (Luke 16:19-31)

Only Luke gives us the parable of the rich man and the poor man, as part of a longer discourse (Luke 16:1-31) about the right use of wealth (cp. 16:1, 9, 13, 14, 19).

> There was a rich man who was dressed in purple and fine linen and who feasted sumptuously every day. And at his gate lay a poor man named Lazarus, covered with sores, who longed to satisfy his hunger with what fell from the rich man's table; even the dogs would come and lick his sores. The poor man died and was carried away by the angels to be with Abraham. The rich man also died and was buried. In Hades, where he was being tormented, he looked up and saw Abraham far away with Lazarus by his side. He called out, "Father Abraham, have mercy on me, and send Lazarus to dip the tip of his finger in water and cool my tongue; for I am in agony in these flames." But Abraham said, "Child, remember that during your lifetime you received your good things, and Lazarus in like manner evil things; but now he is comforted here, and you are in agony. Besides all this, between you and us a great chasm has been fixed, so that those who might want to pass from here to you cannot do so, and no one can cross from there to us." He said, "Then, father, I beg you to send him to my father's house—for I have five brothers—that he may warn them, so that they will not also come into this place of torment." Abraham replied, "They have Moses and the prophets; they should listen

to them." He said, "No, father Abraham; but if someone goes to them from the dead, they will repent." He said to him, "If they do not listen to Moses and the prophets, neither will they be convinced even if someone rises from the dead."

This parable also begins with a sharp contrast, juxtaposing two people: this time a rich man and a poor man. The difference is painted in the starkest colors: the rich man dresses in purple (that is, in outer garments dyed purple). Purple cloth was so costly that only the well-situated could afford garments made of it. The same was true of their undergarments, which were made of byssus, the very finest linen, bleached shining white. The poor man has no garments at all; his body is covered instead by sores.

Within his palace the rich man stages expensive banquets for his guests while the poor man is starving. He lies outside the gate (the rich man's residence has a separate gatehouse) and would have loved to eat the leavings that lay under the tables inside, but no one gives him even those. Instead, dogs lick his sores. The storyteller is by no means describing the sweet-tempered acts of faithful house pets. In Israel, dogs were despised. These are the ownerless feral dogs who run in packs through the streets of Near Eastern cities and devour whatever they can find. They torment the poor man but he hasn't the strength to keep them away from him.

Jesus has said enough to make it clear how hard-hearted the rich man is; nothing more was needed. The rich man lives a life of complete indifference to the misery of the poor; he is not even conscious of the poor man outside his gate. He is guilty of the poor man's death.

This introduction to the parable does not exaggerate in the slightest. In antiquity, when rich people held banquets for invited guests the leavings were, in fact, simply thrown on the floor. Often they consisted of half-gnawed bones or chicken scraps or pieces of the bread people used to clean their greasy hands. Great villas even had floor mosaics in the dining halls that depicted such garbage in highly decorative aesthetic form.[72]

Thus the scenic background for this parable! Then the poor man dies, and so does the rich man. Note the contrast: the rich man "died

---

[72] See the reproduction in Luise Schottroff, *Parables*, vi, and the commentary on p. 167.

and was buried" (the statement could not be simpler), but the poor man is carried by angels "to be with Abraham."[73] Although the expression "as safe as in Abraham's bosom" has become a cliché, the underlying image is usually misunderstood. The poor man is not cuddling in Abraham's lap; the image presupposes an ancient banquet at which pairs of diners recline facing one another—in particular, the guest of honor lies facing the host.[74] Jesus wants his audience to imagine the eschatological banquet at which, as he himself says in another passage, "many will come from east and west, from north and south, and will eat [= recline at table] with Abraham and Isaac and Jacob in the kingdom of God" (cp. Matt 8:11; Luke 13:28-29). So Lazarus is a guest at the never-ending banquet of the reign of God and, moreover, is the honored guest who is privileged to lie at table facing Abraham. He could not find a place at the festal tables of the rich, and now he has the place of honor next to Abraham.

Up to this point everything has run along the usual lines of a parable, but now the expectations harbored by people practiced in listening to parables go off track: what follows is a long dialogue between the rich man, who is suffering in the realm of the dead, and the patriarch Abraham. The dialogue contains no fewer than three exchanges; thus it far exceeds all other dialogues in Jesus' parables.

As unusual as the form of the dialogue is its content. First the rich man pleads for Lazarus to be sent to him to offer at least a tiny bit of coolness in his fiery torment. But that is impossible because he has already enjoyed everything "good" in his lifetime and Lazarus got only the "bad"—that was the trade-off. The situation has been reversed: the rich man is now in misery, and the miserable man is rich. Once again what the Magnificat says has come to pass: the powerful are toppled from their thrones and the lowly exalted; the hungry are filled with good things and the rich sent away empty (cp. Luke 1:52-53). The parable offers an image of what now happens all the time in the reign of God.

---

[73] The Authorized Version's "into Abraham's bosom" much more accurately reflects the Greek, εἰς τὸν κόλπον Ἀβραάμ.—LMM.

[74] See the essential article by Alexey Somov and Vitaly Voinov, "'Abraham's Bosom' (Luke 16:22-23) as a Key Metaphor in the Overall Composition of the Parable of the Rich Man and Lazarus," *CBQ* 79 (2017): 615–33.

In the second exchange the rich man pleads for his family of origin: "my father's house" in this case is the family he comes from. He has five brothers who live just as he did before his death. If Lazarus can no longer come to him where he is, let him at least hasten to visit his brothers; it is urgent that they be warned. (The listeners are probably thinking that he would appear to them in a dream.) But that, too, is impossible. The five brothers should simply hold to the words of Moses and the prophets. There, in the Torah and the prophetic books, they will find everything they need to know about the subject of "how to deal with riches." This, of course, refers to social equality in Israel: enduring solidarity among the people of God, help for the oppressed, the impoverished, the disenfranchised, the day-laborers, the widows, the orphans, the hungry, the sick, the dying.

The third exchange underscores the second: the rich man insists that surely they will listen if someone comes to them from the dead. "No," says Abraham. If they do not pay attention to the social order in Israel that has been given by God they will not listen to a messenger who rises from the dead.

Could this parable, with its long dialogue, come from Jesus? So far we have never seen anything comparable among his parables. The realm of the dead does not appear anywhere—and now, suddenly, we encounter a dialogue between the world above and the world below. Likewise, there is no reference to Moses and the prophets in any other parable. Is the whole thing a later construction placed on the lips of Jesus?

I cannot see any convincing reason for saying so. Only the third exchange (Luke 16:30-31), which really offers nothing new, could be a redactional addition by Luke. In that case the parable would have ended with the second exchange and concluded, altogether effectively, with: "But Abraham said: 'They have Moses and the prophets; they should listen to them.'"

What speaks in favor of the authenticity of this parable? To put it bluntly: its subject! After all, the theme of riches plays an extraordinary role in Jesus' life and teaching. As we have seen, the contrasts between rich and poor had intensified in Palestine at the beginning of the first century of our era. Many farmers in that time could survive bad harvests only by taking out loans, and if they were unable to repay they lost their property. Add to that the weight of taxes. The divide between wealthy feudal lords and dirt-poor wage workers and day-laborers was steadily widening. Jesus experienced these conditions, which no longer bore the slightest resemblance to the biblical social order, every day. Hence his calling the poor blessed! They should rejoice, for the reign of God, now beginning, will put an end to their misery (Luke 6:20).

But above all, Jesus must have repeatedly experienced that it was precisely the lust for wealth and the compulsion to cling to what one had that were preventing people from opening their whole lives to his proclamation of the reign of God. "Keep the commandments," he said to a man who asked him about gaining "eternal life." That was a simple reference to Torah and prophets. But the young man wanted to do more, and Jesus told him: "Go, sell what you own, and give the money to the poor . . . then come, follow me." The man went away sorrowful "for he had many possessions" (Mark 10:17-22). Here wealth was a barrier to discipleship. Jesus certainly had such experiences very often; hence his either-or:

> No one can serve two masters;
> for a slave will either hate the one and love the other,
> or be devoted to the one and despise the other.
> You cannot serve God and wealth [mammon]. (Matt 6:24)

"Mammon" here equals wealth—both wealth and the search for it in a form that is almost demonic and enslaves humanity. Another saying of Jesus is much harsher: "It is easier for a camel to go through the eye of a needle than for someone who is rich to enter the kingdom of God" (Mark 10:25).

What is important about this *logion* is that here wealth is radically contrasted with the realm of God. It brings us quite close to this parable, where the poor share in the eternal feast of the reign of God and the rich do not, where there is an unbridgeable gap between the meal in the reign of God and the world of the dead—as impassable as the eye of a needle is for a camel.

But could we expect that Jesus would point so emphatically to the Torah and the prophets? Wasn't his subject the reign of God? I cannot see the least difficulty on that particular point. The reign of God is not opposed to the Torah, because in the reign of God the goal toward which the Torah and the prophets were aiming has finally come to be: a society that lives altogether for God and in doing so lives altogether for human beings.

Certainly the parable is harsh. Even in the underworld the wealthy Jew appeals to his descent from Abraham, for he calls Abraham his "father." But John the Baptizer had already rejected that appeal: "Do not presume to say to yourselves: 'We have Abraham as our ancestor" (Matt 3:9). In this end-time situation of the people of God the Baptizer is concerned only that they realize what this time demands. Jesus thinks exactly the same way. Now, at this hour, what matters is to abandon everything that stands in the way of the reign of God—and, among other things, that means wealth and its corollary: showing no mercy toward the poor.

Finally: the fact that this parable contains a long dialogue with two (or perhaps even three) exchanges should not surprise us: when telling parables Jesus did not let himself be confined to one particular form. He works with many variations and a great many surprises. We will soon encounter another parable, namely, the one about the foolish wheat farmer (Luke 12:16-20), in which we find an internal monologue with another one slipped inside it: "And I will say to my soul . . ." (Luke 12:19).

This whole parable is an urgent, even a searing warning not to rest on a wealth that not only makes one utterly indifferent to the naked poverty of one's sisters and brothers among the people of God but altogether bars access to the reign of God.

We need not get sidetracked by the two-story construction (underworld here, banquet in the reign of God there). Jesus used the images that were familiar to his listeners so as to illustrate the seriousness of the situation. The question whether the rich man is only in a temporary condition, a kind of "purgatory," or is already in hell is altogether irrelevant to this parable. The text has no interest in that.

## 23. The Ten Virgins (Matthew 25:1-13)

It is probably very clear by now that in his parables Jesus regularly contrasts either individuals or groups:

- a day laborer and a rich merchant (Matt 13:44-46)
- a younger and an older son (Luke 15:11-32)
- a judge and a widow (Luke 18:1-8)
- a Pharisee and a tax collector (Luke 18:10-14)

- two temple officials and a Samaritan (Luke 10:30-35)
- an obedient and a disobedient son (Matt 21:28-31)
- a rich man and a poor man (Luke 16:19-31)
- and here, five wise and five foolish bridesmaids (Matt 25:1-13)

> Then the kingdom of heaven will be like this. Ten bridesmaids took their lamps and went to meet the bridegroom. Five of them were foolish, and five were wise. When the foolish took their lamps, they took no oil with them; but the wise took flasks of oil with their lamps. As the bridegroom was delayed, all of them became drowsy and slept. But at midnight there was a shout, "Look! Here is the bridegroom! Come out to meet him." Then all those bridesmaids got up and trimmed their lamps. The foolish said to the wise, "Give us some of your oil, for our lamps are going out." But the wise replied, "No! there will not be enough for you and for us; you had better go to the dealers and buy some for yourselves." And while they went to buy it, the bridegroom came, and those who were ready went with him into the wedding banquet; and the door was shut. Later the other bridesmaids came also, saying, "Lord, lord, open to us." But he replied, "Truly I tell you, I do not know you." Keep awake therefore, for you know neither the day nor the hour. (Matt 25:1-13)

This parable has fallen on hard times in recent decades, not only from preachers who try to deal with it in humanistic terms but from a whole series of New Testament scholars as well. The bridegroom's "I do not know you"—isn't that hurtful? Why should young women who have made a mistake get the door slammed in their faces? What about a sense of humor? What about generosity? Isn't that vicious response by the bridegroom just absurd and off-putting? Still more: isn't this bridegroom acting like those of whom Jesus said: "You hypocrites . . . you lock people out of the kingdom of heaven" (Matt 23:13)? One can hear or read these and similar questions more and more often.

Certainly the bridegroom's behavior needs explaining! Do we have here a situation similar to the ending of the parable of the banquet (Matt 22:1-14; Luke 14:16-24)? There Matthew had taken the original version that we can still discern in Luke's telling and added the episode of the man without a wedding garment. As far as Matthew 22 is concerned, the protest of today's listeners is understandable. Anyone dragged off the street without warning to attend a royal wedding feast is certainly *underdressed*—and for that the person is bound hand and foot and thrown into the outer darkness?

But we also saw that in the case of the banquet Matthew had expanded Jesus' original parable to make it a picture of the whole of salvation history in light of the destruction of Jerusalem and abuses in the Christian communities. We have to listen carefully to hear what Matthew really means to say.

In the case of the story of the ten bridesmaids the situation could be something similar. Matthew has set the parable in a context in which the subject is, first, Christ's *parousia* (Matt 24:30, 37, 39, 44, 50) and then the judgment of the world (Matt 25:31-46). The bridegroom, who arrives late at night, who has to be awaited with burning torches, and who has the power to say "I do not know you" is the returning Christ.

We even know with a degree of certainty where Matthew got the material about the closed door, the plea "Lord, open to us!" and the "I do not know you." In all probability he found them in the Sayings Source (Q). We know this because Luke presents the same material in an entirely different context (cp. Luke 13:24-27), and there are other echoes of the material in Matthew, within the Sermon on the Mount (Matt 7:13-14, 22-23). The text in question must have appeared in Q more or less like this, with minor variations:

> Strive with all your strength to enter through the narrow door! For many, I tell you, will try to enter and will not be able. When once the owner of the house has got up and shut the door, and you stand outside knocking at the door and saying, "Lord, open to us!" then in reply he will say to you, "I do not know you [and I do not know] where you come from." Then you will begin to say, "We ate and drank with you, and you taught in our streets." But he will say, "I do not know you [and I do not know] where you come from." (cp. Luke 13:24-27)

So there is a good deal of evidence that Matthew knew the parable material I have just quoted, but he did not incorporate all of it in his gospel. Instead, he took the elements cited above and used them to create a striking ending for the parable of the ten bridesmaids.[75]

---

[75] Likewise v. 13, "Keep awake . . .," was added by Matthew.

We should not disparage this new ending or Matthew's redaction overall. Matthew is concerned about the *kairos* that has been missed, the hour that was not seized. The church's history shows us how often Christians have not recognized the hour when they should have acted. Then a door closed, one that would not open soon again. Jesus must have had the same experience: in his time the greater part of the people of God were in danger of failing to recognize the crucial hour in their history.

Certainly we have to ask how the original ending of the ten bridesmaids parable must have looked. The answer could be that the bridal procession with the bridegroom, the bride, and the five bridesmaids with their burning lamps arrived, and the wedding feast began while the foolish bridesmaids were still somewhere else looking for oil. They were not present at the key moment. They had shut themselves out.

Of course a further question then arises: what did the thus-reconstructed parable mean to say? But before we get to that we are confronted with a second objection, again born of modern tolerance, and this one is much more frequently presented nowadays than the concern with the bridegroom's attitude, namely, what kind of miserable "wise bridesmaids" are they who refuse to share their oil with the others? Aren't those young women cold and lacking in solidarity, calculating and without mercy? Instantly the wise bridesmaids become negative figures while the foolish ones embody those driven to the margins, the sufferers and the humbled. All sympathy belongs to them, and we identify with them.

But that kind of attitude completely misses the matter of this parable and reveals ignorance of marriage customs in Jesus' time. It measures a two-thousand-year-old text against our own ideas and makes no effort to understand a narrative from another time and a different culture. To do justice to the parable we have to be clear about what a marriage meant in those times.

1. The wedding was a decisive, indeed *the* decisive event in the lives of people in Israel. It was also an image of the covenant between God and God's people (Isa 62:4-5; Jer 2:2; Ezek 16:8; Hos 2:21-22). Moreover, it was an event that occupied a great deal of space in people's hearts and in reality. A wedding feast could go on for several days (Gen 29:27; Judg 14:12; Tob 8:19), and in rural communities the whole village took part, together with numerous guests. A marriage

was a public event. But it was not only for those reasons that every marriage was elaborate and expensive. It also included the *mohar*, the bride-gift, often a considerable sum, presented by the parents of the bridegroom.

2. For the bride the marriage represented a change in her life such as we can scarcely imagine any more because we do not live in tight family groups. It meant separation from her own family and entry into the husband's family, where she was a stranger (Ps 45:11, 17). Hence the festal manner in which the bridegroom brought the bride into his house. It marked the transit of the bride into the bridegroom's family and it plays an important part in our parable.

3. It seems that the bridegroom's coming late to the bringing-home of the bride is no accident. While we know very little about wedding customs in Israel in Jesus' time we can draw valid conclusions from wedding rituals that can still be observed today in Palestine. It could have been part of the wedding customs that the procession of the bridegroom to the home of the bride was repeatedly held up—by the bride's family. It was no longer a question of negotiating the bride-gift. That had long since been paid, and at that point the marriage was legally completed. Rather, these delays were the occasion for haggling over additional small gifts. The principle was: the lovelier and more valuable the bride, the more numerous should be the gifts to the bride's clan. If we may calculate that the bridegroom's procession to the bride's house was already beset by comparable delays in Jesus' time, the late arrival of the bridegroom was no accident and was most certainly not attributable to his careless behavior. There was method in it, and the bridesmaids knew precisely what was to be expected.

4. Still, bridal customs or no bridal customs, our parable's narrative flow simply presumes that the ten young women could have known what they were supposed to do. They should have expected that it would be a long time before the bridegroom would appear. If they wanted to do right by their honorable office they had to have enough oil on hand to wet their torches (bundles of fasces wrapped in cloth) over and over again. We may even suppose that the torches they carried in the procession to the bride's house would be placed in brackets there to provide festive illumination.

136    *The Forty Parables of Jesus*

5. In any case the role of the torchbearing friends of the bride should not be underestimated. They were of signal importance for the feast. If they all arrived with burned-out torches it would be a profound humiliation for the bride, and the village gossip about it would go on for years. Then in fact "the light would have gone out." We simply cannot imagine nowadays how quickly a bride's honor could be damaged in that time and place. Her honor was a precious thing that absolutely had to be protected—and just so also the honor of the bridegroom! A bridal procession without burning torches—our parable simply presumes—would have been a catastrophe. The wise bridesmaids who refused to share really saved the feast. Refusing to see such things and to override the mentality of the times with modern ideas is nothing but another form of cheap cultural imperialism.

So then, what did Jesus mean to say with this parable? What is demanded of the ten young women is vigilance and readiness, because there is a lot at stake: namely, the feast itself. We certainly may conclude that this is about the marriage feast of God and Israel, the feast of the reign of God. The event the prophets awaited is now present (Mark 2:19)! The time has come. Now everything depends on whether the people of God will recognize the hour and have their lamps lighted. This situation will come only once; it cannot be repeated.

So the parable of the ten bridesmaids is about whether the people of God will recognize the signs of the times and act accordingly. It is similar to the great banquet in Luke 14:16-24: the feast must take place.

### 24. The Barren Fig Tree (Luke 13:6-9)

In the parable of the ten bridesmaids the imagery gave us difficulty. We know too little about marriage customs in Israel at the time of Jesus. The case is different with the next parable, which comes from Luke's special material. Here everything on the image level is clear and simple.

> A man had a fig tree planted in his vineyard; and he came looking for fruit on it and found none. So he said to the gardener, "See here! For

three years I have come looking for fruit on this fig tree, and still I find none. Cut it down! Why should it be wasting the soil?" He replied, "Sir, let it alone for one more year, until I dig around it and put manure on it. If it bears fruit next year, well and good; but if not, you can cut it down." (Luke 13:6-9)

Here we can simply ask: what is normal in the image field of this parable, and what is unusual? It is altogether normal for a fig tree to stand in the middle of a vineyard. In antiquity fruit trees were cultivated within the vineyards; sometimes there were even rows of grain. Fertilization was also normal. Columella, in his work on agriculture, writes at length about the preparation, storage, and correct application of dung.[76]

Likewise normal is the owner's repeated visits to the fig tree to seek fruit beneath its big leaves, because a fig tree bears twice each year—first the early figs and then the summer figs, though these ripen little by little and not all at once.

Finally, it is completely normal that the owner of the vineyard will not tolerate a fig tree in his vineyard if it never bears fruit. After all, fig trees draw nutrients from the soil.

What, in contrast, is altogether unusual—and here we find a certain "extravagance" in the narrative—is that a gardener appears alongside the owner and takes the part of the fig tree. The parable leaves his status open; he is simply called "the gardener." What is important is that he becomes a kind of advocate for the fig tree. He asks that the fig tree be given one more year during which he will not only work the soil around the tree but even fertilize it. That would be unusual, since fig trees were not normally fed; it was simply unnecessary. The owner of the vineyard accepts this extravagant suggestion.

The crucial question here, of course, is again: what did the audience think when they heard this parable? Did they already begin to see something more in the fig tree than just a normal part of the landscape? There are no texts in the Bible in which a fig tree represents

---

[76] E.g., *De re rustica* 2.5.9.15. Cp. also Gustav Dalman, *Arbeit und Sitte in Palästina*, vol. 2, 142–46, and Aryeh Ben-David, *Talmudische Ökonomie: die Wirtschaft des jüdischen Palästina zur Zeit der Mischna und des Talmud*, vol. 1 (Hildesheim and New York: Olms, 1974), 93–97.

God's people Israel so obviously and with the same symbolic weight. There is no broad "field of imagery" involving Israel as God's fig tree, and yet in a very few instances even the fig tree can share in the clear-cut metaphorical character of the vine: for example, in Joel 1:7, or even more clearly in this text from Jeremiah:

> When I wanted to gather them, says the LORD,
>     there are no grapes on the vine,
>     nor figs on the fig tree;
> even the leaves are withered. (Jer 8:13)

This divine speech is about Judah, which was called to repent but refused. Therefore the most profound evil threatens it. Why? "There are no grapes on the vine, nor figs on the fig tree." Here both the fig tree and the vine are metaphors for Israel, and the lack of fruit represents its uselessness.

It is possible, then, that the first hearers of this parable could have sensed that it was about the people of God, that is, themselves. The impression could have intensified when they heard it suggested that the fig tree should be cut down. Above all, those who had heard some of John the Baptizer's preaching must have recalled his radical saying: "Even now the ax is lying at the root of the trees; every tree therefore that does not bear good fruit is cut down and thrown into the fire" (Matt 3:10).

And yet now—to the surprise of the listeners and quite contrary to the Baptizer's preaching—an advocate appears to appeal for a temporary reprieve for the fig tree. Who is this advocate? What is the delay about? How long can it last? Now, at the very latest, the question about the fate of the people of God and likewise the listeners' own fate must have arisen. The parable not only calls for interpretation; that is already present in its metaphors. We are confronted once again with the phenomenon that Jesus speaks about himself in a parable—indirectly and in a concealed way. Isn't he himself the gardener who intercedes on behalf of the fig tree? Is it not he who does everything conceivable for it and still hopes for fruit? In any case, we find here a clearly new angle on the preaching of John the Baptizer.

Nevertheless, the threat of judgment remains, and it is a bitter one. If the people of God does not yield fruit—that is, recognize the signs of the times and repent—it will suffer catastrophe.

It has rightly been pointed out that the fig tree is the silent central figure in this parable.[77] It all begins with the fig tree and everything in the parable revolves around it; it even dominates the last sentence. This is not just about individuals in Israel; it is about Israel itself, which is standing on the brink of catastrophe. Everything depends on its repentance, its turning back. The parable is an imploring appeal by Jesus that Israel not miss its decisive hour, that it not fail to make use of the reprieve that has been granted.

## 25. The Quarreling Children (Matthew 11:16-19)

As we have so often observed, the transition to a parable as well as added interpretations and comments need not have been part of the original. These are for the most part redactional additions. But there are exceptions, and one of these is Matthew 11:16-19. In this case the parable and the subsequent interpretation were probably parts of the same whole from the outset:[78]

> But to what will I compare this generation? It is like children sitting in the marketplaces and calling to one another,
>
> > "We played the flute for you, and you did not dance;
> > we wailed, and you did not mourn."
>
> For John came neither eating nor drinking, and they say, "He has a demon"; the Son of Man came eating and drinking, and they say, "Look, a glutton and a drunkard, a friend of tax collectors and sinners!" (Matt 11:16-19)[79]

Jesus draws on all kinds of sources for his parables: near and far, the little people's nooks and crannies and the broad world of the powerful, the lives of the devout and the criminal milieu, the world of finance and the vegetable garden—and here the sphere of childhood.

---

[77] Cp. Bernhard Heininger, *Metaphorik: Erzählstruktur und szenisch-dramatische Gestaltung in den Sondergutgleichnissen bei Lukas*, NTA n.s. 24 (Münster: Aschendorff, 1991), 123.

[78] This does not apply, however, to v. 19c ("Yet wisdom is vindicated by her deeds").

[79] Matthew 11:16-19 comes from Q (cp. Luke 7:31-35). With only small variations Matthew and Luke are identical. As regards the lesser variations, Matthew usually deserves priority.

Jesus has watched children at play. Some of them want to play wedding and so are blowing a flute for dancing, but others aren't interested and don't join in. Immediately a second scene appears: this time the game is supposed to be a funeral. The women's wailing begins, but here again some others won't join in. Now there is a quarrel; accusations fly back and forth. In the end there is no game at all. The children "take their marbles and go home."

But all that is stated much more concisely. There really are only two snapshots, one after the other. The narrator does not say whether the first scene is about boys (men dance at a wedding) and the second about girls (the wailing at a funeral comes from the lips of women). Above all, the narrator does not say who, exactly, represents "this generation," the concept that initiates the parable.

This has led interpreters astray into a genuine dance of repositionings: Does "this generation" refer to the children who don't want to play, or is the parable comparing "this generation" to the children who do want to play, or is "this generation" likened to all the children involved? All three possibilities have been discussed and go on being considered.

Still, that exegetical confusion is superfluous if we keep in mind how dative beginnings work in parables. "It is with the kingdom of heaven as with a treasure hidden in a field" does not mean that Jesus is comparing the reign of God to a treasure; the comparison is to the whole sequence of actions whereby a day-laborer finds a treasure and makes a fortune. Likewise here: "this generation" is compared to the whole process in which children want to play and never get to play because they cannot agree, so that in the end the spoilers win.

It ought to be clear what Jesus means to say in this parable: "This generation" in Israel who now must answer a question key to its survival, the question of what it really wants, is unable to decide. Those who have to decide are like children who cannot agree and do not know what they want. The fate of God's people is at stake!

But the imagery already conveys all that. Now the speaker leaves the plane of the parable and clarifies its statement with two striking examples: this generation considered John the Baptizer possessed because he was such a strict ascetic; it considers himself, the "Son of Man," to be the opposite, namely, a glutton and a wine-bibber. Jesus quotes sayings about himself and the Baptizer that were in circulation. It is the same as the children's game: people cannot agree. They do not like weeping (that is, the Baptizer's preaching of repentance and his ascetic way of life), but they don't like weddings (namely, Jesus' proclamation and practice of the reign of God) either.

This analogy fits so perfectly with the parable of the quarreling children that we should not question the original relationship between parable and commentary. Jesus' reference to himself as the "Son of Man" is not a valid counter-argument. Just as Jesus always speaks of himself only indirectly in his parables, so here he makes use of the figure of the Son of Man from Daniel 7:13-14 in order to refer indirectly, in the third person, to himself and his mission. Likewise the past tense, "came," need not represent a post-Easter perspective. Still less persuasive is the assertion that references to John the Baptizer and to Jesus allegorize the parable. We have seen over and over again that Jesus' parables can contain metaphorical points of reference even on the level of their imagery. Jesus is not governed by the defined genres that exegetes have invented in order to be able to classify their texts more precisely.

On the whole we may say that the parable of the barren fig tree already revealed the tense and critical situation in which, in Jesus' eyes, the people of God is already living. The parable of the quarreling children again sheds light on that situation. The people of God is in the most profound crisis in its history, and it does not know what it wants.

## 26. Going to Court (Matthew 5:25-26)

We may disagree over whether the following text is a metaphor or a parable. Since it contains no fewer than five "sequential events" I have chosen the parable genre. But no matter how one decides that question, this text also shows what a variety of techniques Jesus commanded and employed in his use of imagery. The parable comes from the Sayings Source Q (cp. Luke 12:58-59), and both Matthew and Luke reworked the model they drew from there. I am (unwillingly) making an exception by offering here not the biblical text but a reconstruction of what might have been the text in the Sayings Source.[80]

---

[80] I am following the reconstruction in Paul Hoffmann and Christoph Heil, *Die Spruchquelle Q. Studienausgabe Griechisch und Deutsch* (Darmstadt: Wissenschaftliche Buchgesellschaft, 2002), 88–89.

> While you are on the way [to court] with your adversary, make every effort to get free of him so that the adversary will not hand you over to the judge and the judge to the bailiff, and the bailiff will throw you into prison. I tell you: you will not get out of there until you have paid back the last *quadrans*.

First let us be clear about the process that is being presented to us here in such brief and concise form. Two people are on their way to appear before the judge: an accuser and an accused. The subject of the dispute is an open question. It could be theft, but more probably it is a lawsuit for the collection of a debt. In any case the accused is assumed to be guilty.

What is unusual about this parable is that it is couched from beginning to end in direct address, and in the familiar form. That in itself gives the utmost urgency to what is said.

Besides this personal address there is a further structural element signaling the urgency of the business: the adversary will hand the accused over to the judge, the judge to the bailiff, the bailiff will throw the accused into prison. Even on the linguistic level it all runs like a well-oiled machine, and it is meant to show that there is great danger here. Paul Ricoeur[81] speaks of an "implacable crescendo from judge to jailer . . . that dramatizes the decision." The accused is enjoined to reach an out-of-court settlement with the accuser *now*, right away, while still on the road: otherwise he will land in jail and will never get out again unless the debt is paid to the last *quadrans*, that is, to the last penny. The *quadrans* was the smallest coin in the Roman monetary system.

It should be noted that there was no such thing in Israel as coercive detention, but evidently it existed in Roman law. We see that Jesus here, as elsewhere, deliberately played on the viciousness of legal systems outside Judaism in order to sharpen the picture.[82]

What meaning did Matthew and Luke assign to this parable? What did they want to say by using it? Matthew locates it within the Sermon on the Mount as the conclusion to the first antithesis, which

---

[81] Paul Ricoeur, "Biblische Hermeneutik," in *Die neutestamentliche Gleichnisforschung im Horizont von Hermeneutik und Literaturwissenschaft*, ed. Wolfgang Harnisch (Darmstadt: Wissenschaftliche Buchgesellschaft, 1982), 248–339, at 327.

[82] Joachim Jeremias, *Parables*, 180, points to execution by drowning (Mark 9:42), the sale of wives (Matt 18:25), and torture (Matt 18:34).

speaks of murder and reconciliation (Matt 5:21-26). For him the parable is a warning to be ready to reconcile at any moment. If Jesus' disciples and the members of the people of God remain unreconciled with one another they are threatened with judgment.

It is altogether different for Luke: in that gospel the parable is located immediately after a small unit that speaks first about the weather. "When you see a cloud rising in the west," Jesus says, "you immediately say, 'It is going to rain' . . . and when you see the south wind blowing, you say, 'There will be scorching heat.'" But, he continues, you are unable to judge the *kairos*, that is, you do not know (or do not want to know) how to interpret what is happening in the present weeks and months, what hour has struck, what is happening now in the eyes of God (cp. Luke 12:54-57).

Luke has hit the original sense of the text much more accurately than Matthew. The parable of going to the judge means to say: there is no time left. Now is the final opportunity; now is the last deadline. The people of God must choose. Thus this parable is very close to those of the quarreling children and the barren fig tree. The next parable belongs in the same context.

## 27. The Foolish Wheat Farmer (Luke 12:16-20)

This parable, too, is about a *kairos*, a crucial moment, an hour one can use one way or another. The "hero" of the parable does not recognize the hour that is offered to him or, to put it bluntly, he ruins it.

> The land of a rich man produced abundantly. And he thought to himself, "What should I do, for I have no place to store my crops?" Then he said, "I will do this: I will pull down my barns and build larger ones, and there I will store all my grain and my goods. And I will say to my soul, 'Soul, you have ample goods laid up for many years; relax, eat, drink, be merry.'" But God said to him, "You fool! This very night your life is being demanded of you. And the things you have prepared, whose will they be?" (Luke 12:16-20)

The parable about going to court presented itself as a "thou" discourse from beginning to end. The one about the foolish wheat farmer is—apart from its introduction and the closing words of God—a pure monologue. There is even a second monologue built into the rich man's speech to himself; it tells us what he is going to say to himself next: "Then I will say to my soul . . ." Jesus plays with many forms in his parables. He possesses an extensive rhetorical repertoire for parable-telling.

Our parable offers no problems as far as the image level is concerned. It is only questionable whether the man really stored his grain in "barns" in the modern sense. If so, it would have been swiftly eaten by mice and rats. People in Israel used dugout rooms under their houses or in nearby cliffs, or else they employed huge clay pots that were filled through a sealable opening at the top and had an arrangement near the bottom through which the grains could be extracted.[83] The Greek word used in our parable is *apothēke*—and *apothēke* not only means "barn" but refers generally to "storage" or a "storeroom."

But Luke is speaking unmistakably of "barns" in the present-day sense. It could be that he introduced circumstances from outside Palestine into the text here; after all, he did something similar in the story of the healing of the lame man (Mark 2:1-12 // Luke 5:17-26). There, according to Mark, the lame man's bearers could not reach Jesus because of the dense crowd, so they "dug" through the Near Eastern flat roof of beams, clay, and woven reeds and lowered the bed through the opening. In Luke's version, though, they let him down "with his bed through the tiles" (Luke 5:19). So Luke was imagining a Greco-Roman tile roof: as he pictured it the bearers only had to remove a single layer of tiles. The "barns" here represent a similar imaginative situation.

That, however, is unimportant. What is crucial is the question: what did Jesus want to say in this parable? Did it have anything to do with the reign of God? Isn't this just common sense about life? Doesn't it speak of the illusion of wealth, sudden death, and the laughing heirs as we meet them also in Psalm 49 and in many other texts of Old Testament wisdom literature? Does this parable come from Jesus at all? Quite a few exegetes raise those questions.

But why shouldn't Jesus use motifs from wisdom literature in a parable? He lived from Scripture in many respects. He repeatedly refers to it—but always in a way that is typical of him: examining, clarifying, making plain. He does that here, too. He doesn't simply portray the foolishness of a rich man who has had a lucky harvest and now wants to live a good life.

---

[83] For details see Gustav Dalman, *Arbeit und Sitte*, vol. 3, 188–206.

What Jesus describes here is a great deal more: a human being who is completely self-absorbed. The linguistic signal of this is that he is presented entirely through internal monologues. This man knows no one but himself. He doesn't ask about anyone else. He presents an image of absolute egocentricity. The moment in which he sees that his fields are producing an abundant harvest could become a *kairos* for him, an occasion to think of others—maybe even to think of God. But his orbit is only himself.

Precisely because of that, what is happening in Israel remains foreign to him. Jesus' sharp words against the rich were grounded not only in the fact that many rich people did not share, that they despised the poor. That would have remained purely on the ethical level. There is a more profound reason why the rich cannot enter the reign of God (Matt 19:24): they live in such self-fixation that they cannot even perceive the reign of God. It is precisely the rich whose estimation of what is happening in Israel with the proclamation of God's rule is utterly false. That is why they are so far from the reign of God.

Still, our parable obtains its ultimate force from the fact that the foolish wheat farmer is by no means portrayed as a figure of fun.[84] He is no more a caricature than the invitees in the parable of the great banquet (Luke 14:16-24), who without exception name rational grounds for not being able to attend. Mustn't a farmer plan carefully? Must one not reckon with bad harvests and therefore also plan thoughtfully for storage?

So our parable shows us that it is not only profound self-fixation that makes it impossible to perceive the coming of the reign of God—no, even a full concentration on the necessities, plans, forces, and cares of everyday life does the same. The wheat farmer wants to avoid those forces once and for all. But he cannot escape.

## 28. The Guest without a Festal Garment (Matthew 22:11-13)

In interpreting the parable of the banquet (Luke 14:16-24) we saw that the Matthean parallel (Matt 22:1-14) is especially off-putting because it is not simply about a festal dinner given by a private citizen

---

[84] See the important point made by Georg Eichholz, *Gleichnisse der Evangelien. Form, Überlieferung, Auslegung* (Neukirchen-Vluyn: Neukirchener Verlag, 1971), 29.

but concerns a wedding feast given by a king for his son. For Matthew as for Luke, indeed, the invited guests absent themselves and are replaced by people from the streets. But then in Matthew comes the bizarre scene in which one of those dragged in from the street is not appropriately dressed and is thrown out. This narrative impossibility is explained by many New Testament scholars by supposing that here Matthew has combined two originally separate parables. There is, indeed, much in favor of that supposition. The parable Matthew attached could have read something like:

> It is with the realm of heaven as with a king who made a wedding feast for his son. But when the king came in to greet those reclining at table he saw one who was not wearing a garment appropriate for a wedding. He said to him: "Friend, how did you get in here without a wedding garment?" But he remained silent. Then the king said to the servants: "Bind him hand and foot and throw him out."

Obviously that is a reconstruction, but it draws on the Matthean text, namely from Matthew 22:2, 11-13a,b. The original parable could have read like that. Does it make any sense?

It certainly makes sense purely in terms of narrative sequence. After the guests who had been invited from the outset have taken their places on their couches the king appears and is presented to the invitees. In the process he arrives at a guest wearing a garment that is utterly unfitting for a banquet. The guest's clothing is regarded as a serious insult and he is thrown out.

Simply as a story, all that is plausible—not in our time, certainly, when everyone can wear whatever occurs to him or her at the time, often even ripped or deliberately damaged clothing. But in previous cultures it was quite different. Then rules for clothing and the right garments for the particular situation played an immense role. Moreover, clothing was a class indicator, revealing at a glance whether a person belonged to the upper class or not, was free or unfree.

Thus the story is plausible in itself, but does it fit Jesus' preaching? I think it certainly does. Already in the Old Testament the coming day of salvation was compared to a wedding (Isa 62:4-5; Jer 2:2-3; Ezek 16:8; Hos 2:18-25). And Jesus used a whole variety of images that employ wedding metaphors to point to the inbreaking time of salvation, the already-appearing of the reign of God: new wine belongs in new wineskins (Mark 2:22); the torches must be kept burning and must not go out (Matt 25:1-13); the wedding has begun, so there can be no more fasting (Mark 2:19).

The new situation that has now arrived requires a new attitude, new behavior, and the guest in everyday clothes does not fulfill it. He has not grasped that this is something new. He has not understood that now it is time to celebrate a wedding.

## 29. The Unforgiving Servant (Matthew 18:23-34)

"Bind him hand and foot and throw him out!" That could have been the ending of the parable about the guest without a wedding garment. A bad end! The parable of the unforgiving servant (called the parable of the wicked servant since Martin Luther's translation appeared) also ends badly. It comes from Matthew's special material; Mark and Luke have not preserved it.

> [It is with the kingdom of heaven as with] a king who wished to settle accounts with his slaves. When he began the reckoning, one who owed him ten thousand talents was brought to him; and, as he could not pay [the debt], his lord ordered him to be sold, together with his wife and children and all his possessions, and payment [of the debt] to be made. So the slave fell on his knees before him, saying, "Have patience with me, and I will pay you everything." And out of pity for him, the lord of that slave released him and forgave him the debt.[85] But that same slave, as he went out, came upon one of his fellow slaves who owed him a hundred denarii; and seizing him by the throat, he said, "Pay what[86] you owe [me]." Then his fellow slave fell down and pleaded with him, "Have patience with me, and I will pay you." But he refused; then he went and threw him into prison until he would pay the debt. When his fellow slaves saw what had happened, they were greatly distressed, and they went and reported to their lord all that had taken place. Then his lord summoned him and said to him, "You wicked slave! I forgave you all that debt because you pleaded with me. Should you not have had mercy on your fellow slave, as I had mercy on you?" And in anger his lord handed him over to be tortured until he would pay his entire debt. (Matt 18:23-34)

---

[85] Literally: the "loan." This is probably just a variant formulation for "debt."
[86] The Greek text here may not be translated "if you owe anything." Cp. Marius Reiser, *Jesus and Judgment: The Eschatological Proclamation in its Jewish Context*, trans. Linda M. Maloney (Minneapolis: Fortress Press, 1997), 275 n. 62.

At first glance this parable offers no difficulties. Problems arising out of a lack of understanding of ancient Near Eastern customs are easily clarified. The "servants" (NRSV "slaves") here portrayed are obviously not body servants or stableboys. In the ancient Near East even the highest functionaries could be called "servants" (cp., e.g., Gen 40:20; Num 22:15-18; 1 Sam 8:14; 2 Sam 9:2). When we speak of "ministers" today it simply means—on the basis of its Latin origins—nothing other than "servants." The "servants" from whom an accounting is being demanded are therefore high officials of the kingdom.[87]

"Settling accounts" must mean a kind of routine "audit." We could call it a review by the royal accountants. This revealed (or perhaps it had already been revealed) that one of the officials owed his master ten thousand talents. The parable does not say how it happened. At any rate, we are talking about a gigantic sum of money. The Greek text speaks of *myrioi*, and *myrioi* (ten thousand) was the highest number that then existed. There was nothing greater. The audience were hearing about a fairytale sum of money: they simply could not imagine more.

We have to suppose that the official in question was in charge of a whole province and its tax revenue, and perhaps he allowed a major share of the income to fall into his own pockets. But here, as is so often the case, the immediate circumstances and background are not detailed; they are left to the hearers' imagination. Only one thing is certain: the official will never be able to repay that much money. His existence is ruined, along with that of his family. After all, we are in the ancient Near East here. Everything he owns will belong to the king and he himself will be sold into slavery, along with his wife and children. They may never see each other again. Incidentally, the prescribed sentence shows that in this parable Jesus is talking about a *Gentile* king or—to put it more cautiously—about Hellenistic legal procedures. Jewish law did not permit the sale of a wife.[88]

---

[87] This is true unless the parable was not originally about a king (cp. Matt 22:2 with Luke 14:16) but perhaps a wealthy tax farmer, an entrepreneur who bought up leases and then had them collected by subordinates. In that case the gigantic sum of ten thousand talents would also be Matthew's redaction. Still, the means used in the course of the parable by the sovereign scarcely fit a private citizen. To that extent this "correction" of Matthew's version is highly questionable.

[88] See H. L. Strack and Paul Billerbeck, *Das Evangelium nach Matthäus*, 798.

In his despair, the official seizes his last chance: he falls on his knees before the king, bows so that his forehead touches the floor (in the Near East this kind of *proskynesis* had become a ritual for petitioners before the royal throne[89]) and begs him pitifully: "Have patience with me!" He is asking for a moratorium on repayment. Obviously that is purely a last-ditch promise that could never have been fulfilled.

But the cry, "Have patience with me!" also implies the plea: "Be generous!" The official thus appeals to a virtue of which rulers in the ancient Near East and in antiquity generally were very proud: in their proclamations on entering into office they promised not only to take care for law and justice; beyond that they loved to surround themselves with a halo of liberality and generosity.

And now, in that very sense, something happens that is unbelievable and yet not entirely outside the realm of possibility for a Near Eastern ruler: the king forgives the official the whole debt: not only the punishment that is called for but the money as well—and not just part of the money but the whole of it! For the hearers, no matter how

---

[89] In the ancient Near East a petitioner's *proskynesis* before a ruler normally proceeded in this fashion: the petitioner approached the throne, knelt, and then bowed until his forehead touched the floor. Often he kissed the king's feet. It was crucial throughout that the petitioner not look at the king. If the ruler accepted the plea, the petitioner could then get up and behold the "face" of the king.

It could also happen, as part of the ritual, that the ruler indicated acceptance of the petition by seizing the petitioner's chin and lifting it so that he could behold the ruler's gracious "countenance."

*Proskynesis* before a superior appears relatively often in the Old Testament, never in such detail but in terms that point in that direction. Falling on one's knees happens with some frequency, as does the full *proskynesis*, bending the forehead to the ground. In this connection the encounter between Jacob and Esau (Gen 33:1-11) is significant. After his *proskynesis* before Esau, Jacob says: "to see your face is like seeing the face of God" (Gen 33:10). Thus Jacob has encountered not only Esau's goodwill and favor; he has seen his "face" light up. Esau has raised him up and shown him his benevolent face. It may be that the statement "You lift up my head" in Ps 3:3 is reminiscent of the ritual lifting of the petitioner's face during the *proskynesis* ritual (cp. also Num 6:25-26).

These reflections are relevant in the present context because the parable of the unforgiving servant so keenly portrays the contrast between the ruler's compassion and the utter absence of compassion on the part of the first official. Might it also be part of the contrast that the ruler touches the chin of the first official to graciously lift him up (the gesture was so familiar that it did not have to be spelled out), whereas the official grabs his colleague by the throat and chokes him?

much they may have heard about royal generosity, this would have sounded like an enormous thing!

Then the scene shifts. As the official is leaving the king's throne room he encounters—on the stairs, so to speak—a minor functionary who in turn owes money to *him*. Compared to the millions that had been forgiven him five minutes previously, the other man's debt to him is positively laughable! Diligent exegetes have calculated that it represents one six-hundred-thousandth of the ten thousand talents.

And that is not all! The story builds up an even greater contrast. The high official grabs the other by the throat, chokes him, and mercilessly demands immediate payment. He acts as if this is altogether a matter of course. He doesn't hesitate for a moment when the other man begs him for mercy in the very same words he had just spoken to the king. The one just now forgiven remains adamant and has the other man thrown into prison.

The story is outrageous, and it outrages listeners even today. It is not only told seamlessly and brilliantly; it is convincing. Anyone who has experienced so much generosity and then acts so heartlessly has forfeited everything. When the king hears of his official's brutality he hands him over to the torturers. That is, he is to be tortured until his relatives pay his debt out of their own pockets and/or until he reveals where he has hidden the stolen money.

Moreover, the story is not only provocative: it is consistent and complete. Whoever hears it grasps it immediately. Still, some interpreters deny that and ask whether the final part of the parable is really authentic, that is, was it part of the original parable Jesus told? These authors see the problem in the final scene, starting with the fellow servants' reporting their disgust to the king over what has happened. Does the parable really need that concluding part? Or at least, couldn't the final sentence (v. 34) be omitted? The following reasons are given for these suggested reductions:

1. The king has shown extraordinary generosity to his official; still more, he has shown him profound mercy. But his sharp reaction would completely destroy that royal behavior.[90] Jewish audiences

---

[90] See, e.g., Hans Weder, *Die Gleichnisse Jesu als Metaphern. Traditions- und redaktionsgeschichtliche Analysen und Interpretationen* (Göttingen: Vandenhoeck & Ruprecht, 1980), 215: "The judgment about to fall on the servant according to v. 34 *must not be told*, because it relativizes the preventative mercy of God."

would necessarily have recognized God in the person of the king, and God forgives all debtors (that is, sinners). Doesn't the harshness the king shows at the end make a farce of his previous mercy? The king is putting himself on the level of his merciless official, and so the parable draws itself out *ad absurdum*. Besides, those who allow the present ending of the parable to stand make the thing that moves God to compassion not divine mercy but fear of punishment. In this line there is even one interpreter who says this is an ending "such as one would be more likely to expect in the sphere of Jewish-legalistic thought."[91]

2. The theme of judgment seems to be extremely important to Matthew. He builds dramatic judgment-scenery into the parable of the banquet (Matt 22:7, 13-14). He also expands the parable of the fishnet by adding a judgment theme (Matt 13:49-50), and he does the same in his interpretation of the parable of the weeds in the wheat (Matt 13:40-43). So was Matthew also at work at the end of this parable (in vv. 31-35)?

3. Were the parable to end with verse 30 (or at least with v. 33) the king's mercy (i.e., God's mercy) would be clearly and simply contrasted with the mercilessness of a subordinate (hence human lack of mercy). Would that not have been a highly effective ending? In that case the parable would end abruptly with the despicable and ignoble attitude of the royal official or (if vv. 31-33 are regarded as authentic) with the king's reproachful question. It would have disgusted its hearers and caused them to reflect on that merciless man— and so also to reflect on their own existence. The rest of the parable would be superfluous because it would only obscure the real subject of the parable: "God is absolutely merciful."

No matter how beautiful that sounds, we may suspect that these interpretations are shaped by current thinking about narrative structures and the tradition history of a text from two thousand years ago, because nowadays Christians very seldom talk about "judgment." After all, God is "tolerant"; God is "tender." Such ideas of course have their effect on exegesis as well. But against this mentality stands the fact that the subject of "judgment" was an integral part of Jesus'

---

[91] Thus Harnisch, *Die Gleichniserzählungen Jesu*, 254.

teaching, as it had been with the Old Testament prophets and John the Baptizer. The fact that now, in this hour, God's mercy is very much in the foreground and exceeds everything else does not change the fact that Jesus also spoke about judgment.

Moreover, as we know, in the Our Father the petition "forgive us [the debt of] our sins" is followed immediately by "as we have forgiven [the debt of] those who sin against us" (Matt 6:12). Unless those praying the Our Father take seriously this mutuality of divine forgiveness of sins and the obligation to forgive our debtors in turn, they bring God's judgment on themselves—or, better, they judge (and condemn) themselves. We would be better advised to allow the parable of the unforgiving servant to end as it does.[92]

I can understand the desire for a more open ending, a happier outcome to this parable. I have sensed it in myself at times. Some years ago, in one of my diaries, I tried to paraphrase the parable of the unforgiving servant. There it ended this way:

> The king's servant left the palace. He couldn't even grasp what had happened to him. He would have liked to skip down the stairs like a little boy, but then one of his fellow servants approached him. This man owed him a hundred denarii. When the official saw the other man lower his eyes and try to avoid him, he approached him, looked at him, and said: "I am giving a banquet this evening, to celebrate with all my family and friends. I want to invite you to join us; bring anyone you want along with you. And forget the money you owe me; your debts are paid. For I was dead and am alive again; I was at an end, and now I can begin anew."

Rereading that text today, I have mixed feelings about it. I say to myself: the idea of the feast to be celebrated and the extension of mercy to the other is certainly biblical, and yet Jesus' parable is better. Quite apart from his style, which is more distanced and less emotional, Jesus speaks more directly to the situation. It is certainly true that we must respond to God's profligate mercy with the same mercy toward others, but that does not say it all. *This is about the people of God.* Now, in this hour when the reign of God is happening, God offers the totality of divine mercy to Israel through Jesus, and the people of God and everyone who hears Jesus' message (and also his

---

[92] For a more detailed treatment of the problem of this de-composition of the parable see Reiser, *Jesus and Judgment*, 275–80.

opponents, who took such offense at his mercy toward sinners) must now, at last, live that divine mercy themselves. They can make their lives correspond to God's action by entering into a new relationship with one another. Empowered by divine mercy they can, for example, live the Sermon on the Mount. If they do not, the world will remain as it is and the history of threats, eruptions of violence, senseless wars, and endless suffering will continue.

In other words: the parable of the unforgiving servant, like all Jesus' parables, offers us no general rules for behavior. It is located in Israel's salvation-historical situation at that moment; obviously, ours is not the same. That situation was (and is) not lovely and not harmonious and not innocuous. For the people of God it demanded a decision of gigantic importance, one that would have consequences—and it has consequences for us, too, depending on how we deal with Jesus and his message. For that reason the parable of the unforgiving servant must not be abridged.

## 30. The Vigilant Slaves (Luke 12:35-38)

"Servants" have appeared from time to time in previous parables: that is, in those cases I have translated the Greek word *doulos* as "servant." Now—as the title given to this parable shows—I am deviating from that rule and suddenly speaking of "slaves," even though it is the same Greek word. That requires explanation.

*Doulos* primarily means "slave," and recent Bible translators have consistently translated *doulos* and its Hebrew equivalent as "slave" wherever it occurs.[93] For example, Martin Luther translated the tenth commandment: "Thou shalt not covet thy neighbour's wife, nor his manservant, nor his maidservant, nor his ass, nor anything that is your neighbour's" (Exod 20:17). Many Bible translations have followed him, speaking of "manservant" and "maidservant" in the tenth commandment. This is true of the Authorized ("King James") Version, the American Standard Version of 1901 as well as its modern revision, and many others. But most newer translations speak at this point of "male slave" and "female slave," and rightly so, for the tenth commandment is about property. In Israel at that time property belonged to *the man*. His property was inviolable, and it consisted of everything

---

[93] This is true of the NRSV (but not of the RSV), as the texts quoted in this book have shown; the same applies to the NABRE.—LMM

in his household, including his wife. Thus it is not appropriate to speak of "manservant and maidservant" here, but only of "male and female slaves."

The situation is similar in many other Old Testament texts. Obviously there were slaves in Israel,[94] either foreigners or Israelites. In the ancient Near East prisoners of war were normally enslaved, and when a city was seized the same usually applied to women and children. Even Israelites could be enslaved in their own land—for example, when they fell into "debt slavery." It is obvious that we must expect to find slaves in Israel from the simple fact that the Torah contains special laws for the treatment of female and male slaves (e.g., Exod 21:2-11; Lev 25:39-55).

As regards the New Testament we must also be aware that in the ancient world of the New Testament texts slaves were a significant part of everyday life. They were merchandise. They were seemingly infinite in number. They were ubiquitous—even in Israel. They were much cheaper to maintain than hired servants. Besides, they were often highly competent and qualified, so that they could be appointed to carry out important functions, even in royal courts. Why, then, should *doulos* not be translated "slave" everywhere it occurs?

I have retained "servant" in this book thus far for the following reason: in the Old Testament people describe themselves in an extraordinary number of places, in relation to those placed above them, God above all, as "your slave" = "your servant." This is a formula of politeness and humility that does not deny the social freedom of the speaker (something that is unavoidable when we use the word "slave").

Hence it is wrong to translate the corresponding terms in principle and universally with "slave." Israel is not "God's slave" but "God's servant," that is, belonging entirely to God and yet free. In such cases Greek offers not only *doulos* (Isa 49:3) but also *pais* (Isa 42:1; 52:13), and that word can also designate slaves.

Isaiah could speak of Israel as the "servant of God" simply because the meaning of *doulos/pais* and its Hebrew equivalents was not restricted to "slave." In the Bible at least, the whole word group refers first of all to someone who is subject to another, and that could be a

---

[94] There is a good overview in Roland de Vaux, *Ancient Israel: Its Life and Institutions*, trans. John McHugh (Grand Rapids: Eerdmans, 1997), 80–90.

servant, a hired hand, a subordinate, an employee, an official, a vassal, or the worshiper of a god. In the gospel parables the individual narrative does not necessarily presuppose the slave relationship everywhere and always. It is a question of service relationships; the precise social status remains open for the most part.

But above all—and this is decisive—all three Synoptic Gospels in many places see "servants" as the disciples or members of the Christian community. The text is *transparent* to the Christian present, case by case. Hence, with certain exceptions, I have held to the familiar tradition of translating *doulos* as "servant," while admitting that the words "servant" and "maid" are increasingly strange to us.

I have just written "with certain exceptions," and those are the "servant parables" that now follow. Within this group of "servant parables" there is one passage that says the returning householder will cut his *doulos* into pieces (Matt 24:51). That text (which will be discussed in detail) presupposes Roman penal law, according to which a slaveowner could punish a disobedient slave with death and could carry out the punishment personally. Here, then, the case is completely clear. And since we are dealing with a "parable group," within the group I will speak of "slaves." That is not an ideal solution, but in principle to translate the word *doulos* as "slave" every time it appears in the New Testament parables is equally subject to challenge. Often we simply do not know what particular social situation the author had in mind.

Here, then, is the text of Luke 12:35-38. The parable is presented in a very clear and considered form. Warnings and benedictions artfully interrupt the parable proper.

> Be dressed for action and have your lamps lit; be like those who are waiting for their master to return from the wedding banquet,[95] so that they may open the door for him as soon as he comes and knocks. Blessed are those slaves whom the master finds alert when he comes; truly I tell you, he will fasten his belt and have them sit down to eat,

---

[95] Literally: "who are waiting for their master to return from a meal, so that when he has arrived and knocked they can immediately open to him."

and he will come and serve them. If he comes during the middle of the night, or near dawn, and finds them so, blessed are those slaves. (Luke 12:35-38)

One example may show how artfully shaped this material is. The second part (vv. 37-38) is "concentrically" structured, according to the following pattern:

(a) Benediction
    (b) Watchful slaves
        (c) The master girds himself, invites them to the table, serves them.
    (b') Watchful slaves
(a') Benediction

Moreover, in Greek the axis of the concentric structure (c) is accentuated by three predicates with a steadily increasing number of words in each and also, of course, by "truly I tell you."[96] It thus becomes clear that the statement's full weight falls on this axis, that is, on the phenomenon that the householder himself serves a slave.

A further observation on the form of this text: it contains a number of fixed formulae that were known to all who were familiar with biblical language. Thus, for example, the instruction "let your loins be girded"[97] is a reference to the first night of Israel's Passover celebration. Watchful, girded, shod, and thus fully ready for exodus: so must Israel, in this night, await the action of God (Exod 12:11).

So we have arrived at the sense Luke has given to our text: for him it is about the return of Christ. The Christian communities must await the hour of their Lord's "return," fully vigilant and constantly ready.[98]

---

[96] See Christine Gerber, "Wann aus Sklavinnen und Sklaven Gäste ihres Herren werden (Von den wachenden Knechten) Lk 12,35-38," in Zimmermann, *Kompendium*, 573–78, at 573.

[97] Thus the Authorized Version; NRSV "be dressed for action" misses the Exodus allusion.

[98] In the parable the "master" returns home during the night. It is no accident that Christian communities later awaited Christ's *parousia* in the night of the vigil of Easter. This is evident, e.g., in Lactantius, *Divinae institutiones* 7.19.3, and Jerome, *In Matthaeum* 4.25.6. On this see especially Wolfgang Huber, *Passa und Ostern. Unter-*

As in the parable of the successful break-in (Luke 12:39), Luke has applied the parable material to Christ's *parousia*.

Naturally the question again arises: what was the original meaning of the material behind Luke 12:35-38? Was it already a *parousia* parable for Jesus? That is highly unlikely. The case is no different from that of the budding fig tree (Mark 13:28-29) or the ten bridesmaids (Matt 25:1-13). It was only after Easter that the texts in question were interpreted as referring to the expected coming of Christ in the near future. So what was the point of the parable of the watchful slaves to begin with?

In order to get closer to that point we would have to pursue the tradition history of Luke 12:35-38 in detail, but that would be terribly difficult. Here the scholarly positions drift far apart. One group sees this as drawn from Luke's special material; another group thinks it comes from Q—and in either case the material is supposed to have been partially combined before it was reworked by the evangelists.

In fact, such exchanges were fairly frequent in the history of the traditional material behind the "slave parables." That is especially clear in the parable of the gatekeeper (Mark 13:33-37), which has a lot in common with our parable. It shows how popular the material about "watchful slaves" or "watchful menials" was in the early communities. That material in particular had to be told often, varied, combined, and enriched.

Hence in this case I will not attempt a reconstruction of the tradition history of the parable. We would get lost in a thicket of hypotheses. Instead I will take as a starting point two motifs that give an impression of originality and even of extravagance: namely, the return of a rich man late at night from an extended wedding feast and the not-to-be-expected phenomenon that, after returning home, the master would reverse the roles of "master and slave" and serve his menials himself.

Around those two central motifs we can reconstruct a story that would have been new and exciting to hearers at that time—and in that respect corresponded to others among Jesus' parable stories. He

---

*suchungen zur Osterfeier der alten Kirche*, BZNW 35 (Berlin: Töpelmann, 1969), 209–28. The model certainly would have been Jewish expectation of the Messiah in the Passover night. On this see Joachim Jeremias, *The Eucharistic Words of Jesus*, trans. Norman Perrin (Philadelphia: Trinity Press International, 1990), 206–7.

must have told it somewhat like this, though much more sparingly and concentratedly than I can:

> A man with a considerable estate participates in a wedding feast. The banquet takes place in the evening, of course. Therefore nothing is said about the first night watch (the hours before midnight) as the time for his return. It is absolutely clear that the man will remain absent until far into the night; hence his slaves must also stay awake. The lamps and torches must remain lighted because it would be difficult to light the little clay lamps again if there was no fire in the stove. The door in the gatehouse had to be locked, and the personnel had to be ready to throw it open and offer a worthy welcome to their master when he returned from the great banquet and to serve him hand and foot. The slaves, both women and men, know that their master wants to be held in esteem, and he wants his comforts. He values being greeted appropriately, not only if it is close to midnight but even long after that.

It seemed at first, certainly, that the parable would run in that direction, and the listeners would have been envious or understanding, but in any case they would have eagerly awaited the end of the story. But then it takes a turn. It by no means describes how the master (slightly tipsy?) makes himself comfortable, how his slaves swarm around him, how he perhaps drinks a last bedtime cordial and then goes to bed. No, exactly the opposite happens: the roles are reversed. The householder binds his long, airy, untailored tunic with a belt so it won't get in his way while he is working; he invites his slaves to take their places on the dining couches; he waits on them and serves their plates, thus making himself a slave and treating his menials as equals—and he celebrates with them.

So the wedding feast is continued at home. We must not ask the story to tell us where the master gets the food and why he does all that, any more than we may ask why the landowner in Matthew 20:1-16 is so attentive and generous.

What did Jesus mean to say with this parable? At any rate it is about watchfulness, in his view. But for what or whom should one be watching? Surely for the inbreaking reign of God, because it is happening already in weary, exhausted Israel. It is possible to sleep through it. With snuffed candles and locked doors one can be oblivious to the hour on which everything depends. One can miss the *kairos*. After all, what Jesus promises is of absolutely no interest to many in

Israel while others oppose it with all their strength—but still others have a watchful heart and receive the new thing with great joy and gratitude. In this case watchfulness means awaiting the fulfillment of the promises, and in that expectation also realizing that they are now being fulfilled.

Those who watch may have an overwhelming experience: Jesus turns all relationships on their heads. Masters now serve others as slaves, and slaves become masters. Precisely what is described in Mary's revolutionary song in Luke 1:46-55 is now taking place:

> He has brought down the powerful from their thrones,
>     and lifted up the lowly;
> he has filled the hungry with good things,
>     and sent the rich away empty. (Luke 1:52-53)

The Magnificat sings of a revolution that began with the liberation of Israel from Egypt and is now making its last and decisive strides in Jesus. It seems that Jesus is the hidden figure behind the householder in the parable, but he himself does not put that into words. His listeners have to discover that concealed background to his words for themselves. Luke will again take up this overturning of all relationships when he tells of Jesus' saying: "[W]ho is greater, the one who is at the table or the one who serves? Is it not the one at the table? But I am among you as one who serves" (Luke 22:27).

## 31. The Slave Keeping Watch (Matthew 24:45-51)

This parable is related in a number of ways to that of the vigilant slaves. Here again the controlling figure in the action is a householder, and here again he commands an imposing property with a large number of female and male slaves. But in contrast to Luke 12:35-38, the "narrative interlocutor" of the householder is not the whole group of slaves but a single one who has been supervising all the rest. Moreover, the householder is not returning from a wedding feast in the evening; it seems that he has been absent for a considerable length of time. But above all, here only *two* possibilities are considered: the story assumes there will be either a good or a bad ending.

Naturally the question immediately arises: did Jesus reuse the material about slaves who await the return of their master in a number of different parables, or was this material so important to the early church, because of its urgent expectation of the *parousia*, that the church itself produced a number of variations? The latter would certainly have been possible. Still, we have to consider that Jesus would probably not have used such striking narrative material as we find here for only one parable.

This parable comes from Q, and Luke 12:42-46 contains a parallel to Matthew 24:45-51, with only minor variations. I have chosen Matthew's version, which seems to be closer to Q:

> Who then is the faithful and wise slave, whom his master has put in charge of his household, to give the other slaves their allowance of food at the proper time? Blessed is that slave whom his master will find at work when he arrives. Truly I tell you, he will put that one in charge of all his possessions. But if that wicked slave says to himself, "My master is delayed," and he begins to beat his fellow slaves, and eats and drinks with drunkards, the master of that slave will come on a day when he does not expect him and at an hour that he does not know. He will cut him in pieces and put him with the hypocrites, where there will be weeping and gnashing of teeth. (Matt 24:45-51)

As with other texts, Matthew has applied this one to Christ's *parousia* and the judgment to follow. Presumably he, like Luke, saw the chief slave as an embodiment of those who held responsibility in the church.[99] If they fulfill their duty they will be richly rewarded; if not, dreadful punishments will fall on them. Matthew added the statement about "weeping and gnashing of teeth" from his repertoire of judgment scenes (cp. Matt 8:12; 13:42, 50; 22:13).

In fact, Q had already interpreted this parable in terms of Christ's *parousia*, and naturally Luke then did so as well. Nevertheless, we would be well advised to keep the theme of Christ's return completely separate from the original parable. What was Jesus talking about when he told it?

Before looking for the answer I need to first examine the *form* of our text. The parable begins with a question that is immediately followed by a benediction, a "beatitude." That is unusual. Certainly a lot of Jesus' parables begin in question form,[100] but here the question

---

[99] Cp. Luke 12:41.

[100] See the summary by Alfons Weiser, *Die Knechtsgleichnisse der synoptischen Evangelien*, SANT 29 (Munich: Kösel, 1971).

is disturbing because we expect that the first part of the parable will speak just as clearly about the opportunities for good behavior on the part of a slave as it will describe the possibilities of bad behavior in the second part. But that does not happen.

It is best not to use possible mistranslations of Aramaic as arguments any more than necessary, but it could be that what we have here is just such a wrong translation.[101] There are good arguments in favor of the proposal that the parable in its Semitic form began with a conditional clause that was misunderstood as a question when it was translated into Greek. The beginning of the parable would have read: "If a slave was appointed by his master to be over the household domestics in order to distribute food to them in a timely manner, he is blessed if the master finds him doing that when he returns. However, if that servant . . . ."[102]

That is a possible reconstruction, based on the grammar. It has the advantage, for one thing, of making the two parts of the parable correspond more closely, as is the case with others of Jesus' double parables (cp., e.g., Matt 7:24-27). This reverse translation has the further advantage of not suggesting that there are two different slaves in view; rather, here we have a description of two possible attitudes on the part of a single slave: correct behavior or misuse of what is entrusted to him. But enough about the original form of the parable!

Certainly it is off-putting today to read that the supervisor-slave is responsible only for distributing food. Didn't he have much more important duties to fulfill while his master was absent? The problem disappears when we consider that slaves were not paid. They had a roof over their heads and food to eat; hence supervision of provisions for the whole domestic crew was the crucial duty of a slave responsible for the household.

So what did Jesus want to say with this parable? Evidently, here again, it is about right behavior—and in an altogether decisive period of time in which heavy responsibility lay on everyone living in "the house of Israel." Each one's whole existence is at stake. Each must decide now, in this very hour, whether to act rightly—rightly, that is,

---

[101] For the following cp. Weiser, *Die Knechtsgleichnisse*, 181–83, as well as Ulrich Luz, *Matthew 21–28*, trans. James E. Crouch, Hermeneia (Minneapolis: Fortress Press, 2005), 222.

[102] Luz, *Matthew 21–28*, 222, citing Klaus Beyer, *Semitische Syntax im Neuen Testament*, vol. 1, part 1, SUNT 1 (Göttingen: Vandenhoeck & Ruprecht, 1968), 287–93.

in light of the reign of God proclaimed by Jesus. But it is possible to misuse the allotted time on which everything depends. It is possible to miss the *kairos*.

This parable, unlike the one in Luke 12:35-38, does not speak of a great many slaves, a whole "household crew" being addressed, but of a single individual who is responsible for all the others. Does that mean that in this parable Jesus was primarily addressing the "responsible people" in Israel?

Under no circumstances can it be denied that Jesus told this parable because the subject of the final judgment plays such a terrible role here, since the subject appears in Jesus' preaching also. When he prayed alone, reciting and meditating on prophetic texts or psalms, he continually came across sayings about judgment, often of the sharpest kind, urging Israel to vigilance and repentance. Are we to assume that Jesus mentally bypassed those sayings about judgment, reinterpreted them, disregarded or even rejected them?

Admittedly, the picture of the slave's being cut to pieces is gruesome. It shows that (as indicated earlier) this is not about a wage-laborer or servant. This can refer only to a slave. In Roman law a slaveowner had life-and-death power over her or his slaves and could carry out the death penalty without any court proceeding. According to Torah, nothing like that was permitted in Israel (Exod 21:20). Moreover, men and women from Israel who had been sold or were forced to sell themselves into slavery had to be offered their freedom after no more than seven years (Exod 21:2; Deut 15:12).

Still, obviously the people in Israel in Jesus' time were constantly confronted with Roman ways of life and pagan abuses. Cities of considerable size had been constructed in Israel, populated by Gentiles who led a Gentile way of life. Jesus quite often refers in his parables to this strange yet familiar world. The material he chose for his parables was neither naïve nor innocuous. It could be incisive.

## 32. A Slave's Wages (Luke 17:7-10)

Here is another parable in which a slave plays the crucial role! But everything is different from the situation in Luke 12:35-38, where the master serves his slaves. Now it is not the owner who comes home but the slave. The master is at home, and the slave is returning after having worked all day. He appears before his master exhausted, sweaty, weary, and hungry. That is the situation the narrator presumes, but he does not describe it. Instead, he simply poses three questions to his listeners:

> Who among you would say to your slave who has just come in from plowing or tending sheep in the field, "Come here at once and take your place at the table"? Would you not rather say to him, "Prepare supper for me, put on your apron and serve me while I eat and drink; later you may eat and drink"? Do you thank the slave for doing what was commanded? So you also, when you have done all that you were ordered to do, say, "We are worthless slaves; we have done only what we ought to have done!" (Luke 17:7-10)

This parable is contained only in Luke's gospel. Similarly to the parable of the importunate friend in Luke 11:5-8, it is artfully structured. We can see that most readily if we drop the three question marks and make the material into a pure narrative. It would look like this:

> A man had a slave who plowed the fields or tended the livestock all day long. When he came home in the evening from his work, his master certainly did not say to him: "Come here at once and take your place at the table!" Rather, he said: "Make my dinner, then gird up your garment and serve me while I eat and drink. Afterward you can eat and drink likewise." And the master was by no means grateful to his slave for doing what he was ordered to do. He saw it as a matter of course. After all, slaves are there to work.

That is precisely the material on which the parable is based, but it is not presented to us in this form. Instead it comes in three questions, so that the hearer is immediately drawn in. This dramatizes the material and enhances its effect. The dramatization is consistent and contains several segments of direct address. This dramatization testifies to the narrator's rhetorical skill.

Still, a whole series of interpreters have laid their literary-critical scalpels on this parable as well: they say the three questions are inconsistent in their structure because the first calls for a negative answer ("no, nobody could imagine that"), the second a positive response ("yes, of course that is the way it is"), and the third a negative again ("no, he would not"). Such a back-and-forth is said to be impermissible. Moreover, the application at the end, they say, does not fit what has been said before, since at first the audience would hear the whole parable from the standpoint of the master, whereas at the end they are suddenly slaves themselves. Thus the text must be radically shortened, dropping the second question as well as the application.[103]

But that trimming of our text is by no means convincing. Rhetorically it is indeed admissible and not at all aberrant for a speaker to pose a series of three questions that are to be answered first negatively, then positively, and then negatively again. Besides, after the first question there is still something unclear. Perhaps the listeners already know the parable about the householder who comes home from the wedding feast, girds up his robes, and serves his slaves (Luke 12:35-38). So it is not all that certain how they would answer the first question. Only the second question creates full clarity; it is therefore absolutely necessary.

Likewise the application at the end fits wonderfully with what has gone before. The change of perspective in verse 10 is not only possible but even represents highly skilled rhetoric: precisely because the listeners first slipped into the role of the master and have regarded the slaves wholly from the master's perspective, even agreeing with it, they must also agree from the slaves' perspective.[104] Besides, it is impossible to imagine this parable without its application—and the reverse is also true: the application cannot exist without the parable.

What we have before us is one of the most moving and perhaps also the most annoying of Jesus' parables. This time what is presupposed is not a rich estate; we are in small, rather poor surroundings. The man has only a single slave who has to work hard and carry out a lot of different roles: herding the livestock, planting the fields, keeping the house in order, and even preparing meals. There is no wife in the picture, not even because she has died or been sent away but because the parable has to be arranged without her. It is just as in Luke 15:11-32, in which the mother of the lost son does not appear at all. Parables have to be simple so that the listeners will not get distracted.

---

[103] Thus, for example, Heininger, *Metaphorik*, 192–93.
[104] Thus rightly Wolter, *Das Lukasevangelium*, 569.

Here again Jesus describes the everyday life of a slave realistically and without any moralizing. It would be ridiculous to demand that he provide a verdict against slavery in his slave parables. His veto of ancient slaveholding society is given in a very different way: namely, that he radically rejects every kind of usurped power relationships within and on behalf of his circle of disciples, whom he has gathered around him as the growth center of eschatological Israel (Mark 10:35-45).

If we want to know what Jesus intended to say with this parable we have to look closely at the situation of the slave in the story. It is true that there were slaves in antiquity who were highly valued by their owners and were therefore allotted considerable freedom. This slave, on the other hand, is entirely dependent on his master and subject to him in all things. He has no control over his life; the owner controls. As a slave, he receives no pay. In place of it he has a roof over his head and his daily bread. He gets no thanks, either. His work is regarded as simply a matter of course.

If we apply these constants to the situation of believers the result is initially alarming. They are altogether dependent on God; they are subject to God in every way. They cannot determine the course of their own lives. God decides. God commands, and God's commands must be obeyed. It is simply assumed that believers will work tirelessly for God's cause and without a thought of payment or even thanks. All they can say is: "We are worthless slaves; we have done only what we ought to have done!"

We must not disguise, certainly we dare not retouch, the picture produced by this material on "God's slaves." It is shocking. Jesus seems here to approach the limits of what can be spoken in order to clarify one particular side of believers' existence. Faith is pure service that makes no demands, no claims, no calls for recognition; it does not insist on its rights but acknowledges the superior rights of "another."

*But*—all that being said, we must add that Jesus can also say exactly the opposite. That opposite is depicted in the parable of the vigilant slaves in Luke 12:35-38. They are certainly rewarded, namely, by the fact that their returning master prepares their meal himself and personally serves them at table. He makes himself their slave. And, as we have seen, in Matthew 24:45-51 the true and faithful slave is rewarded for good behavior by being made manager of his master's whole estate. As manager he can act with great freedom: in fact, his personal initiative is required.

Here, then, within a group of parables that have a lot in common, some arcs of tension are set in place. We could also call them a dialectic: being subject and yet set free; lacking wages and yet rewarded more than abundantly; having to work hard and celebrating together with the master, even being served by him. Evidently Jesus needed these tensions in order to give a right picture of the existence of his disciples. Ultimately it is the tension between grace and freedom, between abandoning every thought of reward and nevertheless receiving a lavish wage.

Still, one thing must necessarily be added: this arc of tension that exists in Israel's experience since Abraham now finds its most powerful manifestation in the rapid approach of the reign of God and is evident above all in the lives of the disciples whom Jesus gathers around him: they leave everything and yet receive it back a hundredfold (Mark 10:29-30); they abandon their freedom and thus become fully free; they no longer expect wages and yet live in profound joy; they seem impoverished and useless and will become a blessing for many.

Jesus brought one extreme of this arc into the picture in the parable about the slave's wages. There is the other extreme, but this parable does not address it in particular. There is much in favor of the idea that it was directed at Jesus' disciples, and obviously it presupposes the situation of the onrushing reign of God that is pure grace and makes us forget all about our own deserving.

### 33. The Money Given in Trust (Matthew 25:14-30)

The next parable is also clearly and compactly structured; indeed, its plan seems almost mathematical. Texts so strictly shaped were easy to retell.[105] In this case the structure is also required because of the numerous formulaic repetitions. The parable has three parts:

1. A rich man travels abroad. Before leaving he entrusts his money to three servants so that they may manage his fortune.

---

[105] Matthew probably had a role in shaping this strict form, but Jesus certainly did as well. The numerous "original" forms of the parable of the "money given in trust" reconstructed in recent decades suffer, at least in part, from a striking absence of form.

2. There is a brief account of what the servants do with the money during their master's absence.

3. After a long time the rich man returns, and the three servants have to give an accounting.

Thus the narrative counterpart to the "sovereign actor" is made up of three servants (here I am reverting to the translation "servant").[106] They appear in all three parts of the parable; obviously they are the narrative representatives of a larger number of servants.

The third part of the parable is by far the longest, and within it the dialogue with the third servant is the most extensive. Hence the parable's accent clearly lies at the end of the third section.

> For it is as if a man, going on a journey, summoned his slaves and entrusted his property to them; to one he gave five talents, to another two, to another one, to each according to his ability. Then he went away.
> The one who had received the five talents went off at once and traded with them, and made five more talents. In the same way, the one who had the two talents made two more talents. But the one who had received the one talent went off and dug a hole in the ground and hid his master's money.
> After a long time the master of those slaves came and settled accounts with them. Then the one who had received the five talents came forward, bringing five more talents, saying, "Master, you handed over to me five talents; see, I have made five more talents." His master said to him, "Well done, good and trustworthy slave; you have been trustworthy in a few things, I will put you in charge of many things; enter into the joy of your master." And the one with the two talents also came forward, saying, "Master, you handed over to me two talents; see, I have made two more talents." His master said to him, "Well done, good and trustworthy slave; you have been trustworthy in a few things, I will put you in charge of many things; enter into the joy of your master." Then the one who had received the one talent also came forward, saying, "Master, I knew that you were a harsh man, reaping where you did not sow, and gathering where you did not scatter seed; so I was afraid, and I went and hid your talent in the ground. Here

---

[106] For the reasons, see the beginning of chapter 30. The NRSV continues to write "slaves."

you have what is yours." But his master replied, "You wicked and lazy slave! You knew, did you, that I reap where I did not sow, and gather where I did not scatter? Then you ought to have invested my money with the bankers, and on my return I would have received what was my own with interest. So take the talent from him, and give it to the one with the ten talents. For to all those who have, more will be given, and they will have an abundance; but from those who have nothing, even what they have will be taken away. As for this worthless slave, throw him into the outer darkness, where there will be weeping and gnashing of teeth." (Matt 25:14-30)

This text has a parallel in Luke 19:12-27. The chief differences between Luke's and Matthew's versions are as follows:

1. In Luke's telling the parable takes place in a space that was originally foreign to it: an aspiring king travels to a distant country to acquire rule over his land. A delegation of his own countrymen follows him in order to prevent him from gaining power over them. Still, the man is promised the throne; he returns home and has his opponents executed. It is absolutely clear that this thread of the narrative was only woven into the story after the fact. It does not match the parable material. That thread is absent from Matthew's version, which clearly offers us the original.

2. In Luke the money is distributed not to three but to ten servants—and the same amount to each. In Matthew there are only three servants and they receive staggered amounts. In Luke's version, however, only three servants appear to give account. Thus the ten servants in Luke are evidently secondary. Whether in Jesus' version the money was evenly distributed among the three servants is a question that must remain open, but it is ultimately unavoidable in the search for the parable's meaning.

3. Luke writes that the first two servants are rewarded by being made proconsuls. In Matthew they are placed "over many things," which sounds more like management of even more wealth, and with even more rights, than before. Thus they will have gone on working to promote their master's business interests. Here again, Matthew's version is probably closer to the original. The appointment of proconsuls in Luke's version must be connected to the story of the master's acquisition of a crown.

4. The amount of money entrusted creates real difficulties. In Luke each of the ten servants receives one *mina*. A *mina* was about a hundred drachmas or a hundred denarii (and a denarius was roughly the day's wages of a laborer). Thus a *mina* is not a huge sum of money. A silver talent, on the other hand, represented six thousand drachmas. Thus Matthew's "talents" are an incomparably greater amount of money than Luke's *mina*s.[107] Most interpreters, by far, regard the "one *mina*" in Luke as original; the reason given is that Matthew loves large sums. But the only evidence that can be adduced for that assertion is the parable of the unforgiving servant, who owed his master ten thousand talents (Matt 18:24). Besides, it seems that the man who goes to another country in Matthew's version is not interested in testing his employees to see which one is the best at handling money. Rather, he wants them to increase his cash reserves while he is away. For the coherence of the narrative, then, the sum in question must be the greater one.

We will have to deal with what I have referred to as the "coherence of the narrative." At this point we may just say that *on the whole* Matthew's version is closer to the original and also more enlightening than Luke's, which is why I have chosen it for treatment here.

Nevertheless, Matthew did make changes to the parable as well. For example: at the accounting the first and second slave are told to "enter into the joy of your master." That is utterly incomprehensible as a reward for good money management, but it becomes abundantly clear when we notice that Matthew has interpreted this parable, too, in terms of Christ's return. The master who goes abroad is Jesus Christ, who has been elevated to the right hand of God. When he returns at the *parousia* he will demand an accounting of everyone, each according to ability. Thus the servants' presentation of accounts is the judgment of the world. Those who withstand the judgment receive a share in the eternal feast of joy ("enter into the joy of your master"). But those who, like the third servant, cannot stand before the judge will lose everything and be thrown into the outermost darkness.

---

[107] For the precise relationship of the sums see Wolter, *Das Lukasevangelium*, 620.

Thus Matthew (and probably other tradents before him) interpreted Jesus' parable in terms of the judgment of the world, in light of the earliest church's expectation of the *parousia*. In doing so they updated the text for their time. This need not prevent us from asking about the meaning of the parable for Jesus. What was this narrative originally about?

In older catechisms this parable is used as the foundational biblical text for the subject of "our spiritual aptitudes and abilities." The catechism says, for example: "We must be especially grateful for our spiritual aptitudes and abilities, improve them and use them rightly. . . . Whoever neglects his or her spiritual aptitudes and abilities through carelessness or laziness commits sin."[108] That interpretation of the parable was, of course, occasioned by the word "talents." The meaning we give to the word "talent" today has its origin in the parable of the money given in trust.

For a long time, in fact, there was a broad current of interpretations that, like the passage quoted, reduced our parable to ordinary moral striving. Here is a second example: According to Adolf Jülicher, Jesus wanted to say in this parable that God rewards only those who use God's gifts faithfully but punishes those who idly waste those gifts.[109] There is not a trace of Jesus' eschatology any longer, to say nothing of his message about the reign of God. "You must always make fruitful the gifts God has given you." Did Jesus really see it as his mission to preach such platitudes?

The exegetes who locate the parable in Jesus' conflicts with his opponents appear at first glance to be much closer to his thinking.[110] The man who buries the good entrusted to him—he represents the Jewish teachers who oppose Jesus. Thus Joachim Jeremias, for example, writes: "God has entrusted them [the leaders of the people, especially the scribes] with much: the spiritual leadership of the nation, the knowledge of his will, the key of the Kingdom of God. Now

---

[108] *Katholischer Katechismus der Bistümer Deutschlands* (Freiburg: Herder, 1955), 115, p. 230.

[109] Jülicher, *Die Gleichnisreden Jesu*, vol. 2, 480.

[110] This line of interpretation apparently began with Martin Dibelius, *From Tradition to Gospel*, trans. Bertram Lee Woolf (Cambridge: James Clarke, 1971), 255. However, Dibelius saw this parable as an accusation against the whole Jewish people, who have neglected the good entrusted to them.

the judgement of God is about to be revealed; now it will be decided whether the theologians have justified or abused God's great trust; whether they have made good use of God's gift, or have turned it to their own advantage and to the imposition of burdens upon their fellow men."[111]

But is the anxiety and inactivity of the third servant really characteristic of Jesus' opponents? The Pharisees and scribes, for example, made great efforts to educate the people, to open the Scriptures to them, and to anchor the Torah in their lives. I cannot see any polemic against the Pharisees and scribes in the parable of the money given in trust. This text must have been about something completely different.

We can most easily gain access to the meaning of this parable if we begin with the figure of the man who entrusts cash to his servants so they can manage his wealth. We have here one of those immoral figures who appear rather often in Jesus' parables. Only when we regard this man as a negative figure does the parable reveal its contours and the narrative become "coherent" in every part. This "master" is among the wealthiest, because he hands his "servants"—that is, slaves in high positions or employees with great responsibilities—extremely large sums of money.

In addition, this man is a braggart, because he calls these huge sums "little things," nothing much. It is inadmissible to conclude from that language that the sums in the reconstructed version of the parable were smaller. This man's words represent a clear understatement. To speak of such quantities of money as "little things" is the same as when a bank president today talks of millions of dollars as "peanuts." Jesus thus characterized the man through his own words as a preening fop.

This rich boaster confirms explicitly that he conducts his business in immoral ways when he says to the third servant: "You knew, did you, that I reap where I did not sow, and gather where I did not scatter?" (Matt 25:26; cp. Luke 19:22). This self-characterization by the mafioso-style "master" must finally be taken seriously. It is a grave mistake to see nothing more than a malicious accusation in the reproach the third servant directs at his master and to regard the

---

[111] Jeremias, *The Parables of Jesus*, 166.

master's answer as an ironic twisting of the words of his subordinate.[112] No, this honorable gentleman is quite proud of being described that way. He agrees wholeheartedly.

But all this means that the man is using tricky business methods. He exploits other people. He may be lending money at exorbitant interest. He extorts; he rakes it in. Probably he also repeatedly speculates on risky ventures. Now he has gone abroad for a while, probably to cultivate his business connections or to make more money.

Employees 1 and 2 are worthy reflections of their chief. While he is abroad they increase the capital entrusted to them 100 percent. A great return! That, of course, could not be achieved with solid buying and selling but only with the kinds of dealings that go on behind closed doors, with daring acts outside the legal limits that, however, were entirely in accord with those of their master.

The third servant is fearful of such practices. He takes on no risk at all, not even putting the money entrusted to him in the bank. After all, even a bank can go bankrupt. He hides his master's money in the locker most commonly used in antiquity: he buries it. This way he loses nothing, but he doesn't earn a cent of profit.

And in just that choice he has lost everything. After all, he is part of a firm that puts value on lightning-fast action, initiative, pleasure in risk, and high returns. The third employee, when his master returns from abroad, is chucked out on his ear. His professional existence is done for.

So in this parable Jesus has used some tension-arousing material that is quite unusual for him. The stuff he uses in this story is neither religious nor moral. Jesus puts his hearers in a world in which affairs are harsh and predatory. Anyone who doesn't go for broke cannot last. He will be fired.

---

[112] We find this, for example, in Harnisch, *Die Gleichniserzählungen Jesu*, 39. He says that the master, in countering his servant, only repeats his statement word for word in order "to discredit the servant's motivation." Such irony would be possible in principle, but then we would have to regard the characterization of the master by his servant in v. 24 as an unjustified attack and malicious slander. There is no reason to do so—above all when we consider the large sums acquired by the first and second servants. They are working with exactly the same business methods as their master. The way the third employee apparently "gives" the money to his master might be seen as rude, but what he says is the truth.

What audacity!—making a statement about the reign of God by using immoral material,[113] a story from the world of the profiteers and speculators! That was so extreme that even the post-Easter tradents could not really deal with this parable material. Still, the self-characterization of the master in the parable was faithfully handed on.

And what a claim underlies this parable! What it wants to say must be clear by now. Jesus is talking about God's plan for the world, the new thing that God wants to create in the midst of the old society. In short: he is speaking of the reign of God. This new world of God's, says Jesus, will not succeed by cowardice, with people who are immovable, who constantly want to make themselves secure, who would rather delay than act. This new society of God's will only succeed with people who are ready to risk, who will wager everything on the turn of a card, who go all out and who, with utter determination, will be "doers."

So in his parables Jesus can say that the reign of God comes as pure grace, as if "by itself" (recall the parable of the seed growing by itself). But he can also say that its coming demands utter commitment. Is that a contradiction? Not necessarily. But it is a paradox. Evidently both those things have to be said if one is to speak appropriately about the reign of God. The paradox must not be resolved—no more than the arc of tension between the present and the future of the reign of God may be broken down.

## 34. The Crooked Manager (Luke 16:1-13)

First let me go back briefly to the preceding chapter—to that firm in which nothing else mattered but making fat profits! Could Jesus really tell such a tale? Could he use a story like that to teach his audience about the reign of God? The answer can only be: he could. That must be clear, because the following parable again has, most certainly, an "immoral hero." That is why Luke, who has preserved this parable, had major problems with it. We can see that from the fact that

---

[113] See the similar argument of A. P. Tàrrech, "La parabole des Talents (Mt 25,14-30) ou des Mines (Lc 19,11-28)," in *A cause de l'évangile. Mélanges offertes à dom Jacques Dupont, O.S.B.*, LD 123 (Paris: Cerf, 1985), 165–93, as well as Tim Schramm and Kathrin Löwenstein, *Unmoralische Helden. Anstössige Gleichnisse Jesu* (Göttingen: Vandenhoeck & Ruprecht, 1986), 158.

Luke (and the tradition before him) attached several "commentaries" to the parable (Luke 16:8-13), all connected to the word "mammon." The task of all these commentaries was to explain the parable, to protect it against misunderstanding, and to make sure that no wrong conclusions would be drawn from it. But Jesus did not "protect" his demanding words. He used daring stories to talk about the reign of God. He told parables that were in no way innocuous. Here it is the story of a manager who unscrupulously uses his master's property to secure his own future.

> There was a rich man who had a manager, and charges were brought to him that this man was squandering his property. So he summoned him and said to him, "What is this that I hear about you? Give me an accounting of your management, because you cannot be my manager any longer." Then the manager said to himself, "What will I do, now that my master is taking the position away from me? I am not strong enough to dig, and I am ashamed to beg. I have decided what to do so that, when I am dismissed as manager, people may welcome me into their homes." So, summoning his master's debtors one by one, he asked the first, "How much do you owe my master?" He answered, "A hundred jugs [*bat*] of olive oil." He said to him, "Take your bill, sit down quickly, and make it fifty." Then he asked another, "And how much do you owe?" He replied, "A hundred containers [*kors*] of wheat." He said to him, "Take your bill and make it eighty." And his master commended the dishonest manager because he had acted shrewdly; for the children of this age are more shrewd in dealing with their own generation than are the children of light. And I tell you, make friends for yourselves by means of dishonest wealth so that when it is gone, they may welcome you into the eternal homes.
>
> Whoever is faithful in a very little is faithful also in much; and whoever is dishonest in a very little is dishonest also in much. If then you have not been faithful with the dishonest wealth, who will entrust to you the true riches? And if you have not been faithful with what belongs to another, who will give you what is your own? No slave can serve two masters; for a slave will either hate the one and love the other, or be devoted to the one and despise the other. You cannot serve God and wealth [mammon]. (Luke 16:1-13)

We may set aside the series of four attached commentaries in verses 8-13. They are presented as words of Jesus; even verse 8a is supposed to be Jesus speaking because obviously the "Lord" who praises the dishonest manager is Jesus and not the rich man in the parable.[114] But as I have said, all these tacked-on sayings try to comment on the parable and protect it against misunderstanding. They don't bring us any further. We have to look at the parable itself—and first, once again, at its structure. This parable, too, has three parts:

1. Exposition: description of the manager's critical situation.

2. The manager's internal monologue: he considers his situation and makes a plan.

3. Resolution of the crisis: the manager speaks with his master's debtors and has them fake their promissory notes.

As in the parable of the money given in trust, the third part is the most extensive. It carries the weight of the narrative and reveals to the hearers, or readers, what the parable means to say. And also, as in many other parables, direct speech plays a prominent role in Luke 16:1-7. In the first part the owner addresses his manager, in the second we hear the manager's internal monologue, and in the third the crime itself takes place: not simply reported to us but conveyed in a dialogue between the manager and certain debtors.

We need to feel the intensity with which the parable becomes palpable and visible at the crucial point. Jesus could have said: "And he had his master's debtors come to him one at a time. He told them to write new promissory notes so that they would owe the proprietor much less oil and wheat." But Jesus does not use such a distant, dry style in his parables. There the many dialogues adopt narrative techniques known in antiquity, especially in the Bible (we only need to read Gen 3:1-5), and yet at the same time they are utterly modern. Good popular literature nowadays—mystery stories in particular—is often half dialogue.

It is of course a deliberate choice to have the manager speak with only two debtors. They are representative of the others. These

---

[114] It is true that the contrary has often been suggested or even asserted. But how can the owner praise someone who is stealing from him? After all, the parable is not a comedy in which the duped master praises his servant in the end because he has so successfully hoodwinked him. Jesus can praise the crook, though, because he has used him to illustrate something about the right attitude toward the reign of God. For the whole problem see, in detail, Reiser, *Jesus and Judgment*, 290–301.

dialogues stand for a whole series of exchanges between the manager and his master's debtors, all of them aimed at the same thing. Here again we may note that parables have to be brief and comprehensible. They show what they want to show by means of examples.

But now we come at last to what this text tells us. It is the story of a clever betrayal carried out by a man who knows how to help himself out of a serious crisis. The listeners do not need to have the scenery and background described for them; they are all familiar with it. In Palestine at that time the really productive land was in the hands of a relatively small group of great landowners. These often lived abroad and their properties were overseen by business managers with extensive authority.

One day it is whispered to such a major landowner that his manager is "wasting" or "squandering" the properties entrusted to him. The Greek word here is *diaskorpizō*, which can be translated in a number of ways. Its basic meaning is "destroy." Thus the text leaves open whether this is simply a case of dubious and careless management or whether the manager has embezzled in a big way. The text even leaves open the question whether the accusations brought to the owner are mere slander or if they approximate the truth. In any case, the owner acts: the manager is invited to a meeting at which he will have to present all his business records. That is the opening situation.

The man knows that he is in a hopeless position, that he is going to lose his appointment and has no chance of finding another. His future appears to be ruined. So now he sinks to the most shameless kind of betrayal, and the coolness with which he does so seems to indicate that he has done it before. But that is not altogether certain. The story leaves the question open for the present. Jesus' listeners would have been left guessing.

But now, at any rate, the situation is clear. The man goes all out. He has all his master's debtors (or perhaps a carefully chosen group of them) come to him, and he has them write new promissory notes that are less favorable to his employer. Obviously the old ones were destroyed. In this way he puts people in his debt, and they will later support him. He creates a "right to hospitality" for himself.[115] Obligations of that kind played an extraordinarily important role in ancient society. There was no such thing as insurance, let alone a "social safety

---

[115] For more on this see Silvia Pellegrini, "Ein 'ungetreuer' οἰκονόμος (Lk 16,1-9)? Ein Blick in die Zeitgeschichte Jesu," *BZ* 48 (2004): 161–78, at 169–71.

net." A network of "friends" could be a lifesaver. Today, of course, such "obligations" exist in more modern guise: among "cronies," for example.

Obviously the treacherous manager has the debtors come to him *one at a time*; no witnesses are wanted for this kind of business. The value of the natural products in question is extraordinarily high: 100 "baths" of oil are equivalent to around 950 gallons, the produce of some 145 olive trees. The quantity of wheat is similarly great.

How does the story end?—or we might ask: how would we end it today? Probably with a high moral assessment such as: the treachery is revealed, and the betrayer loses everything and lands in the jug. Moral: crime doesn't pay! At any rate, that is how it would have been told in the eighteenth or nineteenth century. In recent decades, on the other hand, it might have been given a social touch: the unscrupulousness of the exploitative landowner would be criticized, and the behavior of the manager and the debtors depicted as a bitter act of resistance, so that the story of a crime would become a tale of social heroes. In that case the story would also end in high moral fashion.

What is so stunning here is that Jesus' parable has nothing like a moral ending either in bourgeois or anti-bourgeois terms. We can see how little the story aims at a moral in Jesus' eyes by the fact that the end is simply left out. The outcome remains open; it is of no further interest.

Evidently this story of a scoundrel is about something altogether different. The first commentary added to the parable is still aware of that: Jesus praises the dishonest manager (let me repeat: "the master" is obviously Jesus, as in Luke 18:6, and not the injured landowner), but Jesus does not praise the manager's crime; what he praises is the determination with which he rescues his own existence.

In *his own* terms the manager has acted quite consistently: he had no illusions. He thought through the possibilities quite soberly. He used his reason and imagination, and, once he had thought everything through, he proceeded rapidly and effectively.

You must act in just the same way—Jesus wants his hearers to understand—in light of the reign of God. It is offered to you: now, today. But it will come to you only if you apply your minds, your "smarts," your imagination, your passion—your whole existence. Hence by far the best explanation of the parable is found in the final commentary: "No slave can serve two masters; for a slave will either

178  *The Forty Parables of Jesus*

hate the one and love the other, or be devoted to the one and despise the other" (Luke 16:13).

That is: those who want to live under the rule of God can have none but God as their master. They may serve only God—with their whole will, their whole strength, their whole life. Those who have other masters alongside God are divided, torn back and forth, without direction. They do not really apply themselves; they don't risk; they do things by halves. Then their lives lack the strength that belongs to the reign of God.

The dishonest manager did nothing by halves. He was all in. He acted deliberately. He risked everything and invested everything. For that, and only for that, Jesus admires him and says: If only my disciples, my followers, my friends were just as goal-oriented as that manager—under the presuppositions of the reign of God, naturally!

## 35. The Assassin (*Gospel of Thomas* 98)

The next Jesus parable also tells an immoral story. It is so offensive that it was not even adopted into the canonical gospels. Only the *Gospel of Thomas*, rejected by the ancient church because of its fundamentally Gnostic tendencies, has retained this parable for us, in Coptic. It is understandable that the great-church tradition did not transmit the parable, because it is about preparing for a political murder. There was no appetite either for confusing the members of their own communities or for suggesting to the civil authorities an image of Christian belief that might arouse suspicion.[116]

The parable speaks of the "kingdom of the Father," which in the terminology of the *Gospel of Thomas* is the same as the reign of God.

> Jesus said, "The kingdom of the father is like a certain man who wanted to kill a powerful man. In his own house he drew his sword and stuck it into the wall in order to find out whether his hand could carry through. Then he slew the powerful man."[117]

---

[116] According to Michael Fieger, *Das Thomasevangelium: Einleitung, Kommentar, und Systematik* (Münster: Aschendorff, 1991), 249, in *Gos. Thom.* the "powerful person" represents the material world that in the sense of the parable must be killed. Human beings are to free themselves from all passions so as to be able to recognize the sparks of light in them.

[117] *Gos. Thom.* 98. Translation by Thomas Lambdin, available at http://www.earlychristianwritings.com/text/thomas-lambdin.html.

We may again begin with the "form" of the parable. The text is extraordinarily brief. As is so often the case, here again the question arises: didn't Jesus really tell the parable at much greater length? After all, this is exciting stuff. Is the parable so sparse because its form is derived from a shortening made for catechumens? Or did Jesus tell it so briefly because he wanted to get to the point of some longer remarks about the reign of God (that may have preceded it)? I will leave the question open. Sometimes I lean one way, and sometimes another. But in this particular case we have to ask ourselves whether the extreme brevity here is not due to the author of the *Gospel of Thomas*, who, in fact, often shortened and simplified Jesus' parables known to us from the Synoptic Gospels.

In any case it is astonishing to think of everything the parable does *not* tell. It speaks of a man, but who is he? We never learn. Then we encounter a "powerful person." The Coptic text at this point has adopted the Greek word μεγιστάν without translating it. It seems probable that this word refers to aristocratic, politically powerful people surrounding a king (cp. Mark 6:21), but here we learn nothing more.

Further: why should the powerful person be murdered? Has he committed a serious crime? Has he destroyed someone's whole existence? Was he extremely corrupt? Had he himself committed murder, or ordered it? Is he a symbol for nationwide oppression? That, too, remains open. We are not told.

And then there is the story itself. The listener expects, up to the very end, that everything is now ready and at last the assassination will be described at length. Where does it happen? In a royal palace? In a tight-packed crowd? Has the assassin concealed his short sword or dagger under his cloak? Does he actually thrust it through the cloak? Can he escape, or will he be overpowered immediately? The murderous act is dismissed in the fewest words possible: "Then he killed the powerful one."

This is similar to the parable of the seed growing by itself (Mark 4:26-29). There, too, the harvest is not the important thing. The parable ends simply with: "at once he goes in with his sickle, because the harvest has come." All that was important was the process of growth. There lay the whole weight of the narrative. It is similar here: everything depends on the statement that "He drew the sword in his house (and) stabbed it into the wall to test whether his hand would be strong (enough)." Here, then, we find the point of the parable.

What, then, does the parable mean to say? Evidently the interest lies in the *preparation* for the killing, not the assassination itself. Even so, there are different possibilities for interpretation. For example, it has been said that the point of the parable is the inescapable nature of the murder. Precisely through the description of the careful preparation it means to show that this man is inescapably condemned to death. He doesn't have a chance. And it is just that way with God. The project of bringing about the reign of God must succeed, and it is as certain as the ultimate end of the prominent man.[118]

But that interpretation is highly questionable. Apart from the fact that assassination attempts often go awry, is this parable really saying that God will be successful in the end? That does not do justice to the weight placed on the *preparation* for the killing.

We know from Roman literature that legionaries regularly practiced the mortal thrust with the short sword, using wooden mannequins.[119] It was essential that one not inflict a mere flesh wound on the opponent; one must strike the right place so as to deliver a mortal wound. There could be resistance from cartilage, muscle, ribs, so one's hand had to be accurate and strong. Apparently the assassin in our parable trained in a similar way except that he did not have a wooden figure to aim at, so he used the mud wall of his house. Perhaps he first made a charcoal outline of a human-size figure on the inner wall of the house.

At this point, however, we may again ask: did he train for weeks, like the Roman legionaries or gladiators, so as to make his arm swift and powerful and be able to hit his mark exactly, or is this about a single session "to test whether his arm would be strong (enough)"?

No matter what we decide, in any case Jesus means to say that those who encounter the reign of God and want to gain it must act like this assassin: deliberately, with their whole effort, ultimate conviction, but also clear preparation and the engagement of all their faculties. They cannot afford half measures.

---

[118] Thus Claus-Hunno Hunzinger, "Unbekannte Gleichnisse Jesu aus dem Thomasevangelium," in *Judentum, Urchristentum, Kirche: Festschrift für Joachim Jeremias*, ed. Walter Eltester, BZNW 26 (Berlin: de Gruyter, 1960), 209–20; and especially Schramm and Löwenstein, *Unmoralische Helden*, 54–55.

[119] Cp. Niclas Förster, "Die Selbstprüfung des Mörders (Vom Attentäter) EvThom 98," in Zimmermann, *Kompendium*, 921–26, at 924–25.

If we look at this parable together with the next one about building a tower and making war we may be inclined to see this as a unique, isolated event. In that case the parable of the assassin would not describe strength training over weeks but an all-encompassing focus on the goal: the assassin considers what he wants to do, subjects his plan to a final test, and then plunges his sword deep into the wall of the house. Then he goes to carry out his plan.

## 36. Building a Tower and Making War (Luke 14:28-32)

The following double parable comes from Luke's special material. The evangelist inserted it into a short composition of speech units (14:25-35). Jesus is addressing "a great crowd of people" who are traveling with him (14:25) about the conditions for discipleship and the seriousness of following him.

> For which of you, intending to build a tower, does not first sit down and estimate the cost, to see whether he has enough to complete it? Otherwise, when he has laid a foundation and is not able to finish, all who see it will begin to ridicule him, saying, "This fellow began to build and was not able to finish." Or what king, going out to wage war against another king, will not sit down first and consider whether he is able with ten thousand to oppose the one who comes against him with twenty thousand? If he cannot, then, while the other is still far away, he sends a delegation and asks for the terms of peace. (Luke 14:28-32)

We have already seen several examples of how double parables love contrast. Those about the lost sheep and the lost drachma speak first of a man, then of a woman, each of whom recovers what has been lost (Luke 15:3-10). The parables of the treasure in the field and the pearl speak first of a poor hired worker and then of a wealthy wholesale merchant (Matt 13:44-46).

A contrast is set up here, too, in Luke 14:28-32. The principal figure of the second parable is a king with an army of ten thousand. His opponent is advancing with an army of twenty thousand. Here, then, we are in the world of the great men, the rulers, the powerful who make war on each other.

In the first parable, by contrast, we are in significantly less grand company, that is, in the world inhabited by Jesus' listeners ("which of you?"). So Jesus can address them directly in the first parable: "supposing one of you were to build a tower." Jesus may have been thinking of a vineyard (Isa 5:2). It was common enough that one would build a fairly low round tower of rubble from which to keep watch during the time when the grapes were ripe. The owner of the vineyard had to calculate whether he had the means and the workforce to set up such a tower.

Of course, it is also possible that here Jesus is not thinking at all of a vineyard tower but of a dwelling (cp. *Joseph and Aseneth* 2, 1). But we should not imagine such a tower house as a kind of multistory structure. In Palestine most dwellings were single-story. If someone planned a house with one or two additional stories it could already be called a "tower." It is much more plausible that our parable is speaking about that kind of "tower," since nearly everyone could build a vineyard tower without much financial outlay.[120] It was different with a dwelling tower. The listeners can imagine how the foundations of the planned tower could be seen for years within a neighborhood of dwellings with no further building going on. The builder has overextended himself. One can imagine the jokes in the village or small town. Here, then, we are not in the world of the mighty. These are "bourgeois" conditions. And so the contrast between the two parables is affirmed.

What is the sense of such finely-drawn contrasts? They do not yield much for the interpretation of the double parable, but they do a lot to strengthen the persuasiveness of the whole since it is not only the interrogative structure of our double parable that calls for acquiescence on the part of the hearers. That acquiescence is also achieved by the fact that such double parables are set in different spheres and thus refer to quite different experiences—of men and women, poor and rich, those who are "higher up" in society and those who are "below." Thus in ever new places and with new details we continually come upon the clever storyteller Jesus was.

---

[120] Such a tower was usually "a small building without an inner room and having an outside staircase" (Wilhelm Michaelis, πύργος, *TDNT* 6:954). "Without an inner room" means that the round watchtower consisted of an outer wall of boulders; the interior was filled with rubble. It is hard to imagine that such a building would have been able to bring the farmer who built it into financial difficulties. For watch huts and watchtowers cp. Dalman, *Arbeit und Sitte in Palästina*, vol. 4, 316–29, 332–35.

But now, what about the meaning of this double parable? It is clear as day: before you start something, whether great or small, consider what you are about to do. Ask yourself what the intended action will cost, what burdens it brings with it, what are its consequences, and where you will be when it is finished.

Put that way the meaning of Luke 14:28-32 remains on the level of universal, prudent rules for life. Obviously Jesus had more than that in mind. He does not speak like a wisdom teacher. He addresses a concrete situation: that of the reign of God now in realization. The reign of God is pressing, coming close. It is setting everything in motion and changing everything. Many people hear Jesus' message and see what is happening: the sick are being healed, possessed people freed from the compulsions that shape their lives. The Good News is being preached to the poor. Again and again Jesus encounters women and men who are fascinated by him and want to follow him. And it is precisely in this situation that Jesus not only calls people to discipleship but at the same time has to warn them: "Consider what you are about to do. Do you know what discipleship means? Have you reckoned the costs?"

Thus in the case of our double parable we are in the fortunate position of being able to draw a rather clear picture of the original situation in which it was spoken. There is a whole series of Jesus' sayings that illustrate this situation. Take Luke 9:58, for example: "Foxes have holes, and birds of the air have nests; but the Son of Man has nowhere to lay his head." Jesus called disciples to follow him, but not everyone. He sought out people he considered well suited. He positively warned others who freely volunteered that, in fact, they should not follow him. The double parable in Luke 14:28-32 is evidently one such warning. Indeed, Luke saw that clearly; he created the right context for the two parables.

So Jesus could compare the situation of someone who wanted to follow him with that of a king who has to consider carefully whether he can defend himself against an army double the size of his own. Did Jesus thus legitimate war? Not at all! He merely used a part of the tragic reality of this world in order to draw attention to the calculations that must be made by people who want to be his disciples: the costs and the consequences.

In retrospect that also sheds light on the previous chapter. The parable of the assassin is likewise not a legitimization of murder. It, too, uses the sad realities of this world to show what is demanded of one who follows Jesus: in that case no half measures, but ultimate determination.

Therefore when Jesus forbids his disciples to use violence (Matt 5:39; 26:52) it is no contradiction to the parable of the assassin or the one about making war. The offensive "pictorial material" in Jesus' parables may by no means be set on the same level as the "principles for action" in Jesus' preaching of the reign of God.

## 37. Building a House on Rock or on Sand (Matthew 7:24-27)

The great discourse called the Sermon on the Mount (Matthew 5–7) ends with the parable of building a house; nothing follows but the closing in Matthew 7:28-29. In Luke's gospel the so-called Sermon on the Plain (Luke 6:20-49) corresponds to Matthew's Sermon on the Mount. That discourse also ends with this parable (Luke 6:47-49). Clearly, then, the programmatic discourse in Q that follows Jesus' baptism and temptation must likewise have ended with the parable of building a house. Matthew and Luke each took this closing parable from Q. It seems that Matthew followed the model more closely; therefore I will base what I have to say on Matthew's version:

> Everyone then who hears these words of mine and acts on them will be like a wise man who built his house on rock. The rain fell, the floods came, and the winds blew and beat on that house, but it did not fall, because it had been founded on rock. And everyone who hears these words of mine and does not act on them will be like a foolish man who built his house on sand. The rain fell, and the floods came, and the winds blew and beat against that house, and it fell—and great was its fall! (Matt 7:24-27)

Whereas Luke, in his revision of the parable, seems to have envisioned a great river in flood (Luke 6:48), Matthew held to conditions in Palestine (Matt 7:25): a heavy rain somewhere quite far away could suddenly transform a dry wadi into a rushing riverbed and produce incredible damage. Otherwise, as far as the pictorial level of the parable is concerned, it does not require any extensive explanation. Everyone knows that the very first requirement for building a house is to have a solid foundation. To quote a contemporary expert:

The most important task in laying a foundation is to free the building from stresses and transfer them below ground, without letting the resulting compression of the base disadvantage the building or surroundings. In the case of very tall, narrow buildings there may be horizontal forces resulting from wind pressure.[121]

So the parable-teller could count on his audience's immediate comprehension. Laying a foundation on a rocky base was the ideal; in contrast, building a house on nothing but sand attested to great stupidity or wanton carelessness.

The more important question is what the advancing waters and storm winds signify. Listeners who knew their Bible would inevitably have thought of God's judgment as described in Isaiah 28:14-22. That judgment falls on the mockers and braggarts in Jerusalem. When the flood comes they will be borne away (vv. 18-19) and the hailstorm will sweep away their lies (v. 17). But then God will lay a foundation that is fixed and secure: "in Zion a foundation stone, a tested stone, a precious cornerstone, a sure foundation" (v. 16). Storm and floodwaters, as other Old Testament texts show,[122] are metaphors for judgment.

When Matthew and Luke took this parable from the Sayings Source they also thought about the judgment to come. That is immediately evident in Matthew; there Jesus says: "Everyone then who hears these words of mine and acts on them *will be* like . . ." The future tense is used to point to the impending judgment. Then it will be obvious what kind of foundation the human being has built the house of her or his life upon. Jesus must also have thought of the judgment in telling this parable.

But by far the more important question regarding this parable is: with what is the right way of laying a foundation being compared? As far as Matthew is concerned, the answer is clear: the comparison is with hearing and doing Jesus' words. Here the difficulty is with the word "doing." For Matthew the doing is absolutely decisive; it pervades and dominates the whole of the Sermon on the Mount. "Not everyone who says to me, 'Lord, Lord,' will enter the kingdom of

---

[121] From the article "Gründung (Bauwesen)," *Wikipedia* (German), 20 August 2019. Translated with the assistance of Vincent K. Maloney, M.Arch.

[122] See, e.g., Gen 6:1-9, 29; Ezek 13:10-13; 38:22.

heaven, but only the one who *does* the will of my Father in heaven" (Matt 7:21).

And what about Luke? He also delivers the saying just quoted in the Sermon on the Plain, but in even sharper terms. In his text it applies not to the will of the Father but to Jesus himself: "Why do you call me 'Lord, Lord,' and do not do what I tell you?" (Luke 6:46). That is what this text probably said in Q. And that brings us back to the question of Jesus' own words. Did he himself, as in Luke 6:46, reject just saying, "Lord, Lord," and insist on the doing of his words? And did he understand the parable of the builder in that very sense—that is, that only those who not only hear his words but also follow them can withstand the judgment?

Much depends on the answer to that historical-critical question, for if it is answered positively it means that Jesus has placed his own words above those of the Torah—not as replacing Old Testament commands but as saying that he is now definitively interpreting Torah and thus is, himself, God's final word. In that case Jesus made his own words and the acknowledgment of his person the criterion for judgment. And then for him personally the parable of the builder would be meant to be interpreted not in terms of some judicious way of behaving but as confession of his word—a confession that encompasses one's whole existence.

There is a Jesus saying that is found in a different context and yet points in this very direction:

> And I tell you, everyone who acknowledges me before others, the Son of Man also will acknowledge before the angels of God; but whoever denies me before others will be denied before the angels of God. (Luke 12:8-9; cp. Matt 10:32-33; Mark 8:38)[123]

Jesus uses "Son of Man" as a cloak for himself, and the event taking place "before the angels of God" is the final judgment. "Acknowledging" and "denying," however, refer not only to word and proclamation; they mean confessing (or denying) through doing, through one's life, through one's whole existence.

---

[123] For a more extensive interpretation of Luke 12:8-9 see Gerhard Lohfink, *Jesus of Nazareth*, trans. Linda M. Maloney (Collegeville, MN: Liturgical Press, 2012), 316–17, 345.

We cannot avoid citing this *logion* from Luke 12:8-9 in our search for the original meaning of the parable of the builder. In light of it, Jesus meant to say in this parable: for everyone who hears me, eschatological salvation or judgment depends on obedience to my words.[124]

## 38. The Lamp on the Lampstand (Matthew 5:15)

The parable of the lamp that belongs on the lampstand and nowhere else is found in Matthew, Mark, and Luke—in Luke's case, in two variants (Matt 5:15; Mark 4:21; Luke 8:16; 11:33). Matthew's version is probably closest to the original:

> No one after lighting a lamp puts it under the bushel basket, but on the lampstand, and it gives light to all in the house. (Matt 5:15)

Here again we can ask ourselves whether this is really a parable and not simply a metaphor. But since there is some kind of narrative progress—the lamp is placed on the lampstand, and *then* it lights the house—I count this text among the parables. Nevertheless, it is really a borderline case.

Many people nowadays can no longer picture what a "bushel basket" is. Formerly it was a measure for calculating the quantity of bulk goods such as grain. It was possible, for example, to buy ten bushels of wheat. True, the quantity varied markedly by region; a bushel could be counted as anywhere from seventeen to three hundred liters, but the word "bushel" described not only the quantity it contained but the container with which a bushel was measured. It was (and is) a kind of woven tub.

In his translation of the Bible, Martin Luther rendered the Greek word *modios* as "bushel," and we should hold to that translation, not only because "hiding one's light under a bushel" has become a proverbial expression but also because (at least in Western Europe) there no longer are any baskets of that size in common use that are also used for measurement.[125] The ancient *modios* was much like the

---

[124] Here I am following Hans Klein, *Das Lukasevangelium*, KEK I/3 (Göttingen: Vandenhoeck & Ruprecht, 2006), 266.

[125] In the United States, however, it is quite common to buy apples and other produce by the bushel, and produce for sale at farmstands is often displayed in bushel baskets.

bushel. *Modios* was first a measure of quantity, and then the vessel of corresponding size for measuring.

We know somewhat more about Hellenistic and Roman lamps, most of them made of clay. Basically a lamp was a small bowl with a cover-plate. The plate, often decorated with some kind of ornamentation, had an opening through which olive oil could be poured. The wick was inserted through an extension of the bowl, the so-called lip. The "lampstand" spoken of in this mini-parable was a pedestal of wood or iron placed on the floor; this made it possible to put the lamp on a higher level.

The tradition history of our parable contains a number of variant readings for "bushel." In Mark no one would place the oil lamp under a "bushel basket" or under the "bed" (Mark 4:21). Luke speaks not only of a "jar" and the "bed" (Luke 8:16) but also of a *kryptē*, that is, a "dark hallway," a "hidden corner," or a "cellar" (Luke 11:33). We can see from these variants how often our parable was quoted in the early church and in the process acquired variants. Jesus probably did not speak of a "hidden corner" or a place under the "bed" but of the large vessel for measuring grain, that is, a bushel. Only that corresponds to the sense of reality in his language.

Of course, the discussion of where no one would put a lamp is meaningless for the interpretation of the parable. Much more important is the question: for whom and in what situation did Jesus create this parable?

For Matthew it is addressed to the disciples. They are to let their light shine before everyone (for the determination of the addressees see Matt 5:1, 13, 14, 16). For Mark also the parable is directed at the disciples (cp. Mark 4:10, 13, 21). Luke has it addressed to the disciples (Luke 8:9, 11, 18), but also to a larger audience (cp. Luke 11:14-16, 29).

In this way, it seems, the authors of the gospels have held on to something important. Our parable fits best within the body of instructions for disciples, and perhaps we can determine the original setting even more precisely. Many New Testament scholars rightly hold that Jesus at one time sent the Twelve out two by two to preach the reign of God and heal the sick (Mark 6:6-13). It could not have been easy for the Twelve to be suddenly on their own, commissioned to give witness in Israel. It is not only possible but probable that they raised objections and pled not to have to do it. In that situation Jesus made it clear to them, using the parable of the lamp, that the message of the reign of God cannot remain hidden and most certainly cannot be concealed. It must shed its light on everyone in the house, *that is, everyone in the house of Israel*. The reign of God must be preached; it must be *proclaimed*.

Perhaps—but this certainly is no more than conjecture—this parable was about a still riskier situation. Before his last Passover, at a time when resistance to him had already taken shape, Jesus set out for Jerusalem. The capital city could be dangerous, not only for Jesus but also for his disciples. They therefore tried to persuade Jesus not to go to Jerusalem. There is clear evidence of that attempt; in the course of it Jesus evidently called Simon Peter "Satan," that is, "Tempter" (Mark 8:31-33). It could be that it was precisely in that situation that Jesus used the argument of the light that no one may hide, that must shed its light brightly and openly "for all those in the house [of Israel]." Then the parable would have been a basis for and a defense of his last journey to Jerusalem.

## 39. The Grain of Wheat Dies (John 12:24)

The Jesus of the Fourth Gospel speaks in a wholly different style from the Jesus behind the words of the first three gospels. That is clear simply from a comparison of the Johannine discourses with the parables of the Synoptic Gospels. Jesus' language in John's gospel is a meditation on the language of the historical Jesus, uncovering its deeper dimensions, and for that reason it *must* be different.

Nevertheless, we may suppose that even in the Fourth Gospel there may be fragmentary parables that could be traced to Jesus, not only in substance but in their language as well. The best example is probably the parable of the grain of wheat.

> Unless a grain of wheat[126] falls into the earth and dies, it remains just a single grain; but if it dies, it bears much fruit. (John 12:24)

In the Fourth Gospel this parable is embedded in a curious discourse (John 12:20-36). It takes place in Jerusalem and contains Jesus' last

---

[126] The Greek has "grain kernel" rather than "grain of wheat." But since most of the grain sown in Palestine was wheat we can use the common translation.

public speech (cp. 12:29). The narrative begins with "Greeks" who want to speak with Jesus: they are so-called "God-fearing" Gentiles[127] who have traveled to Jerusalem for the Passover—hence they are depicted as Israel-sympathizers who want to worship the true God in the temple there. They want also to have a conversation with Jesus, and so they approach Philip, who in turn speaks to Andrew (significantly, these are the only two among the Twelve who bear Greek names). Thereafter Philip and Andrew go to Jesus to present the Greeks' request (John 12:20-22). Then, oddly enough, the narrative says nothing about a meeting between Jesus and the Greeks. Instead, without any transition Jesus begins to speak of his glorification—that is, his death. He seems to give Philip and Andrew no response at all, and the Greeks disappear from the story.

This is one of those typical Johannine texts with their own theologically-based logic. Evidently for the author of John's gospel these "Greeks" symbolize the Gentile mission, which had achieved its velocity and impetus only through the "God-fearers," that is, was progressing by way of the many Gentiles who felt themselves drawn to Israel.

The author of the Fourth Gospel does not permit an encounter between these Greeks and Jesus because he wants it to be clear that the whole mission that will lead to the repentance of many in Israel and then make its way to the Gentiles has an unavoidable precondition: the death of Jesus, his surrender of his life. Therefore this text, which evidently dismisses the Greeks altogether, centers on Jesus' words: "unless a grain of wheat falls into the earth and dies, it remains just a single grain; but if it dies, it bears much fruit."

Thus in fact the Gentiles who come from afar and want to speak with Jesus are taken altogether seriously, but for that very reason the text gets to the point immediately and shows what is the precondition for any spreading of the Gospel: the death of the grain of wheat. That, then, is the context in which this enigmatic parable now stands.

Could Jesus himself have spoken it? There are a good many reasons in its favor: (1) It has the brevity and frugality as well as the utter accuracy of many Jesus parables. (2) It is as tightly structured as many

---

[127] It is improbable that they are supposed to be proselytes or Greek-speaking Jews from the Diaspora. Josephus shows in his *Jewish War* (6.427) that "God-fearers" liked to go to Jerusalem for the Passover.

Jesus parables, because it consists of an antithetical parallelism in which "not dying" is contrasted with "dying" and "remaining alone" with "bearing fruit." (3) The parable's content is related to Luke 17:33, "those who try to make their life secure will lose it, but those who lose their life will keep it." (4) Jesus does not speak directly about himself but of a grain of wheat that represents not only Jesus but also whoever follows him—and yet it is quite obviously and primarily about himself. (5) Jesus reflects on a process known to every one of his listeners, something they have before their eyes again and again: the sowing of the grain, the sinking of the seed into the earth, and the rich yield of the field afterward. The parable owes its persuasive power to its everydayness, and that is just what is typical of Jesus' "parables of growth." (6) Jesus does not speak of sowing as a whole and in general terms. Out of the abundance of seed he chooses a single grain. Obviously that recalls another Jesus parable, namely, the one about the abundant harvest (Mark 4:3-9) in which, because of the phenomenon of "tillering," the seed that falls on good ground yields thirty-, sixty-, and a hundredfold.

And in what situation could Jesus have told this parable? Like the one about the lamp on the lampstand, it could have been spoken to his disciples because it affected them—they who had put behind them everything they had, including "wife and children . . . and even life itself" (Luke 14:26). But it applied above all and at the utmost depth to himself, who had given up everything and now must die. He could not hide the light of his life. He had to let it shine, and so it was extinguished.

Is it an accident that, at the end of the peculiar story of the God-fearers who try in vain to speak with Jesus, the metaphor of light that we spoke about in connection with the parable about the lamp on the lampstand reappears? "The light is with you for a little longer. Walk while you have the light, so that the darkness may not overtake you" (John 12:35).

## 40. The Violent Farmworkers (Mark 12:1-12)

We have arrived at our last Jesus parable. It is found in Mark's gospel, and both Matthew (21:33-46) and Luke (20:9-19) have received it from Mark. The Synoptic comparison shows that both have reworked their Markan model. Their redactional alterations can be explained largely on the basis of their desire to give it a better form and a theological explanation.[128]

The apocryphal *Gospel of Thomas* contains a short version of this parable as well.[129] This brief text has played an important part in the discussion about the earliest form of the parable, as a supposed confirmation of the fact that originally it was much briefer and less offensive. But in fact the author of the *Gospel of Thomas* already had Matthew's, Mark's, and Luke's versions of the parable[130] and deliberately eliminated all the salvation-historical motifs because they did not fit his Gnostic view of redemption. He thus substantially shortened the traditional form of the parable.[131] What follows is based on Mark's version.

> "A man planted a vineyard, put a fence around it, dug a pit for the wine press [in a stony place], and built a watchtower; then he leased it to tenants[132] and went to another country.

---

[128] There are so-called minor agreements between Matthew and Luke in contrast to canonical Mark. We may leave the explanation of those out of the picture here.

[129] The version in *Gos. Thom.* 65 reads: "He said, 'There was a good man who owned a vineyard. He leased it to tenant farmers so that they might work it and he might collect the produce from them. He sent his servant so that the tenants might give him the produce of the vineyard. They seized his servant and beat him, all but killing him. The servant went back and told his master. The master said, "Perhaps they did not recognize him." He sent another servant. The tenants beat this one as well. Then the owner sent his son and said, "Perhaps they will show respect to my son." Because the tenants knew that it was he who was the heir to the vineyard, they seized him and killed him. Let him who has ears hear.'" Translation by Thomas Lambdin, available at http://www.earlychristianwritings.com/text/thomas-lambdin.html.

[130] Cp. Michael Fieger, *Das Thomasevangelium. Einleitung, Kommentar, und Systematik*, NTA 22 (Münster: Aschendorff, 1991), 192. Cp. Gerd Lüdemann, *Jesus after 2000 Years: What He Really Said and Did*, trans. John Bowden (Amherst, NY: Prometheus Books, 2001), 637, quoted at http://www.earlychristianwritings.com/thomas/gospelthomas98.html.

[131] Cp. W. R. Schoedel, "Gleichnisse im Thomasevangelium. Mündliche Tradition oder gnostische Exegese?" in *Gleichnisse Jesu. Positionen der Auslegung von Adolf Jülicher bis zur Formgeschichte*, ed. Wolfgang Harnisch, WdF 366 (Darmstadt: Wissenschaftliche Buchgesellschaft, 1982), 369–89, at 384–89. One indicator of *Gospel of Thomas*'s gnosticizing tendency is the statement "Perhaps they did not recognize him."

[132] The text has *geōrgoi*, "farmers." Our modern agricultural specializations played no part in ancient Israel. Those came somewhat later, in the large estates in the Roman style such as are presumed by Columella in *De re rustica*. Probably what is meant here is a group of former farmers who had cultivated their small plots for subsistence but then lost them to the great barons of the *latifundia*. Now they work as tenants in

When the season came, he sent a slave to the tenants to collect from them his share of the produce of the vineyard. But they seized him, and beat him, and sent him away empty-handed. And again he sent another slave to them; this one they beat over the head and insulted. Then he sent another, and that one they killed. And [so it was with] many others; some they beat, and others they killed. He had still one other, a beloved son. Finally he sent him to them, saying, 'They will respect my son.' But those tenants said to one another, 'This is the heir; come, let us kill him, and the inheritance will be ours.' So they seized him, killed him, and threw him out of the vineyard. What then will the owner of the vineyard do? He will come and destroy the tenants and give the vineyard to others. Have you not read this scripture:

> 'The stone that the builders rejected
> has become the cornerstone;
> this was the Lord's doing,
> and it is amazing in our eyes'?"

When they realized that he had told this parable against them, they wanted to arrest him, but they feared the crowd. So they left him and went away. (Mark 12:1-12)

This, then, is one of Jesus' most difficult and disputed parables. Why is it disputed? There are two primary reasons.

First is the horrifying history of Christian anti-Judaism, supported and nourished by a false theology, namely, one that saw it simply as a matter of course that Israel had been rejected by God and the church had taken the place of God's once-chosen people. That was a theology of the salvation-historical rejection, replacement, and disowning of Israel. We find statements pointing in that direction from a very early period in the church's history. To take only one example: in the second century the great theologian Irenaeus of Lyons, a pioneer for future centuries, wrote his important work *Against All the Heresies* (*Adversus haereses*), in which he said of this parable:

> For inasmuch as the former [i.e., the Jews] have rejected the Son of God, and cast Him out of the vineyard when they slew Him, God has justly rejected them, and given to the Gentiles outside the vineyard the fruits of its cultivation. This is in accordance with what Jeremiah

---

a vast vineyard. Only to that extent can we call them "vine-growers" (or "grape-pickers").

194   *The Forty Parables of Jesus*

says, "The Lord has rejected and cast off the nation[133] which does these things; for the children of Judah have done evil in my sight, says the Lord." (*Adv. haer.* 4.36.2, quoting Jer 7:29-30)[134]

We could go on and on with quotations of that kind. Christian theologians wrote repeatedly of the rejection and hence the salvation-historical disowning of Israel. In this way the church had a profound share in the guilt for the anti-Judaism that existed already in pagan antiquity but has flared up over and over again throughout history. Only the Holocaust at last opened our eyes to what was happening. Repentance—including theological repentance—is in progress, and it *must* take place. So can we trust a parable that apparently establishes the disowning of Israel by speaking of the "destruction" of the farmers and also says that the vineyard will be "given to others"?

A second reason why this parable is debated is its Christology. According to Isaiah 5:1-7, a text to which the parable alludes at the very beginning, the vineyard is the house of Israel and the vineyard's owner is God. In that case, must we not read the whole parable of the violent farmworkers metaphorically at its heart? Then we cannot avoid seeing the "beloved son" as Jesus himself. But in that case this would be the only one among all Jesus' parables in which he spoke clearly and decisively *about himself.* Can we really suppose so?

Both objections are serious. The result, in recent decades, has been a series of bold and daring interpretations of this parable, all characterized by the fact that they seek to escape the problems just described. Either they deny altogether that Jesus uttered this parable[135] or they remove every metaphorical feature. For example, some interpreters place it among the parables featuring "immoral heroes" and assert that the farmers' violent actions are simply meant to illustrate a wise grasp of the situation and a decisive risking of everything on one throw of the dice for the sake of the reign of God.[136] Or the par-

---

[133] The Greek text of *Adversus haereses* is accessible to us only through a very early Latin translation and from quotations in the works of the Greek fathers. At this point the Latin translation reads *gentem;* the corresponding Greek quotation, like the LXX, has *genean* = generation.

[134] Text at https://www.newadvent.org/fathers/0103436.htm.

[135] So, for example, Joachim Gnilka, *Das Evangelium nach Markus,* EKK II/2 (Zürich: Benziger; Neukirchen-Vluyn: Neukirchener Verlag, 1979), 148–49.

[136] See, for example, John Dominic Crossan, "The Parable of the Wicked Husbandmen," *JBL* 40 (1971): 451–65; also Schramm and Löwenstein, *Unmoralische Helden,* 22–42.

able is given a social-critical interpretation: it is said to depict the hopeless situation of small farmers in Israel who have lost their farms to the big landowners and now have to work as tenants but who nevertheless cannot produce the high rents and so resort to violence. "The victims of economic violence become murderers." The parable is said to condemn that situation in the hope of bringing the leaders of the people to repent, together with "those among the people who react with hatred and violence against their own powerlessness."[137]

But do not interpretations of this kind likewise commit violence against the text? Doesn't the parable go in a different direction? Is its purpose really to change the miserable situation of small farmers in Israel and bring mutually hostile social groups to repentance? Are the farmers really "immoral heroes," that is, models of determined action for the reign of God? Or is it really impossible that Jesus might have used a parable to interpret his situation and that of the people of God in expectation of his own death?

This last question is the most important: can we suppose that, in an entirely *new* situation, Jesus might have said something *new*? But before I turn to that question let us for a moment consider the addressees of this parable. Who are they?—at least in the eyes of Mark, Luke, and Matthew? Is the parable addressed to the whole people of Israel?

As I said before, there can be no question that this parable has played a decisive and catastrophic role in Christian theology of Israel. But was that right? Or has the parable been pressed into a false position, indeed misused? Let us look more closely! This parable is part of a discourse that begins with Mark 11:27-28: "Again they [Jesus and his disciples] came to Jerusalem. As he was walking in the temple, the chief priests, the scribes, and the elders came to him and said, 'By what authority are you doing these things? Who gave you this authority to do them?' Jesus said to them . . . ."

The question of Jesus' authority refers to the action previously described.[138] Now a brief dialogue develops between Jesus and the chief priests, scribes, and elders. The dialogue leads directly to our parable, introduced by "Then he began to speak to them [i.e., the leaders of the people] in parables" (Mark 12:1). Mark could not have

---

[137] Thus Schottroff, *Parables*, 21, 24.
[138] That is, the so-called cleansing of the temple, Mark 11:15-17.

been more clear about the subjects to whom the parable of the violent farmworkers was directed, but even that clarity is strengthened once again after the conclusion of the parable by the closing notice: "When they realized that he had told this parable against them, they wanted to arrest him, but they feared the crowd. So they left him and went away" (Mark 12:12).

Thus it is clear that for Mark, and probably for his source as well, this parable was not addressed to the people, and therefore it does not speak about Israel and its rejection. It is about the leaders of the people. They are the "builders" who have rejected the cornerstone; it is they who are threatened with judgment.

The question remains: what did it mean for Mark that the vineyard would be "given to others"? He would have been thinking of the Gentile mission. Whether originally the statement referred to the Gentile mission—indeed, whether it was even part of the original parable—remains uncertain.

The situation is not very different for Luke. In his telling the parable is, indeed, told to the *laos*, the "people" (Luke 20:9, 16), but their leaders are present (Luke 20:1-2), and, as in Mark, they understand that they are the target of the parable (Luke 20:19).

The speaker's situation in Matthew is exactly the same as in Mark; the whole speech in Matthew 21:23-46 is directed to the high priests and elders (Matt 21:23), and Matthew also adopts Mark's closing remark that they know it is about themselves (Matt 21:45-46). Otherwise, Matthew has expanded and sharpened Mark's observation that the vineyard will be "given to others." In Matthew it now reads: "Therefore I tell you, the kingdom of God will be taken away from you and given to a people that produces the fruits of the kingdom" (Matt 21:43).

From whom will the reign of God be taken away? From the leaders of the people, of course. We have to admit that at this point it is very easy to make the leap to thinking of the whole people Israel because of the immediate reference to "another people." Besides, Matthew's passion account contains a text in which "the people as a whole" cry out to Pilate: "His blood be on us and on our children" (Matt 27:25)—that is: "we accept responsibility for his death." What is crucial here is the expression "the people as a whole." Matthew inserted this passage into Mark's passion account.

It is understandable that on the basis of this Matthean presentation later theology developed the idea of Israel's disinheritance. Even if

Matthew saw things differently, he produced a formulation that was all too easily misunderstood.

Still, all that has taken us far from the question of the historical Jesus and the original meaning of our parable. We have gotten mixed up in the question of the line of thought that colors the whole of Matthew's gospel (and, correspondingly, the whole of Mark's gospel and all of Luke's two-volume work). So let me linger on this question for a moment. Let us suppose the worst-case scenario: that Matthew really represented a theology of disinheritance. In that case we ought not to hear only the voice of Matthew's gospel in regard to this question, because there is a very different voice that speaks to it—namely, what Paul says in Romans 9–11 about whether Israel has been ejected from salvation history or whether its divine election is irrevocable. The voice of Romans is weightier here than all others because Paul poses this probing question explicitly, categorically, and at great length. For Paul, Israel's calling is irrevocable (Rom 11:29).

In other words: if we ask the theological question about God's enduring fidelity to God's people, or about the possibility of Israel's rejection, we have to listen to the whole of the New Testament, above all Romans 9–11. Still more: the Old Testament has to be heard as well, because the question whether God could reject this people and seek a completely different one was already treated at length in the Old Testament (especially in Exod 32:7-14). Thus the whole question can be answered "canonically," that is, by applying the whole of Sacred Scripture. That seems obvious enough, but regrettably it is often forgotten, and always at the moment when Scripture is seen not as a single book but as a collection of individual books that have nothing to do with each other.

All that needs to be said at this point, but my question takes a different tack: I am asking about the original meaning of our parable on the lips of Jesus. We have to address that question now. Certainly it is connected with the search for the oldest version of the parable. How might we imagine that original form?

The parable begins with an allusion to Scripture: "A man planted a vineyard, put a fence around it, dug a pit [in a stony place] for the wine press, and built a watchtower." That is not a literal quotation, but clearly it refers to Isaiah 5:1-2. Some interpreters regard that allusion as a secondary addition, inserted later in order to expand the parable and give it biblical coloring. It is said that this expansive description of the laying-out of the vineyard is unnecessary to the narrative framework. It does not in any way contribute to the action of the parable itself; therefore it is certainly secondary.

Still, it could be altogether different. Undoubtedly the scribes, the teachers of the law who were in Jesus' audience, knew Isaiah's parable of the vineyard. They knew that the vineyard is Israel and that the vineyard parable is about God's profound disappointment with this, God's people. Still more: it speaks of a dreadful judgment on Israel: God tears down the protecting wall around the vineyard, and God's model estate becomes a wasteland.

Moreover, it was not only the scribes in the audience who knew the text of Isaiah; quite certainly there were others among the listeners who were familiar with it. Therefore the allusion to the text could very well have been part of the introduction to this parable because with the reference to Isaiah Jesus had pronounced the theme for the narrative to come, and its meaning: "My story will be about Israel and the profound crisis into which it has fallen, and with the following parable I will explain to you what is happening now, in these days, in your midst." So let us allow the parable its allusion to Isaiah 5![139]

After this indicator has been given to the listeners, the exposition of the parable is completed: the vineyard thus prepared, more magnificent than anyone can imagine, is leased to tenants who no longer have farms of their own. The man who owns the vineyard is an estate owner. Probably he lives somewhere abroad. Once the vineyard is laid out, he returns to his foreign home.

Two or three years pass before the vineyard produces its first harvest. Nothing need be said about that; all Jesus' listeners knew it.

---

[139] Peter Stuhlmacher is correct when he writes: "Jesus' parables include repeated *allusions to biblical traditions*. Hence the parable of the wicked tenants in Mark 12:1-11 par. refers to Isaiah 5:1-2, 5; the parable of the growing seed in Mark 4:26-29 alludes to Joel 4:13 [ET 3:13]; the parable of the mustard seed in Mark 4:30-32 has in view Psalm 104:12 and Daniel 4:9, 18 [ET 4:12, 21]; etc. The metaphorical linguistic world of Jesus' parables also includes many preformulated expressions: hence 'king' and 'shepherd' stand for God (and the Messiah), the 'meal' symbolizes the kingdom of God, 'sowing' stands for proclamation, the 'planting' or 'herd' stands for God's congregation, etc. . . . It is therefore no longer advisable to continue interpreting the parables according to the simplistic dictum that all the authentic parables of Jesus were originally purely pictorial sayings which the post-Easter church interpreted allegorically and supplied with Scripture references." Peter Stuhlmacher, *Biblical Theology of the New Testament*, trans. Daniel P. Bailey (Grand Rapids: Eerdmans, 2018), 92.

This whole length of time is bridged in the narrative by the simple "when the season came." That means: "when the time had come for the first harvest to be gathered."

So now comes the day when the tenants must deliver. The estate owner sends an agent to collect the rent—probably not in coin but in produce[140]—and of course not in grapes but in the first production of wine. It is also possible that the agent is supposed to sell the harvest locally. The parable leaves such things open.

Then comes the first surprise in the narrative: the tenants seize the agent, beat him, and chase him away. Of course the listeners are shocked, because they could not have anticipated this turn in the story; they know how risky the stated action would be. Still, they understand it; such things happened repeatedly in those times, or at least they were "in the wind."[141] Usually the rent was set too high, and the tenants were always on the ragged edge of existence. A bad harvest could also cause them major difficulties.

The narrator does not pause to insert a critique of social conditions. He is on the side of the owner, not that of the vineyard workers. Their violent deed is neither prettified nor condoned. It remains there—a violent act—and the story goes on. The estate owner sends another agent, perhaps equipped with greater authority. It is possible that the first agent was a slave, but hearers have to imagine that for themselves. The narrative goes on inexorably.

The second messenger is treated just like the first one, but the mistreatment is worse: this man is struck on the head. Such a blow could be mortal. Then comes a verb that is usually translated "insulted," but it can also mean "degraded" (cp. Rom 1:24). Was the man raped?

Still the narrator does not pause or comment. A third agent appears, and now the narrative finally enters into the realm of what parables research, following Paul Ricoeur, calls "extravagance": the whole thing becomes improbable. What estate owner would send a third agent to follow the first two?

But we might put it better: it is not that these things are historically improbable or impossible; the narrative simply goes to the extreme.

---

[140] Remember that in those days the vineyards contained not only grapevines but also olive trees and other useful plants.

[141] Cp. esp. Martin Hengel, "Das Gleichnis von den Weingärtnern. Mc 12,1-12 im Lichte der Zenonpapyri und der rabbinischen Gleichnisse," *ZNW* 59 (1968): 1–39.

Everything becomes so tense that the hearers are breathless. Now all they want to know is what comes next. And what comes next is even more terrifying: the third agent is not only raped and beaten but killed.

At this point it is worth taking a look at narrative technique.[142] From the point of view of content we see that the violence increases in three stages: (1) beating; (2) hitting on the head, possible rape; (3) murder. At the same time the number of verbs used decreases steadily:

> First stage: seizing, beating, driving away;
> Second stage: bashing, raping (?);
> Third stage: killing.

So, as with a pyramid or a cone we see here a "sharpening" or intensification accompanied by a reduction in volume. Obviously that is masterful narrative technique; it is no accident.

In accordance with the law of popular narrative we have already observed in a number of Jesus' parables there have now been three cases, and the fourth (3 + 1) must bring the turning. It does—but probably not as the listeners expect. The horror only increases: now the master of the vineyard sends his own son and he, too, is killed and further dishonored by being thrown out of the vineyard so that his corpse is delivered over to the dogs, the jackals, and the birds of prey. That was the worst thing anyone could do to a dead person in those days. To the minds of eastern peoples, and most especially of Jews, it was altogether unbearable!

With this murder of the only[143] son the narrative has become still more "extravagant." The listeners must long since have asked themselves: Why does the vineyard owner do all that? Why does he even

---

[142] For the following observations on style cp. Hans Weder, *Die Gleichnisse Jesu als Metaphern. Traditions- und redaktionsgeschichtliche Analysen und Interpretationen*, 2nd ed. (Göttingen: Vandenhoeck & Ruprecht, 2015), 148.

[143] Mark 12:6 has "beloved son," but the Hebrew OT and especially its translation in the LXX show that "beloved son" could be a circumlocution or equivalent for "only son"; cp. Gen 22:2; Amos 8:10; Judg 11:34, and frequently elsewhere. Many interpreters consider "beloved" as a resumption of Mark 1:11 ("You are my beloved son") and a redactional expansion by Mark, but that is by no means certain since the original version of this passage could also have spoken of an "only" son, and that was important to the "fable" of the parable since the vineyard workers hope, by getting rid of the "only" son, to obtain possession of the vineyard.

send his own son? What are we hearing? What is it really about? What is actually happening here?

But now, back to the course of the narrative! We have observed four cases or phases in the narrative in which the violence increases and the event becomes more and more brutal; the murder of the son is just one step worse than the murder of the third agent. The narrative is shocking, but it has its own logic. Still, the logic is skewed by the expansion in the third case (v. 5b): "And so it was with many others; some they beat, and others they killed." That is clearly a note that upsets the balance of the narrative. It comes either from Mark or from the tradition before him. The readers/hearers are directed to note what the murder of the third agent means: the murder of Israel's prophets, to which the Old Testament refers in many places (1 Kgs 18:13; 19:10; 2 Chr 24:20-22; Jer 26:20-24; Zech 13:3, and frequently elsewhere).

That expanded commentary was unnecessary, and it must have been absent from the earliest version of the parable. The audience, and above all the scribes, would in any case have already grasped what Jesus was alluding to in speaking of the three servants: the murder of prophets in Israel. Not only the beginning of the parable, with its reference to Isaiah 5:1-7, would have made them alert to its metaphorical features. Beyond that, Sacred Scripture very frequently, and in formulaic fashion, has God referring to Israel's prophets as "my servants the prophets" (2 Kgs 9:7; Jer 25:4; Ezek 38:17; Amos 3:7; Zech 1:6, and frequently elsewhere). Moreover, in this parable Jesus has now spoken three times about violent actions against a "servant" or "agent." The expansion in verse 5b was certainly not necessary. It is there for the benefit of Gentile Christian readers unfamiliar with Scripture.

With the shameful murder of the "son" the narrative has reached its climax. Did Jesus have to explain who he meant? Probably not. No further explanation was required. Jesus could let the story work on his hearers.

On the other hand: maybe Jesus did say something more, because in Isaiah's "song of the vineyard" things are likewise named at the end for what they are. Remember: "for the vineyard of the Lord of hosts is the house of Israel, and the people of Judah are his pleasant planting; he expected justice, but saw bloodshed; righteousness, but heard a cry!" (Isa 5:7).

So did Jesus, like Isaiah, reveal everything at the end, to make it clear to the last hearer that he was talking about the possibility that he himself would be eliminated? Perhaps not. Maybe Jesus really did end his parable with the question, "What then will the owner of the vineyard do?" On the other hand, he could have ended it with:

> What then will the owner of the vineyard do? He will come and destroy the tenants and give the vineyard to others. (Mark 12:9)

In this instance also it would obviously not have been simply about establishing an unavoidable fact: for example, "Yes, Israel is rejected and disinherited and another people will take its place." To read the text that way is, at the very least, to completely misunderstand *Jesus'* intent. He did not talk about unchangeable facts. His real desire was that those facts should *not* become reality. With his parable he wanted to uncover what was going on with Israel's leaders. He wanted to lay everything open. He wanted to warn. Maybe he even threatened—but only so that, after all, things would turn out differently.

In this way he did what Israel's prophets had always done. He warned Israel, and above all its leaders, not to miss an all-determining hour in the divine will. There is no possible hint of anti-Judaism in this; it was about conflicts within Israel, about Jesus' ultimate, extreme, extravagant effort to bring his people, at last, to listen to its God and do God's will.

At the end of his life it was then evident that Jesus had no thought of excluding Israel from God's faithfulness. At his last meal, when it was clear to him that they would kill "the son," Jesus interpreted his death as one of surrender on behalf of Israel, and beyond Israel for the "many" (cp. Mark 14:24; Isa 53:11). Perhaps Matthew was even alluding to that interpretive word spoken in the room where the Last Supper took place when he portrayed "all the people" as shouting, "His blood be on us and on our children" (Matt 27:25). In that case the evangelist was wanting to say that they did not know the blood of which they spoke was the liberating, pardoning blood of Jesus' surrender of his life.

But however that may be, and however Mark, Matthew, and Luke understood the parable of the violent farmworkers, on the lips of Jesus the parable was not about disinheriting Israel. It was a sharp, pointed warning to the people, above all to its leaders, not to squander their election as God's people. Its point was that the reign of God is rushing nearer; Jesus says that whoever rejects him, the one who proclaims the reign of God, rejects the reign of God. And rejecting the reign of God is the same as rejecting God.

Did Jesus understand himself as the "son"? Why would he not? Who dares to say that is impossible, and for what reasons? Those who eliminate the possibility of such a self-concept on Jesus' part from the outset claim the right to decree what Jesus might have thought and how he could have understood himself. Although in the parable of the violent farmworkers Jesus puts himself in the picture, even here he speaks of himself only in a concealed way, in hidden fashion. "[The vineyard owner] had still one other, a beloved son." That is not yet the same thing as the later christological title "Son of God," and the listeners at that time could not have heard that later statement in a story that ended with the death of the "son." But they could glean, with alarm, that there was one among them through whom Israel's path and their own would be decided. They could ask themselves, in dismay, whether it could be true that, in Jesus, God was speaking to them directly—as directly as never before.

# Part Three

## What Is Different about Jesus' Parables

## 1. The Material

Looking back, we are first astonished at the variety and color of the material Jesus uses for his parables.

Jesus tells of how a householder is unable to prevent a thief from breaking into the house by night (Luke 12:39); how a day-laborer comes across a buried treasure while plowing (Matt 13:44); how a wholesaler discovers a precious pearl (Matt 13:45-46); how a woman kneads leavening into a huge quantity of flour (Luke 13:20-21); how a moneylender forgives the whole debt of two of his debtors (Luke 7:41-42); how a poor woman turns her house upside down to find a gold coin she has lost (Luke 15:8-10); how a shepherd abandons his whole flock to look for one lost sheep (Matt 18:12-14); how a young man demands his inheritance, quickly plays it all away, and gets into deep trouble (Luke 15:11-32).

Jesus recounts how a field produces a rich harvest in spite of many obstacles (Mark 4:3-9); how a vineyard owner pays the same wage to workers hired at the last hour of the day as to those who have worked since early morning (Matt 20:1-16); how a corrupt judge gets fed up with the pleas of a poor widow (Luke 18:1-8); how, right before a great banquet, all the guests send excuses and the householder fills the hall with street people (Luke 14:16-24); how fishers draw their nets to land and sort out the useless fish (Matt 13:47-50); how someone who is initially indifferent finally does the will of his father (Matt 21:28-31).

Jesus tells how weeds are sown among a farmer's wheat during the night (Matt 13:24-30); how a Pharisee and a tax collector pray simultaneously in the temple and how their prayers differ (Luke 18:10-14); how a man underway between Jerusalem and Jericho is attacked and how a priest and a Levite pass the wounded man without noticing him (Luke 10:30-35); how a poor man starves before a rich man's door (Luke 16:19-31); how the arrival of the bridegroom is delayed on the evening of the marriage (Matt 25:1-13); how a barren fig tree is given an additional year (Luke 13:6-9); how children cannot agree whether to play wedding or funeral (Matt 11:16-19); how, after an unexpectedly rich harvest, a farmer deliberates on the kind of comfortable life he will live in future and how he dies a few hours later (Luke 12:16-20).

Jesus recounts how someone appears in inappropriate dress at a royal wedding feast and is thrown out (Matt 22:11-13); how a high official who has just been forgiven a gigantic debt has a fellow worker thrown into prison for owing him a much smaller sum (Matt 18:23-34); how a gentleman returns late at night from a wedding, goes on celebrating with his male and female servants, and serves them as if he were their slave (Luke 12:35-38); how a rich man who uses Mafia-like business methods entrusts his employees with large sums of money and how they all double their capital except for one who buries the money entrusted to him (Matt 25:14-30).

Jesus relates how an assassin prepares to murder an influential man (*Gos. Thom.* 98); how a manager threatened with dismissal calls in his master's debtors and, with their cooperation, falsifies their promissory notes (Luke 16:1-7); how an estate owner lays out a vineyard and entrusts it to tenants, but when the rent is due they beat the first agent sent to them, shame the second, kill the third, and, when the man finally sends his own son, kill him too (Mark 12:1-12).

But that is by no means all the material found in Jesus' parables. It is only the stuff of those that more or less "tell a story." Besides those we have all the other parables that do not narrate but simply "discuss" something.

Jesus discusses the fact that bandits who are planning to plunder a property first have to make sure that they can overpower the owner (Mark 3:27); that the buds on a fig tree show that summer is near (Mark 13:28-29); that a tiny mustard seed can produce a tree-like bush, bigger than everything else growing in the garden (Mark 4:30-32); that seed grows and ripens without human assistance (Mark 4:26-29); what happens when someone is asked by his neighbor, in the middle of the night, for bread to feed an unexpected guest (Luke 11:5-8).

Jesus considers how appropriate it is for someone faced with sentencing to negotiate an extrajudicial agreement with the opponent while they are on the way to see the judge (Matt 5:25-26); how a slave ought to deal with fellow slaves when given responsibility for the whole household (Matt 24:45-51); how a slave who has worked outdoors all day and in the evening still has to do the household chores and should not expect any thanks from the master (Luke 17:7-10).

Jesus discusses how a house built on rock has a sure foundation while, in contrast, a house built on sand collapses under the weight of rain and storm (Matt 7:24-27); how someone who wants to build an expensive house should first calculate the cost, just as a king who wants to defend against an approaching army must take account of whether he has enough soldiers (Luke 14:28-32).

Finally, Jesus proposes that a lamp in a small, windowless house belongs on a lampstand, not under a bushel (Matt 5:15), and that a grain of wheat can bear fruit only if it is first sown in the earth and dies (John 12:24).

Note: this long list was by no means intended to summarize the content of the individual parables, most certainly not to formulate their "sense." Such a thing would not have been possible for the longer parables anyway, because they are "narratives." One simply cannot do justice to such stories under the categories of "sense" or "crucial point." But it would also be impossible in the case of Jesus' shorter parables, some of which are close to being simple metaphors, because their "sense" depends on their context or on the situation in which they were originally spoken. Rather, the listing above is only intended to give a short sketch of the *world of imagery* within which Jesus' parables move.

It is a full, colorful world filled with sorrows and joys, everydays and feastdays, normal life and escapades, banalities and adventures, crimes and profound humanity. There are inside and outside, near and far, the ordinary and the unique, nature and society, those "high up" and those "on the bottom."

Here we find the worlds not only of adults but also of children. We encounter poor and rich, women and men, criminals and the pious, slave and free, lost and found, lenders and debtors, judges and petitioners, impoverished tenants and estate owners, day-laborers and merchants, viticulturists and housewives, a priest and a Levite, a Pharisee and a tax collector, kings and a swineherd.

We cast an eye into the contours of major capital and the banquet halls of the very rich, but also into the little world of people who have to live in a single room that lacks even a window. We experience how hard people have to work in vineyards threatened by the *chamsin*, how leaven is kneaded into a huge quantity of bread dough, how bridal parties see their torches flickering out, how wheat tillers itself, and how a house built on sand is always in danger of being washed away.

I dare to say that there was no storyteller in antiquity from whom we have received so many authentic parables and whose parables offer so much rich, colorful material. This wealth of material and world-encompassing character of Jesus' parables were not attained anywhere else in the ancient world.

## 2. The Form

When we look back at these forty parables from Jesus, though, we are struck not only by their breadth and world-encompassing nature. We ought to have equal admiration for the *form* Jesus gave his parables. That is the subject of this chapter.

Obviously Jesus did not invent the form of his parables and the rules according to which they are composed. The genre of "parables" had existed long before him, and with it a great number of formal rules for popular narrative. I need to expand on that somewhat.

Beginning in the eighteenth century, a scholarly interest in popular forms of narrative awakened in Europe, and that interest grew rapidly. Its first object was sayings and fairy tales, but then it came to include short forms such as fables, legends, examples, anecdotes, riddles, funny stories, and jokes. All these narrative genres increasingly entered the scope of poetics and literary criticism. The formal rules for such texts were more closely examined and described. Especially important for biblical scholarship in that regard was an essay by the Danish scholar Axel Olrik that appeared in 1909 in the *Zeitschrift für deutsches Altertum und deutsche Literatur* under the title "Epische Gesetze der Volksdichtung [Epic Laws of Popular Poetry]." The article soon exercised influence on the emerging fields of biblical "form criticism" and "genre criticism," especially in the hands of Hermann Gunkel (1862–1932), Martin Dibelius (1883–1919), and Rudolf Bultmann (1884–1976).[1]

Olrik wrote, among other things, about the "rule of repetition," the "rule of three," the "rule of stage duality," the "rule of contrast,"

---

[1] The first works thus influenced include Martin Dibelius, *From Tradition to Gospel*, trans. Bertram Lee Woolf (Cambridge: James Clarke, 1971), and Rudolf Bultmann, *The History of the Synoptic Tradition*, trans. John Marsh (Oxford: Basil Blackwell, 1963).

and the "rule of centralization [focus on a leading character]." In what follows I will refer to Olrik's article but also and especially to the continuation and deepening of his observations by Rudolf Bultmann in his *History of the Synoptic Tradition*.

In that influential book Bultmann states the first formal rule of Jesus' parables as the *"conciseness* of the narrative."[2] He thus seized immediately on one of the most crucial points. In part 2 of this book we repeatedly found ourselves facing the question: why did Jesus formulate his parables so tersely and with such tight organization?

For example, there was the double parable of the treasure in the field and the pearl (Matt 13:44-46). A longer narrative with a detailing of the circumstances under which the treasure and the pearl were found would have been utterly enthralling and exciting, but the parable dispenses with such. We are spared the circumstances. We asked ourselves whether the striking brevity of this double parable was due to later catechetical schematization of two originally longer parables. I toyed with that idea, but in the end I rejected it. The brevity of the form has a deeper significance here: the parable develops only the things that are important. Every external, everything that is only decorative and distracting, is deliberately left out. The parable is meant to tell how one gains access to the reign of God; it hews to that thought, says all that is essential, keeps the story as brief as possible so that what is decisive in the event is illuminated and touches the hearts of the hearers.

All that was even clearer in the parable of the two different sons (Matt 21:28-31). Here it was absolutely clear that this parable, with its carefully curled structure, could in no way be lengthened.

The same can be shown for many other Jesus parables. Jesus knew precisely when he must narrate briefly and when at greater length, when the greatest brevity was appropriate and when a longer narrative thread was called for, when he should "discuss" and when he should "narrate." So it is that he simply omits quite a lot: for example, the mother in the parable of the lost son (Luke 15:11-32) or the wife in the parable of the importunate friend (Luke 11:5-8). Here, as in so many other parable narratives, only the necessary persons are introduced. As far as the population of the stories is concerned, the strictest economy is called for.

---

[2] Bultmann, *History of the Synoptic Tradition*, 188.

To take one other example: in the parable of the banquet (Luke 14:16-24) three invitees excuse themselves, saying they are prevented from attending. But "many" were invited (14:16), and obviously they have all made excuses, without exception. The three who are named represent the whole group—as in the Old Testament parable of the bramble (Judg 9:8-15) the olive and fig trees and the vine stand for all the trees. Bultmann says correctly: "In this case two would be too scanty, more than three superfluous."[3]

But it is not only the number of persons who appear in Jesus' parables that is strictly limited. The same is true of the event itself. In the parable of the leaven (Luke 13:20-21) the lengthy and arduous kneading of the dough goes unmentioned. The woman kneads the leaven into the flour—end of story. Nothing is said about the necessary water and salt or the highly important rising of the dough. There are many similar examples to be found.

The "conciseness of the narrative" also includes the phenomenon that the persons are seldom described. Their character expresses itself in their actions. Thus in the parable of the lost son the nature of the father emerges wholly from what he says and does (Luke 15:20-24), and in the parable of the rich man and the poor man the character of the rich glutton is apparent from the fact that he lets the poor man starve at his door (Luke 16:19-31). Even the Pharisee and the tax collector are characterized solely by the way they appear in the temple and by their prayers (Luke 18:10-14).

We can add to the "conciseness" and thus "simplicity" of the narrative what Olrik calls the rules of "stage duality" and "centralization." By "stage duality" he means that in popular stories a *single* scene contains only *two* people who speak and act. If another person appears, that leads to a new scene. So in the parable of the money given in trust the employees appear sequentially before their master to be rewarded or punished (Matt 25:20-28). The rule of "stage duality" can be quite clearly seen in that parable.

To take another example: in the final scene of the parable of the workers in the vineyard, in the evening the dissatisfied workers meet the estate owner and his manager (Matt 20:10-15), but the manager and the crowd of grumbling workers remain completely in the back-

---

[3] Bultmann, *History of the Synoptic Tradition*, 190.

ground. The estate owner speaks only with a single worker: "Friend, I am doing you no wrong."

Closely related to the "rule of stage duality" is the "rule of the single perspective." The classic novel as it has emerged since the eighteenth century can develop a highly complicated association and interaction of various narrative threads and constellations of characters. Not so in popular literature as analyzed by Olrik. Here there is only one narrative thread at a time—and so it is with Jesus' parables. Never do we hear of two locations at the same time. In the parable of the lost son the first half is told in a single strand, from the viewpoint of the younger son (Luke 15:12-24). Then, clearly distinct, comes the second half of the parable, told from the viewpoint of the older son (Luke 15:25-32). What goes on at home during the absence of the younger son is completely out of the picture.

Besides the "rule of the conciseness of the narrative" we have that of "clear structuring." In this the number three plays a significant role. In the parable of the abundant harvest we first encounter three enemies of the seed: the birds, the rocky soil, the thorns (Mark 4:4-7). Only then, following the pattern of 3 + 1, is the abundant harvest described. In the parable of the money given in trust (Matt 25:14-30) large sums are given to three employees. Their work with that money and the successive conversations between them and their master organize the parable as a whole. The violent farmworkers (Mark 12:1-12) first disgrace themselves by their treatment of three emissaries of the vineyard owner and then kill his son. Here again the sequence of 3 + 1 structures the parable. Finally, we may mention the parable of the merciful Samaritan (Luke 10:30-35). Here three men encounter the victim of the attack: a priest, a Levite, and a Samaritan.

Jesus' parables are also structured by their many repetitions, a feature likewise characteristic of popular types of narrative. We saw such stereotypical repetitions at the very beginning of this book in the parable of the bramble (Judg 9:8-15): the olive tree, the fig tree, and the vine reject the idea of becoming king, and they do so in nearly identical words. Similarly stereotypical are the excuses offered in the parable of the banquet (Luke 14:16-24) and, in the parable of the money given in trust, the dialogue of the master with his employees; the same is true of the forging of the promissory notes in the parable of the crooked manager (Luke 16:1-7).

According to Axel Olrik the "rule of contrast" also plays an important part in popular stories. This means that in these narratives contrasting figures are repeatedly presented together. That same rule dominates many of Jesus' parables. Think only of the contrasting pairs:

> day-laborer—wholesale merchant (Matt 13:44-46)
> big debtor—little debtor (Luke 7:41-42)
> younger son—elder son (Luke 15:11-32)
> judge—widow (Luke 18:1-8)
> rich invited guests—street people (Luke 14:16-24)
> good fish—useless fish (Matt 13:47-48)
> Pharisee—tax collector (Luke 18:10-14)
> priest and Levite—Samaritan (Luke 10:30-35)
> obedient son—disobedient son (Matt 21:28-31)
> rich man—poor man (Luke 16:19-31)
> five wise bridesmaids—five foolish bridesmaids (Matt 25:1-13)
> wedding—funeral (Matt 11:16-19)
> faithful slave—wicked slave (Matt 24:45-51)
> increased sum of money—money buried in the earth (Matt 25:14-30)

Finally, the technique of popular narrative includes frequent "direct discourse." That, too, is characteristic of Jesus' parables. Of the forty parables discussed in this book, more than half contain "direct discourse"—occasionally in the form of "internal monologues" or "soliloquies" that appear in the form of direct discourse. It is clear why this type of popular literature would so often contain such discourse: it lends the narrative concreteness, vividness, and drama.

Everything thus far listed obeys the rules of popular narrative, which are not only found in parables but also shape legends, fables, anecdotes, jests, and jokes. Jesus skillfully applied the repertoire of such narrative techniques in his parables. He didn't have to invent it; it already existed. We need only to study the numerous animal fables that circulated in antiquity under the name of Aesop to discover, almost without exception, the narrative structures here de-

## What Is Different about Jesus' Parables 215

scribed. There are extremely short fables but also longer ones: we again encounter economy in the number of actors, the rule of two to a scene, the frequent direct discourse, and even internal monologues. Particularly striking is the constant contrasting of the animals: "The Wolf and the Lamb," "The Horse and the Donkey," "The Eagle and the Fox," "The Donkey and the Goat," "The Stag and the Lion."

It is not legitimate to argue that Jesus would have had no notion of ancient fables. We cannot suppose that people in Israel were so out of the loop. But in any case Jesus knew his Bible, and there one can find not only the masterfully well-constructed fable of the bramble but also the parable of the poor man's lamb and the parable of the vineyard.

Still, Jesus was not familiar with popular literature only through those three parables. He of course knew all the numerous other stories in Scripture, and he could have learned from them how a good, strong narrative should go. In Scripture he encountered a great variety of texts demonstrating everything we have discussed above: simplicity, frugality, unity of purpose, contrasts, direct discourse, repetitions. Of course, he also encountered narrative complexes that used extremely refined—one might almost say "modern"—narrative techniques: for example in the book of Deuteronomy. There, too, he could have learned intuitively.

Naturally, the question remains: Did Jesus find everything he needed for the structuring of his parables ready to hand? Did he adopt all the narrative techniques in his parables from somewhere else? Was there nothing original with him as far as "formal rules" are concerned?

If that were the case, the vividness and freshness as well as the constant surprises in his parables would be inexplicable. At the beginning of this chapter I spoke of the extreme terseness of his parables. Nothing about that needs to be withdrawn, and yet that characteristic must necessarily be augmented by the observation of the striking concreteness that repeatedly blazes forth within Jesus' stories.

Jesus did not say "The younger son suffered hunger in a foreign land," but "He would gladly have filled himself with the pods that the pigs were eating" (Luke 15:16).

Jesus did not say "unless he has first overpowered the strong man," but "without first tying up the strong man" (Mark 3:27).

Jesus did not say "The woman searched the whole house for her lost drachma," but "Does [she] not light a lamp [and] sweep the house [so she can hear the coin rattle]?" (Luke 15:8).

The harvesters do not say "We have worked all day," but "[We] have borne the burden of the day and the scorching heat" (Matt 20:12).

The man who has invited his acquaintances to a great banquet, after they have all made their excuses, does not say to his servant "Go into the city and bring in the poor," but "Go out at once into the streets and lanes of the town and bring in the poor, the crippled, the blind, and the lame" (Luke 14:21).

Jesus could have said "No one puts a lamp in a remote corner of the house." Instead, he said "No one after lighting a lamp puts it under the bushel basket" (Matt 5:15).

In the parable of the seed growing by itself it would have been enough to say "The earth produces fruit all by itself," but Jesus added "first the stalk, then the head, then the full grain in the head" (Mark 4:28).

The parable of the quarreling children (Matt 11:16-19) does not say "We wanted to play funeral and you wouldn't join in," but "We wailed, and you did not mourn [strike yourselves on the breast]."

And how vividly Jesus constructs contrasts: for example, in the parable of the rich man and the poor man (Luke 16:19-31): "There was a rich man who dressed in purple and fine linen and who feasted sumptuously every day. And at his gate lay a poor man named Lazarus, covered with sores." The rich man is clothed in purple and fine linen, the poor man only in sores, Jesus says here.

We must appreciate this sensuous concreteness that appears again and again in Jesus' parables if we are to do justice to the frugality of his narration. The two belong together: the utmost brevity and full visibility. It may be precisely the interplay of the two that is the "mark of originality" in Jesus' parables.

It seems there is a second special feature in Jesus' parables: simply, so it seems to me, the *multitude of forms* in which he told them. There are parables introduced with the formula "it is with the reign of God as with . . ."—that is, the classic beginning with the dative, the form in which many Jewish parables begin. Others of Jesus' parables simply begin with the nominative: "A man was going down from Jerusalem to Jericho." Still others begin with a question: "Which of you, intending to build a tower, does not first sit down and estimate the cost?" In the parable of the importunate friend the question form is sustained almost to the end of the parable.

But the forms of the parables are still more variable: the one about going to court is formulated in thou-address from beginning to end: "While thou art on thy way to court with [thine accuser]." And the parable of the foolish wheat farmer, except for its beginning and end, consists almost exclusively of an "inner monologue" on the part of the farmer, much as does the one about the judge and the widow. Then there are parables that are open-ended even though the listeners really might have expected that, given the beginning, they would hear the ending. That is the case with the parable of the lost son, and in a sense also with the one about the judge and the widow, although in the latter case the ending is anticipated in the judge's inner monologue. But precisely that anticipation of the outcome in a speech between the judge and himself shows the freedom and variability with which Jesus organized his parables.

Another point should also be mentioned here, one that may show most clearly what is "special" about Jesus' compositional power: the so-called immoral heroes. I am thinking of the parables of the money given in trust, the dishonest manager, and the assassin. Here it is not just a matter of a limited motif in the *content*. When Jesus told parables with "immoral heroes" the whole structure of the parable in question was involved. What do I mean by that?

Let me illustrate the point in terms of Aesop's fables. There we regularly meet animals who do violence to other animals—above all the lion and the wolf. Their appearance is always for the purpose of illustrating how things are in society: the weaker are oppressed and betrayed, and in the end they are devoured. Consider the parable of the wolf and the lamb: a tiny lamb is devoured by the wolf because both are slaking their thirst at the same stream and the little lamb—so the wolf says—supposedly muddied the water for him. In reality the wolf is standing upstream. He was the one who muddied the water. So it goes in the human world, says the parable: the stronger push their way ahead in brutal fashion; moreover, they ground their actions in lies and disinformation.

Jesus can also depict such types: for example, the corrupt judge or the rich man who allows a poor man to starve in front of his door. But in the parables with "immoral heroes" things are different. Here the criminals are not part of the inventory of the particular parable; rather, the behavior of scoundrels is turned into parables that, as a whole, tell how one must seize the reign of God: with ultimate persistence and daring initiative. These are extremely cool and daring constructs that were not understood even by the early church.

But perhaps at this point we should mention that stylistic device in Jesus' parables whereby the familiar and ordinary suddenly shifts into something surprising and unheard-of: the owner of the vineyard pays the last as much as the first; a king forgives one of his slaves his whole debt; a sinful tax collector goes home justified but a Pharisee does not; a banqueting hall is filled with the blind, the crippled, and the lame; it is not the servants of the temple who help the beaten man but a questionable Samaritan; an unfruitful fig tree is given another chance; and after rebellious farmers have already beaten one emissary, shamed a second, and murdered a third, the owner of the vineyard sends his own son. Confusing and disturbing events of that kind are also part of the narrative style of Jesus' parables and contribute to their uniqueness.

However, we must immediately add that, on this point also, Jesus learned a great deal from Scripture. The joke of Jotham's fable (Judg 9:8-15), the deceiving of David by the prophet Nathan (2 Sam 12:1-4), the capture of the listeners in the song of the vineyard (Isa 5:1-7), the narrative skill in the story of the binding of Isaac (Gen 22:1-19), the masterful art of presentation in the complex of the succession history (2 Sam 9:1–20:26; 1 Kgs 1:1–2:46), the clever metaphors in the book of Psalms: all that and a great deal more has entered into Jesus' parables. Here again, he completed what had existed before him.

## 3. The Tradition

Still, can we really suppose that in everything we have said in the first two chapters we are talking about authentic Jesus parables? Hasn't it become clear in part 2 that the authors of the first three gospels worked over their models again and again?

In fact there were such interventions, and in many forms. Jesus' parables were often supplied with an "application" or a "commentary." Likewise "parable beginnings" and "introductory formulae" may be secondary. Beyond that, Matthew, Mark, and Luke repeatedly undertook massive rewritings of the "narrative framework" of the parables. That happened—to mention only two such cases—in the parable of the banquet (Matt 22:1-14) and the one about the money given in trust (Luke 19:12-27). In this book interventions of that sort were discussed where they appeared.

Obviously we must also expect that there were similar changes and expansions in the tradition phase *before* the composition of the Synoptic Gospels. Must we not even assume that often we are looking not at Jesus' narrative style but at that of his tradents and then ultimately that of the evangelists? So are the observations in the first two sections of part 3 standing on clay feet? That is certainly not the case. Let me offer some notes:

1. In reconstructing Jesus' parables in this book I have largely ignored parable openings and commentaries and other attachments. That is, I have not rested my discussion on the elements in the text that most frequently come from the evangelists' hands.

2. Expansions of the narrative framework itself or of the course of events in the parables (in technical terms, their "fable") were relatively easy to discern. Take as an example the parable of the abundant harvest (Mark 4:3-9). Three enemies of the seed appear there: birds that pluck the seed, the rising sun that singes the seed, and finally the thorns and briars that choke it. In these three initial parts of the parable, however, the *second* is unusually expansive and awkward in its formulation, in contrast to the first and the third. A literal translation reads:

> And other fell on rocky ground, where it did not have much soil, and it immediately began to sprout because it had no depth of earth, and when the sun arose it was scorched, and because it had no roots, it dried up. (Mark 4:5-6)

Here Mark evidently wants to give a clearer explanation for his hearers, and in doing so he delivers too much of a good thing. Hence I simplified the text on the model of the first and third parts of the parable as follows:

> And other seed fell on rocky ground, and when the sun arose it was scorched because it had no roots.

So the first three parts of the parable, each of which names an "opponent" of the seed, reveals an equal increase in Greek word content. But above all, each of the three parts strictly corresponds to the structure:

1. Placement of the seed

2. Coming of the opponent(s)

3. Destruction of the seed

Such correspondences in structure are important because it is precisely those things that guarantee a correct retelling of the parable. So in all probability Mark, at this point, expanded the version of the parable he had received; the briefer model is relatively easy to reconstruct.[4]

It is similar with the parable of the violent farmworkers (Mark 12:1-12). Here it can easily be shown that Mark has expanded the treatment of the third agent beyond the realism of the image level:

> Then he sent another, and that one they killed. And so it was with many others; some they beat, and others they killed.

In writing "and so it was with many others . . ." Mark wants to remind his readers of the murders of the prophets in Israel's history. But "and so it was with many others" does not fit the structure of the parable. Quite a few interpreters go so far as to strike the whole of verse 5, including the murder of the third agent. Their reasoning is that otherwise the point of the subsequent murder of the son is weakened. I have not gone that far in my reconstruction, since the murder of the son is sufficient in itself to present the hearers with a shocking escalation. But it is obvious that the reference to the many murders of prophets is disruptive.

The case is similar with the parable of the banquet in Matthew 22:1-14. The murder of the slaves sent with invitations and the king's wrath as he sends out his army to kill the murderers and lay their city in ashes (Matt 22:6-7) obviously does not fit the context of the original parable. Here Matthew has inserted a brief sketch of salva-

---

[4] For a fuller grounding of this shortened reconstruction let me refer to Gerhard Lohfink, "Das Gleichnis vom Sämann (Mk 4,3-9)," BZ 30 (1986): 36–69, at 37–42.

tion history, but in fairly clumsy fashion. The thread of the narrative is palpably broken by Matthew's interpolation. The readers notice right away that something does not fit, and they react indignantly. In almost every case textual alterations of this kind are expansions, and they are relatively easy to pinpoint.

3. But what about reworkings during the period of oral traditioning, that is, the time between Jesus and the authors of the Synoptic Gospels? Here, in the nature of things, individual indicators of redaction are much more difficult to pursue methodologically, but we may always suspect redaction when it can be shown that a parable does not reflect Jesus' situation but instead touches typical problems in the early communities. In part 2 of this book we repeatedly encountered such examples. Each time it turned out that Jesus' theme of the "reign of God" had shifted to the post-Easter "return of the Son of Man." Certainly such new accents did not change much in the narrative framework of the parable itself. To recall one such example: in the parable of the budding fig tree (Mark 13:28-29) the contextual shifting of the theological point was absolutely clear, but almost nothing in the wording of the parable had changed.

Moreover, at this point we should also recall that many of Jesus' parables were strictly and clearly constructed so that, because of their catchy structure, they could easily be retold. Thus insertions or changes are quickly apparent to the exegete. We should also not fail to notice that people regarded Jesus' parables, like all his *logia*, that is, his individual sayings, as precious and unalterable. Therefore they were carefully handed on, as faithfully as possible. Expansion through commentary was more probable than shortening or major changes in the material.

4. Finally, we have to ask whether Jesus' parables were not shaped by the *stylistic* talents of the tradents and then later by the individual styles of the three Synoptic evangelists. Certainly we cannot rule that out in advance.

To that problem, however, I would say: Jesus' parables testify to an author of genius who possessed the techniques of storytelling to an astonishing degree. And not only that! A great many things come together in these parables—not only a narrative technique that is not easily applied, but also wordplays, richness of imagination, precision in imagery, and breadth of material. Likewise worth noting is the "intent of the utterance": justification, attack, consolation, empowerment to freedom, and always the silent petition to the listeners to let themselves be carried by the narrative out of their own calcified situation into the altogether new one of the reign of God, now coming to be.

Those who deny Jesus the authorship of some of his parables, or at least their narrative style, must at the same time posit narrators and theologians of like genius for the parables in question. In that case one may ask them why they do not think first of Jesus before bringing hypothetical storytellers into the picture: people who are not even known to have existed. As for Jesus, we know he existed. From him we have not only parables but a great number of extremely brief sayings that speak in the same powerful, polished, image-rich, and often disturbing style.

Moreover, we must not overlook the fact that for a long time, as regards the question of authenticity of Jesus texts, people talked in positively grotesque ways about the formative power of Christian communities. In the first half of the twentieth century "community composition" was a concept that shaped itself, in corresponding investigative essays, into a kind of *cantus firmus* or sustained melody. The concept of community composition rested on the idea of a community possessing the utmost in language skills and excellent theological competence. Out of the depths of its collective soul, so to speak, and employing a supreme creative skill, such a community regularly generated new Jesus texts. This romantic idea, which for a certain period of time also played a part in folk-culture studies, being applied to fairytales and sagas, is now long outdated. It was a phantom. Great texts are always created by individuals. They do not emerge from the linguistic talents of a collective.

## 4. The Subject

The subject, or theme, of Jesus' parables, without exception, is the coming of the reign of God or kingdom of God. I hope to demonstrate that in what follows.

But why do we need a whole section for that? Doesn't it mean wasting space on something obvious? Most certainly not, because the idea that the reign of God is the subject of all Jesus' parables is by no means generally accepted.⁵ To take just one example: many exegetes believe that the parable of the rich man and the poor man (Luke 16:19-31) is by no means about the reign of God, and that is the main reason why they deny that Jesus told it.⁶ Thus it is worthwhile to take a closer look at the theme of the "reign of God" in Jesus' parables. I will divide my reflections into four steps.

1. The "reign of God" is the clear and unmistakable central theme of Jesus' work. When he preached before crowds (Mark 1:14-15), in the context of his healing of the sick (Luke 11:20), in his call to discipleship (Luke 9:59-62), when teaching his disciples (Luke 18:29), again and again Jesus speaks of the "reign of God." The significance of that idea for him is evident from word statistics alone. Here is a table showing the frequency of *basileia tou theou* (reign of God/kingdom of God) or the Matthean equivalent *basileia tōn ouranōn* (kingdom of heaven) in the New Testament writings and letters (column 2).⁷ Then, in column 3, in order to show the real proportions, I have given the corresponding numbers of pages in the *Novum Testamentum Graece* (Nestle-Aland²⁶) for the document or collection. The fourth column shows the resulting relationship—more precisely, the occurrences of the concept per one hundred pages in the *Novum Testamentum Graece*.

---

⁵ In the important and well-balanced book *Gleichnisse—Fabeln—Parabeln*, Kurt Erlemann writes: "The idea of the 'matter' of the parable cannot be applied one-dimensionally to the reign of God. Many parables get by without that 'framing metaphor.' The 'matter,' that is, what it is really about, is instead a bundle of religious experiences. That bundle includes experience with God (theological aspect), experiences with Jesus Christ (christological aspect), experiences of reality (eschatological aspect), and even experience with productive, salvific actions (ethical aspect)." (Kurt Erlemann and Irmgard Nickel-Bacon, *Gleichnisse—Fabeln—Parabeln: exegetische, literaturtheoretische und religionspädagogische Zugänge*, UTB [Tübingen: Francke, 2014], 27. [Trans. LMM.]) But those are precisely the exceptionless and interwoven central elements of Jesus' proclamation of the reign of God: God's *eschatological action* is *now* revealed *in and through Jesus* and open for all who believe in the promised and hoped-for space of *salvation*.

⁶ Cp., e.g., Hans Klein, *Das Lukasevangelium übersetzt und erklärt* (Göttingen: Vandenhoeck & Ruprecht, 2005), 552: "We may ask whether the parable goes back to Jesus. The answer is more likely to be in the negative because the idea of the *basileia* is entirely absent."

⁷ Based on the numbers in William F. Moulton and Alfred S. Geden, *A Concordance to the Greek New Testament* (Edinburgh: T & T Clark, 2002).

| Biblical Book | βασιλεία τοῦ θεοῦ / βασιλεία τῶν οὐρανῶν | Pages made up by book in the NTG | Occurrences per 100 pp. |
|---|---|---|---|
| Matthew | 37 | 87 | 43 |
| Mark | 14 | 62 | 23 |
| Luke | 32 | 96 | 33 |
| John | 2 | 73 | 3 |
| Acts | 6 | 89 | 7 |
| Pauline corpus | 9 | 179 | 5 |
| Catholic letters | 0 | 44 | 0 |
| Revelation | 1 | 49 | 2 |

The numbers alone show that the notion of the "reign of God/kingdom of God" is characteristic of the three Synoptic Gospels; the usage falls off sharply in the remainder of the New Testament writings. The reason is obvious: the idea of the "reign of God" was central for the historical Jesus and for the Jesus traditions on which the Synoptic Gospels drew, but it was less and less useful in the early church tradition. Other ideas moved to the fore. Conclusion: speaking about the "reign of God" was characteristic of Jesus. It was central to his message and his practice. *And if that is so, then it must have been central to his parables also.*

2. It follows that it is no accident that a whole series of parables begins with introductory formulae on the pattern of "It is with the reign of God as with . . . ." Matthew is especially fond of that formula, but since it is attested in Mark (4:26, 30-31) and also in Q (Luke 13:18-19 // Matt 13:31; Luke 13:20-21 // Matt 13:33) it must be that Jesus sometimes began a parable with such a formula. In that case the theme of the "reign of God" was explicitly named at the beginning of the parable, though not necessarily in every case. Luke found a striking number of parables in his special material that had a "nominative beginning" of the type "a man was going down from Jerusalem to Jericho" (Luke 10:30; cp. also 13:6; 15:11; 16:1, 19).

3. But even if this introductory formula with the key words "reign of God" did not exist it would still be clear that the body of Jesus' parables, just like the rest of his preaching, was about the "reign of

God," because the "tensions" that shaped his preaching are all found in his parables too.

For example, there is the tension between "already and not yet." The double parable of the treasure in the field and the pearl (Matt 13:44-46) shows that one may come across the reign of God already today; one may own it and take hold of it. The parable of the budding fig tree (Mark 13:28-29), on the other hand, shows that it is near, it is just at the door, but it is not here yet.

Another tension characteristic of Jesus' preaching appears in the parables: human beings cannot bring about the reign of God, much less force its coming. They can lie down at night and rest peacefully (Mark 4:26-29), and yet they must do everything, radically and with ultimate commitment, in order to win it (Matt 25:14-30; Luke 16:1-7; *Gos. Thom.* 98).

Let me point to still another tension: Jesus repeatedly promises rich reward to those who believe his words or even follow him. That reward is a share in the reign of God (cp., e.g., the Beatitudes in Matt 5:3-12). But at the same time the reward far surpasses everything the human being can hope for because it is pure grace. That tension appears also in Jesus' parables. The watchful slaves are rewarded surprisingly and more than richly: a feast begins when the master returns, a feast in which they themselves become the masters and mistresses, and their real master serves them like a slave (Luke 12:35-38). But the parable of the slave's wages (Luke 17:7-10) stands in stark contrast: the slave has to work until his tongue is hanging out and has no claim to wages, let alone deserving anything. He can only say: "I am a useless slave."

Consider a final tension: that between mercy and judgment. Jesus not only preached God's forgiveness; he could also speak about judgment—when the Gospel is rejected (Luke 10:13-15). The human creates her or his own judgment. This tension also, which shows that one dare not make light of the Good News, is found in Jesus' parables: God's incomprehensible mercy (Luke 15:11-32) but also the threat of judgment (Luke 13:6-9; 16:19-31).

4. And now the ultimately decisive point: Even those among Jesus' parables that seem to be altogether about other things and at first glance have nothing at all to do with the reign of God do indeed speak of it. I will choose four that are especially controverted in this regard.

(a) The rich man and the poor man (Luke 16:19-31). The first thing uncovered in this parable is the danger of wealth. Riches can cause a person to leave poor people to starve outside one's door and even to suffer having dogs slobber on them before they die. Here we are already on the level of "social critique of riches."

But for Jesus such wealth has a still more dangerous aspect: he must have experienced over and over again how it was precisely the desire for riches or stubborn fixation on one's own property that prevented people from opening themselves to his proclamation of the reign of God (cp. Mark 10:17-22). Hence his radical either-or: one cannot simultaneously serve the true God and make riches one's god, that is, a thing that governs one's whole life (thus Matt 6:24).

The crucial aspect is that this "serving the true God" by no means refers to a timeless worship. Rather, it is the acceptance of the reign of God that Jesus is preaching. But the acceptance of this new thing is precisely what is obstructed by wealth, because "it is easier for a camel to go through the eye of a needle than for someone who is rich to enter the kingdom of God" (Mark 10:25).

The poor have an easier time of it with the reign of God: they are called blessed (Luke 6:20). That is, they can rejoice because the reign of God, now beginning, will put an end to their misery. How so? Because then, finally, the solidarity with the poor in Israel that is demanded by the Torah will become a reality.

All of this clearly forms the background for the parable of the rich man and the poor man. In it Lazarus obtains a share in the eternal banquet of the reign of God; the rich man does not. And there is an unbridgeable chasm between the meal in the reign of God and the world of the dead—a chasm as impassable as the eye of a needle is for a camel.

The parable of the rich man and the poor man, which at first reading seems like an "illustration" of Wisdom-style morality, thus has its proper location in Jesus' proclamation of the reign of God. Now, at this hour, everything depends on giving up all that stands in the way of the reign of God—and that includes precisely the way many rich people take their sated and pleasing life for granted and do not even notice the poor before their own doors.

(b) The foolish wheat farmer (Luke 12:16-20). The situation here is similar to that in the parable of the rich man and the poor man just discussed. Here again, as we saw in part 2, we are not presented simply with generalized advice for living—for example, moral instruction about the burden of wealth and the perils of sudden death and laughing heirs.

Luke 12:16-20 is not about things that happen all the time; it speaks of a very specific circumstance: a piece of good luck, an abundant harvest. In doing so it brings a *kairos* into view, a decisive moment, a situation the wheat farmer could have made use of in different ways. He could have put his unhoped-for wealth to use in aid of the poor among the people of God, but he does not even perceive the opportunity that is offered to him. He is completely caught up in his self-centeredness. He doesn't even engage in conversation with anyone else. Throughout the whole parable he only talks to himself.

Because of his "self-focus" he cannot perceive the reign of God, and so he becomes the embodiment of the people who remain blind to the hour of Jesus' appearance. They were exclusively occupied with themselves, and precisely for that reason what was happening around them was opaque to them.

Thus we must not make the parable an instruction on *memento mori*, as in medieval mystery plays, or an illustration of Old Testament Wisdom rules for living. The parable can be located without any difficulty in real life. The *kairos* Jesus has in view in telling his tale is not the hour of death but the hour of the reign of God, and self-centeredness can cause one to miss that hour.

(c) The merciful Samaritan. In part 2 of this book we saw that the interpretation of Luke 10:30-35 in commentaries and most certainly in parish sermons is often dominated by such phrases as "hour of human fellow-feeling," "common concern for fellow human beings," "universal ethos of helping," "global love for humanity." Or it is said that here all "particular boundaries" of love of neighbor are demolished. If that were true, then the parable would indeed not have the least relevance to Jesus' preaching of the reign of God.

After all, in his preaching of the reign of God Jesus does not speak about humanity in general and most certainly not about universal human understanding. For him the reign of God cannot be separated from the people of God. It has a concrete and definable point to which it adheres, and that point is Israel. For Jesus it is clear that, because the reign of God is coming, it is time for the fulfillment of what the prophets had always demanded. Now, at the very latest, the unity between worship of God and love of neighbor must become reality—and that must happen in Israel. The people of God must thus become the "light for the world," the "salt of the earth," and a sign for the nations (Matt 5:13-16).

We can find no trace of this inner unity between worship and love of neighbor in the priest and the Levite, but with the Samaritan it is different. Here, as we have seen, is the real point of the parable: Jesus wants to gather all Israel—wants to do so for the sake of what is now in preparation: the reign of God. It appears that for him the despised Samaritans are part of the people of God. Jesus refuses to accept the existing separation and hatred between the two groups. He wants to overcome divisions in Israel.

This restoration of the unity of the people of God is, for Jesus, an elementary part of the proclamation of God's reign. That is why, for example, Jesus places among the Twelve—for him the real symbol of the Israel that is to be gathered—people from very different groups, from the tax collector Matthew (Matt 10:3) to Simon the Zealot (Luke 6:15).

If the parable of the merciful Samaritan speaks not only of the exemplary mercy and solidarity of someone who in Israel is a hated outsider but, beyond that, of Jesus' will to gather Israel, then this parable is eminently about the reign of God, even though that is not named at all.

(d) The two different sons. Again, the reign of God is not mentioned at the beginning of this parable, so that some interpreters have asked what Matthew 21:28-31 can have to do with Jesus' genuine preaching. For us the crucial starting point was the consideration of what could be meant here by "the will of the father." Is it just about obedience to God in a general sense? Concretely: is it solely about keeping everything prescribed in the Torah?

Another text—namely, the story in Mark 3:31-35—can show us that for Jesus "the will of God" has a different meaning, because here Jesus separates himself from his own family who want to stop him from working and take him back home. Moreover, he not only separates legally from his family; at the same time he creates a "new family." His new family—his mother, brothers, and sisters—from now on is made up of all those who "do the will of God" (Mark 3:35). Here the "will of God" certainly cannot be the Torah (which was most assuredly being faithfully fulfilled by his natural family) but is what God is now setting in motion: God's intention, God's cause, God's plan, or, more concretely, what God is now accomplishing in Israel through Jesus. They do "the will of God" who in this hour hear "the word of God" from the lips of Jesus "and obey it" (Luke 11:28); that is, they are those who open themselves to the reign of God.

Adolf Jülicher still thought, in the framework of his parables theory, that the parable of the two different sons was about an evaluation of the discrepancy between "speaking and doing."[8] In that he did justice neither to the vineyard motif nor to the situating of the parable in Jesus' conflicts with his contemporaries. The point here is not some timeless ethic ("human speech should always correspond to human action") but right attitudes in light of the reign of God. That is the right "obedience" to God that is now demanded. The parable of the two different sons is an urgent warning not to miss the signs of the times but to surrender oneself to the call of the present hour.

So much, then, to the thesis proposed at the beginning of this chapter: *Jesus' parables, without exception, have as their subject the coming of the reign of God.* That is true even for those parables that at first glance appear to have nothing to do with the theme of the "reign of God."

But how can we give a more exact description of the theme "reign of God" that dominates all Jesus' parables? What do his parables tell us about the reign of God?

First, they tell us that it is happening *now*. It is not somewhere above the clouds or waiting somewhere in the future. It is happening among those who listen to Jesus (and therefore among us also), and its coming is as close as summer is near when the fig tree's shoots are full of sap.

Still, the coming of the reign of God is an event filled with tension. If we were to say simply that it is coming "soon" we would miss the

---

[8] Adolf Jülicher, *Die Gleichnisreden Jesu*, vol. 2 (Freiburg: Mohr [Siebeck], 1886), 385.

tension, because we have to say simultaneously "it is already here." One may encounter it the way the day-laborer stumbles over the clay jug full of silver coins, and one can pick it up the way the wholesale merchant acquires the precious pearl. We must even say: the reign of God has already broken in, like a burglar who broke into a house. One would like to have prevented it. One would not have admitted it into the house of Israel and the rituals of one's own life, but it came like a thief in the night.

The comparison with the thief in the night signals that the reign of God does not come simply as everything in nature grows, ripens, and gets bigger and stronger. It is something that happens in "history"—and "history" means obstacles, resistance, enemies, threats, difficulties, denunciations. Still, Jesus can also speak of those forms of resistance to the reign of God with images drawn from agriculture: birds pluck up the seed; the sun dries up the soil so that the seed is scorched; thorns and thistles choke the shoots; an evil enemy sows weeds; a fig tree produces no fruit.

On the other hand, despite these barriers and threats, the coming of the reign of God cannot be prevented. Despite all the obstacles, good ground brings forth abundant fruit, the tiny mustard seed grows into a great bush, a huge quantity of bread dough is thoroughly leavened.

It is true that the coming of the reign of God involves the whole world, but the proximate place of the reign of God, its presence, its homeland, is Israel. That is why Jesus repeatedly uses the image of a vineyard, and that is why he speaks of a fig tree, a banquet, and a wedding. The people of God are confronted with a grave decision: Will the different brothers work in their father's vineyard, or will they refuse? Will those invited to the evening banquet participate or excuse themselves? Will everyone come wearing a wedding garment or insult the host? Will the people of God greet the bridegroom with burning torches? Will they be awake when the master of the house returns from the wedding? The peril of missing the decisive hour is great: it is the danger of quarreling like children who cannot agree what to play. It is the danger of remaining blind to the signs of the times—as the rich who are occupied with themselves and their good life do not even see what is right before their eyes.

In light of this critical situation every individual among the people of God is called to act. It is a matter of grasping the new thing with the utmost effort, with passion, desire, imagination, and eagerness—the way terrorists and major capitalists do business. But it must also be done with wisdom, care, and balance—like builders who have to calculate ahead of time whether they can finance the house-tower they are planning. At the same time it is paradoxically true that human beings by themselves cannot bring about the reign of God; they can sleep quietly at night because God brings that reign, and no one can prevent God from working.

This now-already-happening reign of God is the offer of an incomprehensible affection and love on the part of God. It is as great as the love of a father who embraces his debauched son and doesn't even hear his confession of sin all the way through, and it is as great as the graciousness of the feudal lord who orders that the last be paid as much as the first. As a shepherd rejoices at finding a lost sheep and a woman exults at finding her lost drachma, so God rejoices over every sinner who repents. God forgives all sin and guilt but likewise demands that from now on all sin and guilt within the people of God must be forgiven. God cancels all debts but also requires that from now on all debts must be forgiven within the people of God. Those who do not grasp that law, who mercilessly demand repayment from others even though God has just forgiven them everything, become subject to judgment.

Oh yes, Jesus' parables also speak of judgment; we cannot expel that apparent contradiction from them. The practice of the reign of God inevitably demands the gathering of Israel, but that gathering of the people of God at the same time leads to a division that runs right through the middle of God's people: not only are the good fish gathered into baskets, but the useless ones are discarded. And if the fig tree, despite the grace period granted it, still does not produce fruit it will be cut down. It is impermissible to pull up the darnel growing in the wheat field, but in the end it will be separated out.

Certainly it is true that gathering and division, mercy and judgment, nearness and distance of the reign of God are not blind fate that seizes people and sets its iron claws into them willy-nilly. The coming reign of God radically intensifies what was already the case in Israel: the intimacy of trust between human beings and God. Now all the people of God are empowered to rely with infinite trust, with an insistent immediacy, on God's action—like the importunate friend who can securely rely on getting bread for his guest and like the poor widow who will, after all, receive help. When, in this world, people even get up in the middle of the night to help each other, and when even corrupt judges finally do their duty—then certainly and in every case God will act as well.

*All this has been an attempt to describe, to paraphrase, to show through metaphors[9] what "the reign of God" conveys in Jesus' parables.* It is impossible to capture these parables in formulae. For that reason I also cannot, in any real way, distill any abstract basic ideas from these forty parables. I could not do anything but constantly refer back to Jesus' narratives and creative imagery. Jesus' parables simply do not tell simple people in pictorial illustrations what could really be formulated much better and more precisely in theological language. They say *in parables* what the reign of God is and how it comes. *The parable form is irreplaceable for that purpose.*

The fact that Jesus repeatedly spoke in parables is connected with the fact that ultimately one can talk of the reign of God only in this form: still more, that the reign of God itself comes to the listeners in the parables themselves, very much as it was already happening in Jesus' miracles. If those who listen to Jesus' parables allow themselves to be carried away and changed by a parable they are near to the reign of God; then it is already "present."

Thus the intent to determine the central theme of Jesus' parables is a rather helpless effort to paraphrase what Jesus said, not in formulae, but in parables. The exegete can only reconstruct the historical situation of the parables, investigate their structure, describe the world in which their imagery is situated, and uncover the organic context they depict—but then, at the latest, the texts must speak for themselves.

Let me add one final note about the subject of this section! Attentive readers will have noticed that my interpretation of Jesus' parables has spoken again and again about the "todayness" of the reign of

---

[9] Hans Weder, *Die Gleichnisse Jesu als Metaphern. Traditions- und redaktionsgeschichtliche Analysen und Interpretationen*, 2nd ed. (Göttingen: Vandenhoeck & Ruprecht, 1980), 65, rightly emphasizes that Jesus' parables cannot be replaced by any kind of formulae. What they mean to say can at best be "paraphrased."

God—that it is "now" coming, in fact that with Jesus' appearance it has already broken in and has begun to change the world. In technical language that is called "present eschatology." The end-time events do not begin in the future but in the present. They have already begun; they are here now.

So is there no "future eschatology" for Jesus—namely, what is still awaited, what has not yet come, what is still to be expected and hoped for from God? Obviously all that is also part of his proclamation. He certainly speaks in the future tense of the fulfillment of all history, the coming of the Son of Man for judgment, the perfection of the world, the day—to use Paul's expression (1 Cor 15:28)—when God will be "all in all." I have repeatedly pointed to the tension between "already and not yet."

But it appears that especially in Jesus' *parables* the "has-already-come" of the reign of God plays a more important role than the still-to-be-awaited future. It is easy to understand why that is: every pious person in Israel believed in the rule of God; they only needed to read Psalm 145 to know that

> All your works shall give thanks to you, O Lord,
>   and all your faithful shall bless you.
> They shall speak of the glory of your kingdom,
>   and tell of your power,
> to make known to all people your mighty deeds,
>   and the glorious splendor of your kingdom.
> Your kingdom is an everlasting kingdom,
>   and your dominion endures throughout all generations.
> (Ps 145:10-13)

But what is so shocking in Jesus' words and actions is precisely *not* this obvious faith in the always-already-existing, eternal rule of God or the coming of that reign in the future. No, what is unique in his appearance is that the reign of God is coming now, in his person, in his preaching, and in his miracles. That is what is special about him, and therefore he had to put before his hearers precisely *that*, declare it to them, put it into words. And that he does, first and foremost, in his parables. Evidently they were best suited to the purpose.

So with Jesus we have both—"already" and "not yet"—and the tension between the two is maintained. But in his parables the emphasis is clearly on the "already," the "today," the "now." And that very thing is connected with the mystery of his person. I must speak of that now.

## 5. The Theme within the Theme

At the end of the preceding section I attempted to describe or paraphrase the theme or subject of Jesus' parables, but the crucial point I left aside: when Jesus speaks in his parables about the reign of God he is at the same time speaking about himself. In part 2 of this book we discovered such indirect self-references by Jesus in a number of parables. At this point let me refer again to four of them as representative of the rest.

1. The abundant harvest (Mark 4:3-9). We have seen the dynamic that develops in this parable. In its first three parts the destructive power of the opponents increases, and the annihilation of the seed likewise expands tragically: first it is only the seeds themselves that are affected, by the birds' attack, but then the blazing sun scorches the first shoots; finally the thorns and thistles choke the stalks that are beginning to shape the grain. Despite all that, the seed that falls on good ground grows and produces fruit.

It is clear that Jesus is speaking here about the reign of God. It indeed meets great opposition but it resists all its enemies. Despite the number of its opponents, in the end the stem bears rich fruit.

It was ever so: those among Jesus' hearers who were familiar with Scripture had to picture the sower as God, for in the Old Testament God is depicted as the one who sows seed again and again—more precisely: the one who sows people of God among the Gentiles (i.e., scatters them among the Gentiles) or who, in the time of salvation that is to come, will sow them anew in the Land (Zech 10:9; Hos 2:1-3, 25; Jer 31:27-28).[10]

But does the parable refer only to God? That is hard to imagine. Jesus speaks here, indirectly and with restraint, about himself. He is the sower who sows the word of proclamation. He is thus also the one who sows people (cp. Mark 4:16); that is, he wins people over

---

[10] Cp. Gerhard Lohfink, "Die Metaphorik der Aussaat im Gleichnis vom Sämann (Mk 4,3-9)," in *Studien zum Neuen Testament*, SBAB 5 (Stuttgart: Katholisches Bibelwerk, 1989), 131–47.

for the sake of God's reign and gathers them around himself. He is the one who has had to bear the attacks of his opponents from the beginning of his ministry. He is the one who has had to experience over and over again how his opponents paint a scary picture of him and destroy their faith in his mission. And he is the one who can see how, despite it all, the seed is growing. All that echoes in this parable, like the "overtones" produced when a musical instrument is played. One can hear them as soon as one becomes aware of the reality of Jesus' working.

But Jesus does not paint that unmistakable background explicitly. It is his art to leave his own role unspoken. It is true that the parable genre did not allow for open and explicit reference to Jesus (except at the end), but even there Jesus did not make direct reference to himself. As regards his own person he remained reticent. We might even say: he protected his secret.

2. The lost son (Luke 15:11-32). Something similar can be said about this parable: when Jesus told his listeners how the father embraced his returning son, many must have thought of God. They may have recalled the verse they had heard or recited, again and again, from the book of Psalms: "As a father has compassion for his children, so the Lord has compassion for those who fear him" (Ps 103:13), and they would have recalled other texts from Scripture: for example, the well-known passage in Exodus in which God reveals the very Self of God to Moses with the words "The Lord, the Lord, a God merciful and gracious, slow to anger, and abounding in steadfast love and faithfulness" (Exod 34:6).

In the parable of the lost son Jesus put before them the image of a father such that, if they accepted it, they had to respond: "God is like that." God looks lovingly on even the guilty and the lost. God is overcome with joy when a lost one returns.

They may even have noticed that, in fact, this parable goes far beyond God's self-revelation in the book of Exodus; here a father is portrayed who holds nothing against anyone, not even "to the third and the fourth generation" (Exod 34:7). This father completely forgets what has happened. He forgives unconditionally and without stipulation. He forgives even when humans no longer do so. The father in the parable of the lost son mirrors God.

Yet even to say that is inadequate—just as it would not have been sufficient for the parable of the abundant harvest—because at the same time this father represents Jesus. After all, in this parable Jesus is defending his attitude toward sinners against the reproaches of his opponents. He is justifying his own practice (Luke 15:1-2). The dialogue between the father and the elder son (Luke 15:28-32) shows that unmistakably. Thus we may say that in this parable Jesus justifies his actions, namely, his acceptance of sinners, by speaking about God. What he does is fully transparent with respect to God. There is no way of separating Jesus' actions from the working of God.

3. The Pharisee and the tax collector (Luke 18:10-14). When they heard this parable, many of Jesus' hearers must at first have been altogether on the Pharisee's side because—at least at first glance—he completely matched the God-fearing speakers of Psalm 1 who "do not follow the advice of the wicked, or take the path that sinners tread, or sit in the seat of scoffers; but their delight is in the law of the Lord" (Ps 1:1-2). They would initially have identified the tax collector with the "wicked" who do not belong to the "congregation of the righteous" and whose way "will perish" (Ps 1:4-6).

But their identification of the two must have wobbled when they heard the Pharisee speak so self-righteously and with such self-reliance, in contrast to the humility and fear of God expressed by the tax collector. Still, even if they did not waver in their evaluation of the two, at the end of the parable they heard Jesus' conclusion: "This man went down to his home justified rather than the other" (Luke 18:14). We saw what that means: the tax collector was justified by God, freed from divine judgment; the Pharisee was not.

We could not avoid asking ourselves: Who gave Jesus the right to talk that way? Is he not speaking, in this parable, as if he stood in the place of God? He—he himself—judges and acquits. He himself utters divine judgment. That was just as unfathomable as the fact that the tax collector was acquitted by God in spite of his altogether false way of life.

4. The violent farmworkers. Mark 12:1-12 has been shown to be one of the most disputed of all Jesus' parables. Many interpreters doubt that it comes from Jesus at all. The crucial point introduced in this connection was that if Mark 12:1-12 is really supposed to be from Jesus, then here in this parable for the first time he speaks about himself—and apparently even uses the later christological title "the Son."

Those who deny that this parable comes from Jesus must be clear about the fact that they are involving themselves in a fundamental "prior decision"—namely, asserting or denying that, as things were coming to a head in Jerusalem, Jesus could have interpreted his own situation in a parable. If we presuppose that Jesus had a fixed canon of statements that he constantly repeated, so that it would have been impossible for him to say something novel in new situations—that is to say, if we suppose that in essence he lived an ahistorical life—then this parable really could not be his. But that presupposition is not only false but also ungodly: it denies Jesus his historical existence and makes him a "timeless" voice.

After his action in the Jerusalem temple Jesus must have known that from then on it was a case of life or death for him: still more, that everything was coming to a crisis for the people of God. In this situation he spoke his—possibly last—parable, meant to uncover the game being played by Israel's leadership. In this parable Jesus wants to reveal what is really going on in Jerusalem. What he says achieves its explosive power through what his allusion to Isaiah 5:1-2 makes clear from the outset: this is about God, the owner of the vineyard, and thus it is about Israel. In that light, when the word "son" appears in the further development of the narrative Jesus is placing himself in an unbelievable nearness to God.

Certainly that was not entirely outside Jesus' previous preaching. He had appeared not only as the proclaimer but as the representative of the reign of God. Whoever rejected him likewise rejected God.

Moreover: although in the parable of the violent farmworkers Jesus brings himself into the picture more than in any other parable, here also he speaks of himself in a veiled and hidden way. "[The vineyard owner] had still [or: only] one other, a beloved son" (Mark 12:6). As we have seen, that is by no means the same as the later christological title "Son of God," because in the contemporary situation in Palestine, extremely unsettled and in part lawless as it was, one cannot rule out the possibility that the owner of a *latifundia* living abroad might send his own son, the only person with full "legal capacity," to settle legal questions regarding his property with the local judges.[11]

---

[11] Cp. Hengel, "Das Gleichnis von den Weingärtnern," 25–31.

Thus in this parable we also have both: Jesus' unheard-of claim that he was sent to call the people of Israel to an ultimate decision, and to do so as one who stands in the place of God, and at the same time a concealment wrought by the garment of parable that secures theological discretion.

In the preface to this book I quoted the well-known Lutheran theologian Eberhard Jüngel: "The parables not only draw us into the center of Jesus' proclamation; at the same time they point to the person of the proclaimer, the mystery of Jesus himself." That really says it all. Jesus' parables lose their situation and their whole excitement if we do not grasp Jesus' enormous underlying claim.

After all, Jesus does not preach *about* the reign of God; he proclaims it.[12] He not only proclaims it; he says "It is present now." He says not only "It is present now," but "It is present in me"—in my words, in my miracles. Jesus himself therefore brings the reign of God. But how? Jesus allows God to reign, so that the holy God is now finally and forever present in this world—in Jesus himself. Jesus has become the place where people will decide for or against God, and not only decide, for Jesus has become the place where one may see who God is and what God wants. In that sense the later words of John's gospel, "Whoever has seen me has seen the Father" (John 14:9), are a fully legitimate and indeed necessary interpretation of what was veiled in Jesus' parables.

In that sense Jesus' parables already contain an "implicit Christology," and therefore every "explicit Christology" such as is ineluctably required of the church must really have its starting point in Jesus' parables, because in them we are standing on solid historical ground, and Jesus' whole claim is already present there.

The literary circle spoken of at the beginning of this book still exists. Now it is discussing Jesus' parables. Of course it is impossible for me

---

[12] In what follows I am drawing on Gerhard Lohfink, *Das Geheimnis des Galiläers*, 252–53.

to produce a log of the stimulating dialogues that take place there. Still, I take the liberty of giving a short sketch of our last meeting.

The older woman who argued so energetically about the interpretation of the "lion, the bear, and the serpent" (Amos 5:18-20) as the inevitability of death said this: "I do not deny that there must be a judgment. Still: I would simply like to forget those parables that talk at the end about 'wailing and gnashing of teeth.' I want to die with the wonderful parable of the lost son in my heart." She added: "I would also like to forget the parable about the poor girls who did not have enough oil for their torches. I find it horrifying that the door is shut in their faces. I cannot and I will not imagine a Jesus who is so unmerciful."

The psychotherapist responded: "But you have to realize that the 'foolish virgins' and the 'closed door' and the 'weeping and gnashing of teeth' are images representing what is dark in the world—the shadows within ourselves, our refusals, what is sluggish and undecided in us, the doors we ourselves have closed; that they are images for the things we have not dealt with, not clarified, the things that run riot so destructively in our depths. Why are you so afraid to deal with such images? Why, after all, are you so afraid of the judgment? I myself profoundly desire that eventually everything that is dark, confused, and evil in the world will be brought to light—even if it exists in myself."

Then the professor of classical philology spoke up. His words were directed at me, but I got the idea that they were also a quiet corrective to what the psychotherapist had just said. The philologist said: "It is a good thing that you have recently put the problems of structuralism into words. When some interpreters speak of Jesus' parables as 'purely aesthetic constructions' and 'autonomous works of art,' that has its limits. Obviously structuralist methods can play an extremely important role in the interpretation of texts, but an absolute set of structural laws that deliberately refuses to inquire about the author, the historical situation, and the interaction of a particular text with time and place is something I would see as nothing more than an aesthetic game. That kind of structuralism would tear Jesus' parables out of their rootedness in Israel and the life of Jesus. It would amputate the feet with which Jesus' parables stand on the ground of history. Charles Harold Dodd and Joachim Jeremias, in their books on parables, already showed us how to situate Jesus' parables on their true

240   *The Forty Parables of Jesus*

soil.[13] That was their great historical legacy. In particular, Jeremias's book on parables should continue to be highly honored."

Then came a long speech from the doctoral student who was working on a dissertation on seventeenth-century moral theologians. He said: "You know, sometimes I imagine I'm not going to write on people from the seventeenth century but about Jesus' parables instead. That's what really interests me." He went on to talk about hermeneutical principles, parables as metaphors, rhetorical provocation, narrative analysis, surface and deep structures, informative and performative speech, the connections between syntactical and semiological actants, the differences among parables, similitudes, and exemplary narratives, Jesus' parables as speech events—and a lot more.

The woman whose child had died and whose husband had cheated on her was silent. She looked at the doctoral student with big, puzzled eyes.

And the seventeen-year-old who had so often made her mark with provocative but intelligent remarks spoke only a single sentence. She said: "I want to find the hidden treasure and the precious pearl."

---

[13] The professor of classical philology is speaking of C. H. Dodd, *The Parables of the Kingdom*, rev. ed. (New York: Scribner, 1980), and Joachim Jeremias, *The Parables of Jesus*, trans. S. H. Hooke, rev. ed. (New York: Charles Scribner's Sons, 1962).

# Acknowledgments

My special thanks go to Professor Dr. Marius Reiser, who read the entire manuscript and who, with his philological skill and theological passion, offered me many useful suggestions.

Frau Antje Bitterlich likewise, as always, worked through everything and with her diligent attention preserved this book from quite a few orthographical mistakes, instances of questionable syntax, and stylistic stumbles.

As with all my previous publications, Hans Pachner selflessly and knowledgeably assembled all the necessary literature.

And then there were the many who encouraged me with their interest, their questions, and their suggestions—let me mention especially my brother Norbert, then Volker Zehetbauer, Carmelita and Gerd Block, Kristina and Dr. Johannes Hamel. Raphael Jaklitsch was a swift and knowledgeable helper when computer problems arose.

Dr. Bruno Steiner accompanied this book, like so many others, in friendly fashion, with his professional advice and publishing experience. And while I am speaking of the Herder publishing house I must offer very special thanks to Frau Francesca Bressan in the foreign rights division, whose charm and international connections have made possible so many translations of my books.

Thanks also, once again, to the Rev. Dr. Linda M. Maloney, who has carefully and reliably translated this book into English, like so many others. The same hearty thanks go to Mr. Hans Christoffersen, academic publisher at Liturgical Press, for his interest and fruitful cooperation.

*Gerhard Lohfink*

# Works Cited

*The following bibliography cannot and is not intended to give an overview of the most important literature on Jesus' parables. It contains only the literature cited in this book.*

Aland, Kurt. *Synopsis quattuor evangeliorum.* 8th ed. Stuttgart: Deutsche Bibelgesellschaft, 1973. English: *Synopsis of the Four Gospels.* New York: American Bible Society, 2010.

Ben-David, Arie. *Talmudische Ökonomie: Die Wirtschaft des jüdischen Palästina zur Zeit der Mischna und des Talmud.* Vol. 1. Hildesheim and New York: Georg Olms, 1974.

Berger, Klaus. *Formen und Gattungen im Neuen Testament.* UTB 2532. Tübingen and Basel: Francke, 2005.

Beyer, Klaus. *Semitische Syntax im Neuen Testament.* Vol. 1: *Satzlehre Teil 1.* 2nd ed. Göttingen: Vandenhoeck & Ruprecht, 1968.

Brox, Norbert. *Der Hirt des Hermas.* KAV 7. Göttingen: Vandenhoeck & Ruprecht, 1991. For English see: Carolyn Osiek, *Shepherd of Hermas: A Commentary.* Hermeneia. Minneapolis: Fortress Press, 1999.

Buber, Martin. *Tales of the Hasidim.* New York: Schocken Books, 1991.

Bultmann, Rudolf. *The History of the Synoptic Tradition.* Translated by John Marsh. New York: Harper & Row, 1976.

Crossan, John Dominic. "The Parable of the Wicked Husbandmen." *JBL* 40 (1971): 451–65.

Dalman, Gustav. *Arbeit und Sitte in Palästina.* Vol. 2: *Der Ackerbau.* Hildesheim: Olms, 1964.

———. *Arbeit und Sitte in Palästina.* Vol. 3: *Von der Ernte zum Mehl: Ernten, Dreschen, Worfeln, Sieben, Verwahren, Mahlen.* Hildesheim: Olms, 1964.

———. *Arbeit und Sitte in Palästina.* Vol. 4: *Öl und Wein.* Hildesheim: Olms, 1964. For portions of these works in English see: Gustav Dalman. *Work and Customs in Palestine: The Course of the Year and the Course of the Day.* Vol. 1: *Autumn and Winter*; vol 2: *Spring and Summer.* Translated by Nadia Abdulhadi-Sukhtian. Ramallah: Dar al Nasher, 2013.

De Vaux, Roland. *Das Alte Testament und seine Lebensordnungen.* Freiburg: Herder, 1960. English: *Ancient Israel: Its Life and Institutions.* Translated by John McHugh. 2nd ed. London: Darton, Longman & Todd, 1965.

Dibelius, Martin. *Die Formgeschichte des Evangeliums.* Tübingen: Mohr, 1919; 6th ed., 1971. English: *From Tradition to Gospel.* Translated by Bertram Lee Woolf. Cambridge: James Clarke, 1971.

Dithmar, Reinhard, ed. *Fabeln, Parabeln und Gleichnisse. Beispiele didaktischer Literatur*, dtv 4047. 2nd ed. Munich: Deutscher Taschenbuch-Verlag, 1972.

Dodd, C. H. *The Parables of the Kingdom.* Rev. ed. London: Collins, 1961.

Dormeyer, Detlev. "Gleichnisse als narrative und metaphorische Konstrukte—sprachliche und handlungsorientierte Aspekte." In *Kompendium der Gleichnisse Jesu: Methodische Neuansätze zum Verstehen urchristlicher Parabeltexte*, edited by Ruben Zimmermann, 420–37. 2nd ed. Gütersloh: Gütersloher Verlagshaus, 2015.

Eagleton, Terry. *Literary Theory: An Introduction.* Oxford: Basil Blackwell, 1983.

Eichholz, Georg. *Gleichnisse der Evangelien. Form, Überlieferung, Auslegung.* Neukirchen-Vluyn: Neukirchener Verlag, 1971

Erlemann, Kurt, and Irmgard Nickel-Bacon. *Gleichnisse—Fabeln—Parabeln: exegetische, literaturtheoretische und religionspädagogische Zugänge.* UTB. Tübingen: Francke, 2014.

Fiebig, Paul. *Altjüdische Gleichnisse und die Gleichnisse Jesu.* Tübingen and Leipzig: Mohr (Siebeck), 1904.

Fieger, Michael. *Das Thomasevangelium: Einleitung, Kommentar und Systematik.* Münster: Aschendorff, 1991. For English see: Richard Valantasis. *The Gospel of Thomas.* London and New York: Routledge, 1997.

Förster, Niclas. "Die Selbstprüfung des Mörders (Vom Attentäter) EvThom 98." In Zimmermann, ed., *Kompendium*, 921–26.

Gerber, Christine. "Wann aus Sklavinnen und Sklaven Gäste ihres Herren werden (Von den wachenden Knechten) Lk 12,35-38." In Zimmermann, ed., *Kompendium*, 573–78.

Gnilka, Joachim. *Das Evangelium nach Markus*. EKK II/2. Zürich: Benziger; Neukirchen-Vluyn: Neukirchener Verlag, 1979.

Gross, Walter. *Richter*. HTKAT. Freiburg: Herder, 2009.

Harnisch, Wolfgang. *Die Gleichniserzählungen Jesu. Eine hermeneutische Einführung*. UTB 1343. Göttingen: Vandenhoeck & Ruprecht, 1985.

———, ed. *Die neutestamentliche Gleichnisforschung im Horizont von Hermeneutik und Literaturwissenschaft*. WdF 575. Darmstadt: Wissenschaftliche Buchgesellschaft, 1982.

———, ed. *Gleichnisse Jesu. Positionen der Auslegung von Adolf Jülicher bis zur Formgeschichte*. WdF 366. Darmstadt: Wissenschaftliche Buchgesellschaft, 1982.

Heininger, Bernhard. *Metaphorik, Erzählstruktur und szenisch-dramatische Gestaltung in den Sondergutgleichnissen bei Lukas*. NTA 24. Münster: Aschendorff, 1991.

Hengel, Martin. "Das Gleichnis von den Weingärtnern. Mc 12,1-12 im Lichte der Zenonpapyri und der rabbinischen Gleichnisse." *ZNW* 59 (1968): 1–39.

———, and Anna-Maria Schwemer. *Jesus and Judaism*. Translated by Wayne Coppins. BMSEC. Waco, TX: Baylor University Press; Tübingen: Mohr Siebeck, 2019.

Hoffmann, Paul, and Christoph Heil. *Die Spruchquelle Q. Studienausgabe Griechisch und Deutsch*. Darmstadt: Wissenschaftliche Buchgesellschaft, 2002. For English see, e.g., John S. Kloppenborg. *Q, the Earliest Gospel: An Introduction to the Original Stories and Sayings of Jesus*. Louisville: Westminster John Knox, 2008.

Huber, Wolfgang. *Passa und Ostern. Untersuchungen zur Osterfeier der alten Kirche*. BZNW 35. Berlin: Töpelmann, 1969.

Hunzinger, Claus-Hunno. "Unbekannte Gleichnisse Jesu aus dem Thomasevangelium." In *Judentum, Urchristentum, Kirche: Festschrift für Joachim Jeremias*, edited by Walter Eltester, 209–20. BZNW 26. Berlin: de Gruyter, 1960.

Jeremias, Joachim. *The Eucharistic Words of Jesus*. Translated by Norman Perrin. London: SCM, 1966.

———. *The Parables of Jesus*. Rev. ed. Translated by S. H. Hooke. Philadelphia: Trinity Press International, 1990.

Jülicher, Adolf. *Die Gleichnisreden Jesu. Zwei Teile in einem Band. Erster Teil: Die Gleichnisreden Jesu im Allgemeinen. Zweiter Teil: Auslegung der Gleichnisreden der drei ersten Evangelien*. Freiburg: Mohr [Siebeck], 1886.

Jüngel, Eberhard. "Die Problematik der Gleichnisrede Jesu." In Harnisch, ed., *Gleichnisse Jesu*, 281–342.

*Katholischer Katechismus der Bistümer Deutschlands.* Freiburg: Herder, 1955.

Klein, Hans. *Das Lukasevangelium.* KEK I/3. Göttingen: Vandenhoeck & Ruprecht, 2006.

Linnemann, Etta. *Gleichnisse Jesu. Einführung und Auslegung.* 4th ed. Göttingen: Vandenhoeck & Ruprecht, 1966. English: *Parables of Jesus: Introduction and Exposition.* Translated by John Sturdy. London: SPCK, 1966.

Lohfink, Gerhard. *Das Geheimnis des Galiläers. Ein Nachtgespräch über Jesus von Nazaret.* 2nd ed. Freiburg: Herder, 2019.

———. "Das Gleichnis vom Sämann (Mk 4,3-9)." *BZ* 30 (1986): 36–69. Repr.: *Studien zum Neuen Testament,* 91–130. SBABNT 5. Stuttgart: Katholisches Bibelwerk, 1989.

———. "Die Metaphorik der Aussaat im Gleichnis vom Sämann (Mk 4,3-9)." In *À cause de l'Évangile. Études sur les Synoptiques et les Acts. Mélanges offerts à Dom Jacques Dupont,* 211–28. LD 123. Paris: Cerf, 1985. Repr.: *Studien zum Neuen Testament* (1989), 131–48.

———. *Im Ringen um die Vernunft. Reden über Israel, die Kirche und die Europäische Aufklärung.* Freiburg: Herder, 2016.

———. *Jesus of Nazareth: What He Wanted, Who He Was.* Translated by Linda M. Maloney. Collegeville, MN: Liturgical Press, 2012.

———. "What Does the Love Commandment Mean?" In *No Irrelevant Jesus: On Jesus and the Church Today,* translated by Linda M. Maloney, 64–74. Collegeville, MN: Liturgical Press, 2014.

Luz, Ulrich. *Matthew 8–20.* Translated by James E. Crouch. Hermeneia. Minneapolis: Augsburg Fortress, 2000.

———. *Matthew 21–28.* Translated by James E. Crouch. Hermeneia. Minneapolis: Fortress Press, 2005.

Merz, Annette. "Jesus lernt vom Räuberhauptmann (Das Wort vom Starken), Mk 3,27." In Zimmermann, ed., *Kompendium,* 287–96.

Moenikes, Ansgar. *Die grundsätzliche Ablehnung des Königtums in der Hebräischen Bibel.* BBB 99. Weinheim: Beltz Athenaeum, 1995.

Moulton, William Fiddian, Alfred Shenington Geden, et al. *A Concordance to the Greek Testament.* Edinburgh: T & T Clark, 2002.

Nestle, Eberhard, Erwin Nestle, Barbara Aland, Kurt Aland, et al. *Novum Testamentum Graece.* 26th ed. Stuttgart: Deutsche Bibelgesellschaft, 1979.

Olrik, Axel. "Epische Gesetze der Volksdichtung." *Zeitschrift für deutsches Altertum* 51 (1909): 1–12.

Pellegrini, Silvia. "Ein 'ungetreuer' οἰκονόμος (Lk 16,1-9)? Ein Blick in die Zeitgeschichte Jesu." *BZ* 48 (2004): 161–78.

Poplutz, Uta. "Eine fruchtbare Allianz (Weinstock, Winzer, und Reben), Joh 15,1-8." In Zimmermann, ed., *Kompendium*, 828–39.

Rad, Gerhard von. *Genesis: A Commentary*. Translated by John H. Marks. OTL. Philadelphia: Westminster Press, 1972.

Reiser, Marius. *Bibelkritik und Auslegung der Heiligen Schrift. Beiträge zur Geschichte der biblischen Exegese und Hermeneutik*. WUNT 217. Tübingen: Mohr Siebeck, 2007.

———. *Jesus and Judgment*. Translated by Linda M. Maloney. Minneapolis: Fortress Press, 1997.

———. "Numismatik und Neues Testament." *Bib* 81 (2000): 457–88.

———. *Sprache und literarische Formen des Neuen Testaments. Eine Einführung*. UTB 2197. Paderborn: Schöningh, 2001.

Ricoeur, Paul. "Biblische Hermeneutik." In Harnisch, ed., *Die neutestamentliche Gleichnisforschung*, 248–339.

Schoedel, W. F. "Gleichnisse im Thomasevangelium. Mündliche Tradition oder gnostische Exegese?" In Harnisch, ed., *Gleichnisse Jesu*, 369–89.

Schottroff, Luise. *The Parables of Jesus*. Translated by Linda M. Maloney. Minneapolis: Fortress Press, 2006.

Schramm, Tim, and Kathrin Löwenstein. *Unmoralische Helden. Anstössige Gleichnisse Jesu*. Göttingen: Vandenhoeck & Ruprecht, 1986.

Somov, Alexey, and Vitaly Voinov. "'Abraham's Bosom' (Luke 16:22-23) as a Key Metaphor in the Overall Composition of the Parable of the Rich Man and Lazarus." *CBQ* 79 (2017): 615–33.

Stemberger, Günter. *Mekhilta de-Rabbi Jishma'el. Ein früher Midrasch zum Buch Exodus*. Berlin: Verlag der Weltreligionen, 2010.

Strack, Herman L., and Paul Billerbeck. *Kommentar zum Neuen Testament aus Talmud und Midrasch*. 4 vols. in 5. 3rd ed. Munich: Beck, 1961.

Stuhlmacher, Peter. *Biblical Theology of the New Testament*. Book 1: *The Origin and Character of the New Testament Proclamation*. Edited and translated by Daniel P. Bailey. Grand Rapids: Eerdmans, 2018.

———. "Der Kanon und seine Auslegung." In IDEM, *Biblische Theologie und Evangelium. Gesammelte Aufsätze*, 167–90. WUNT 146. Tübingen: Mohr Siebeck, 2019.

Tàrrech, A. P. "La parabole des Talents (Mt 25,14-30) ou des Mines (Lc 19,11-28)." In *À cause de l'Évangile* (1985), 165–93.

Via, Dan Otto, Jr. *The Parables: Their Literary and Existential Dimension*. Philadelphia: Fortress Press, 1967.

Weder, Hans. *Die Gleichnisse Jesu als Metaphern. Traditions- und redaktionsgeschichtliche Analysen und Interpretationen*. 2nd ed. Göttingen: Vandenhoeck & Ruprecht, 1980.

Weiser, Alfons. *Die Knechtsgleichnisse der synoptischen Evangelien*. SANT 29. Munich: Kösel, 1971.

Wolter, Michael. *Das Lukasevangelium*. HNT 5. Tübingen: Mohr Siebeck, 2008.

Zimmermann, Ruben, ed. *Hermeneutik der Gleichnisse Jesu. Methodische Neuansätze zum Verstehen neutestamentlicher Parabeltexte*. WUNT 231. Tübingen: Mohr Siebeck, 2008.

———, ed. *Kompendium der Gleichnisse Jesu: Methodische Neuansätze zum Verstehen urchristlicher Parabeltexte*. 2nd ed. Gütersloh: Gütersloher Verlagshaus, 2015.

———. "Parabeln—sonst nichts!" In *Hermeneutik der Gleichnisse Jesu*, 383–419.

# Scriptural Index

## Old Testament

*Genesis*
| | |
|---|---|
| 1 | 28 |
| 1:28, 30 | 58 |
| 2:19 | 58 |
| 3:1-5 | 175 |
| 6:1-9 | 185n122 |
| 6:7 | 58 |
| 22 | 120 |
| 22:1-19 | 218 |
| 22:2 | 200n143 |
| 22:9-10 | 120 |
| 22:9 | 185n122 |
| 29:27 | 134 |
| 33:1-11 | 149n89 |
| 33:10 | 149n89 |
| 40:20 | 148 |
| 48:15 | 77 |

*Exodus*
| | |
|---|---|
| 12:11 | 156 |
| 20:2-17 | 28 |
| 20:2 | 46 |
| 20:17 | 153 |
| 21:2-11 | 154 |
| 21:2 | 162 |
| 21:20 | 162 |
| 22:21-23 | 96 |
| 23:4-5 | 122 |
| 32:7-14 | 197 |
| 34:6 | 235 |
| 34:7 | 235 |

*Leviticus*
| | |
|---|---|
| 5:3 | 121n65 |
| 11:9-12 | 107 |
| 19:18, 34 | 122 |
| 21:1-6 | 121n65 |
| 25:39-55 | 154 |

*Numbers*
| | |
|---|---|
| 6:25-26 | 149n89 |
| 18:21 | 116 |
| 22:15-18 | 148 |

*Deuteronomy*
| | |
|---|---|
| 6 | 74 |
| 14:22-27 | 116 |
| 15:12 | 162 |
| 20:3 | 109 |

*Judges*
| | |
|---|---|
| 7 | 5 |
| 9:4-5 | 6 |
| 9:5 | 6 |
| 9:6 | 6 |
| **9:8-15** | **6–11**, 27, 103, 124, 212, 213, 218 |
| 11:34 | 200n143 |
| 14:12 | 134 |

*1 Samuel*
| | |
|---|---|
| 8:10-18 | 10 |
| 8:14 | 148 |

248

## Scriptural Index

| 2 Samuel | |
|---|---|
| 3:2-5 | 12n7 |
| 5:13-16 | 12n7 |
| 9:1–20:26 | 218 |
| 9:2 | 148 |
| **12:1-4** | **11–14**, 27, 71, 218 |
| 12:3 | 88 |
| 23:8, 39 | 11n6 |

| 1 Kings | |
|---|---|
| 1:1–2:46 | 218 |
| 1:8 | 11n6 |
| 18:13 | 201 |
| 19:10 | 201 |

| 2 Kings | |
|---|---|
| 9:7 | 201 |
| 17:5-6, 24 | 119 |

| 2 Chronicles | |
|---|---|
| 24:20-22 | 201 |
| 28:15 | 122 |

| Ezra | |
|---|---|
| 4:10 | 119 |

| Esther | |
|---|---|
| 6:14 | 104 |

| Job | |
|---|---|
| 24:3 | 96 |

| Psalms | |
|---|---|
| 1:1-2 | 86–87, 236 |
| 1:4-6 | 236 |
| 3:3 | 149n89 |
| 8:8 | 58 |
| 23:1 | 77 |
| 35:10 | 35 |
| 45:11, 17 | 135 |
| 49 | 144 |
| 66:17 | 101 |
| 79:2 | 58 |
| 80:2 | 77 |
| 80:8-16 | 125n70 |
| 80:9-17 | 17 |
| 80:10, 12 | 8 |
| 94:6 | 96 |
| 103:10-12 | 87 |
| 103:13 | 235 |
| 104:12 | 58, 198n139 |
| 107:27 | 8 |
| 119 | 116 |
| 121:5 | 9 |
| 129:7-8 | 90 |
| 145:10-13 | 233 |

| Song of Songs | |
|---|---|
| 1:6 | 15 |
| 2:11-13 | 56 |
| 2:15 | 15 |
| 7:8, 13 | 15 |
| 8:11-12 | 15 |

| Isaiah | |
|---|---|
| 1:23 | 96 |
| **5:1-7** | **14–18**, 22, 27, 71, 88, 125n70, 194, 201, 218 |
| 5:1-2 | 197, 198n139, 236 |
| 5:5 | 198n139 |
| 5:7 | 201 |
| 5:24 | 67 |
| 9:3 | 5 |
| 10:1-2 | 96 |
| 24:20 | 8 |
| 25:6-8 | 105 |
| 28:14-22 | 185 |
| 28:23-25 | 64 |
| 32:2 | 9 |
| 40:11 | 77 |
| 42:1 | 154 |
| 49:3 | 154 |
| 52:13 | 154 |
| 53:11 | 202 |
| 62:4-5 | 134, 146 |

| Jeremiah | |
|---|---|
| 2:2-3 | 146 |

| | | | |
|---|---|---|---|
| 2:2 | 134 | 2:1-3, 25 | 234 |
| 3:1-13 | 21 | 2:18-25 | 146 |
| 7:29-30 | 194 | 2:21-22 | 134 |
| 7:33 | 58 | 6:6 | 121 |
| 8:13 | 138 | 10:1 | 17 |
| 23:1 | 77 | | |
| 25:4 | 201 | *Joel* | |
| 26:20-24 | 201 | 1:7 | 138 |
| 31:10 | 77, 109 | 4:13 [= ET | |
| 31:27-28 | 234 | 3:13] | 64, 198n139 |
| 31:27 | 70 | | |

*Lamentations*

| | | *Amos* | |
|---|---|---|---|
| 2:1 | 20 | 2:7 | 5 |
| 2:13 | 20 | 3:7 | 201 |
| 4:20 | 9 | 3:15 | 5 |
| | | 4:1 | 5 |
| *Ezekiel* | | **5:18-20** | **3–6**, 239 |
| 13:10-13 | 185n122 | 5:21-23 | 5 |
| 16 | 21–23, 33 | 6:4-6 | 5 |
| **16:1-63** | **18–22** | 8:4 | 5 |
| 16:8 | 134, 146 | 8:10 | 200n143 |
| 17:22-24 | 59 | | |
| 20:34-38 | 109 | *Micah* | |
| 22:7 | 96 | 2:12 | 77 |
| 31:3-6 | 58n13 | | |
| 31:6 | 58, 60 | *Zechariah* | |
| 31:10-13 | 59 | 1:6 | 201 |
| 34:1-16 | 77 | 10:9 | 234 |
| 34:13 | 77 | 13:3 | 201 |
| 34:13, 16 | 77 | | |
| 36:22-28 | 108 | *Tobit* | |
| 38:17 | 201 | 8:19 | 134 |
| 38:22 | 185n122 | | |
| 44:25-27 | 121n65 | *Wisdom* | |
| | | 9:13-18 | 125n71 |
| *Daniel* | | | |
| 4:7-9 | 58n13, 59 | *Sirach* | |
| 4:9, 18 [= ET | | 35:15-26 | 96 |
| 4:12, 21] | 198n139 | 35:15-19 | 97 |
| 7:13-14 | 141 | | |
| | | *2 Esdras* | |
| *Hosea* | | 4:26-32 | 72n28 |
| 1–3 | 21 | 7:30-36 | 72n28 |

# New Testament

## Matthew

| | |
|---|---|
| 3:9 | 131 |
| 3:10 | 138 |
| 4:18 | 107 |
| 5:1, 13, 14, 16 | 188 |
| 5:3-12 | 225 |
| 5:13-16 | 228 |
| **5:15** | **187–89**, 209, 216 |
| 5:21-26 | 143 |
| **5:25-26** | **141–43**, 208 |
| 5:38-42 | 93 |
| 5:39 | 184 |
| 6:12 | 74, 152 |
| 6:24 | 130, 226 |
| 7:3 | 36 |
| 7:13-14, 22-23 | 133 |
| 7:21 | 186 |
| **7:24-27** | 161, **184–87**, 209 |
| 7:28-29 | 184 |
| 8:11 | 128 |
| 8:12 | 107, 160 |
| 10:3 | 228 |
| 10:32-33 | 186 |
| 10:39 | 52 |
| **11:16-19** | **139–41**, 139n79, 208, 214, 216 |
| 12:30 | 107 |
| 12:43-45 | *xii* n3 |
| 13:1-53 | 107 |
| 13:22 | 51 |
| **13:24-30** | **109–14**, 207 |
| 13:31-32 | 57n11 |
| 13:31 | 224 |
| 13:33 | 224 |
| 13:36-43 | 37, 224 |
| 13:40-43 | 151 |
| 13:41-42 | 107 |
| 13:42, 50 | 160 |
| **13:44-46** | **47–54**, 131, 181, 211, 214, 225 |
| 13:44 | 207 |
| 13:45-46 | 207 |
| **13:47-50** | 24, **106–109**, 207 |
| 13:47-48 | 101, 214 |
| 13:49-50 | 151 |
| 16:6 | 62 |
| 18 | 75n29 |
| 18:1-35 | 76 |
| 18:6-10 | 75 |
| 18:10 | 75n30 |
| **18:12-14** | **75–77**, 207 |
| 18:14 | 125n71 |
| **18:23-34** | **147–53**, 208 |
| 18:24 | 169 |
| 18:25 | 142n82 |
| 18:27 | 73 |
| 18:34 | 142n82 |
| 19:24 | 145 |
| **20:1-16** | **89–95**, 158, 207 |
| 20:10-15 | 212 |
| 20:12 | 216 |
| 21:23–23:39 | 106 |
| 21:23-46 | 196 |
| 21:23, 45-46 | 103 |
| 21:28-32 | 122n69 |
| **21:28-31** | **122–26**, 132, 207, 211, 214, 228 |
| 21:28 | 13 |
| 21:43 | 196 |
| 21:45-46 | 196 |
| 22:1-14 | 132, 145, 219, 220 |
| 22:1-10 | 102 |
| 22:2, 11-13 | 146 |
| 22:2 | 148n87 |
| 22:6-7 | 220 |
| 22:7, 13-14 | 151 |
| **22:11-13** | **145–47**, 208 |
| 22:13 | 107, 160 |
| 23:13 | 132 |
| 23:37 | 107 |
| 24:30, 37, 39, 44, 50 | 133 |
| 24:30 | 55 |
| 24:43-44 | 42n1 |

| | | | |
|---|---|---|---|
| 24:43 | 112 | 8:38 | 186 |
| **24:45-51** | **159–62**, 165, 208, 214 | 9:38-39 | 113n55 |
| 24:51 | 155 | 9:40 | 114n60 |
| **25:1-13** | 101, **131–36**, 147, 157, 207, 214 | 9:41 | 113n53 |
| | | 9:42 | 142n82 |
| **25:14-30** | 114n58, **166–73**, 208, 213, 214, 225 | 10:17-22 | 130, 226 |
| | | 10:25-30, 36-37 | 118 |
| 25:20-28 | 212 | 10:25 | 130, 226 |
| 25:30, 41 | 107 | 10:29-30 | 166 |
| 25:31-46 | xii, 133 | 10:31 | 89 |
| 26:52 | 184 | 10:35-45 | 165 |
| 27:25 | 196 | 11:15-17 | 195n138 |
| | | 11:27-28 | 195 |
| *Mark* | | **12:1-12** | 124, **191–203**, 208, 213, 220, 236 |
| 1:11 | 200n143 | | |
| 1:14-15 | 223 | 12:1-11 | 198n139 |
| 2:1-12 | 144 | 12:1 | 13, 195 |
| 2:13-17 | 76 | 12:6 | 200n143, 237 |
| 2:15 | 85, 108 | 12:18 | 108 |
| 2:16 | 113 | 13:5-23 | 55 |
| 2:17 | 85 | 13:26 | 55 |
| 2:19 | 136, 147 | **13:28-29** | **54–56**, 157, 208, 221, 225 |
| 2:22 | 146 | 13:28 | 36 |
| 3:13-19 | 108 | 13:33-37 | 157 |
| 3:20-21 | 108 | 14:3-9 | 73 |
| 3:22 | 46, 112 | 14:24 | 202 |
| **3:27** | **45–47**, 208, 216 | | |
| 3:31-35 | 228 | *Luke* | |
| **4:3-9** | 57, **65–72**, 103, 124, 191, 207, 219, 234 | 1:46-55 | 159 |
| | | 1:52-53 | 128, 159 |
| 4:4-7 | 213 | 2:34 | 108 |
| 4:5-6 | 219 | 5:17-26 | 144 |
| 4:8 | 66n20 | 5:19 | 144 |
| 4:10, 13, 21 | 188 | 6:15 | 108, 228 |
| 4:16, 18, 20 | 70 | 6:20-49 | 184 |
| 4:16 | 234 | 6:20 | 130, 226 |
| 4:21 | 187, 188 | 6:39 | 37 |
| **4:26-29** | 57, **63–65**, 114n57, 179, 198n139, 208, 225 | 6:46 | 186 |
| | | 6:47-49 | 184 |
| 4:28 | 216 | 6:48 | 184 |
| **4:30-32** | **56–61**, 198n139, 208 | 7:22 | 55 |
| 6:6-13 | 188 | 7:31-35 | 139n79 |
| 6:21 | 179 | 7:36-50 | 73 |
| 8:15 | 62 | **7:41-42** | **73–74**, 207, 214 |
| 8:31-33 | 189 | | |

| | | | |
|---|---|---|---|
| 8:1-3 | 113n52 | 13:30 | 89 |
| 8:9, 11, 18 | 188 | 13:34 | 107 |
| 8:16 | 187, 188 | 14:1 | 108 |
| 9:54-55 | 121 | 14:15 | 105 |
| 9:58 | 183 | **14:16-24** | **101–106**, 124, 132, 136, 145, 207, 212, 213, 214 |
| 9:59-62 | 223 | | |
| 10:13-15 | 225 | 14:16 | 13, 148n87, 212 |
| 10:23 | 61 | 14:21 | 216 |
| 10:25-30, 36-37 | 118 | 14:25-35 | 181 |
| | | 14:26 | 191 |
| **10:30-35** | 34, 108, **118–22**, 132, 207, 213, 214, 227 | **14:28-32** | **181–84**, 209 |
| | | 14:28-30, 31-32 | 75 |
| 10:30 | 13, 224 | 15 | 85 |
| 11:2-4 | 101 | 15:1-3 | 76 |
| 11:2 | 42 | 15:1-2 | 75, 236 |
| **11:5-8** | **99–101**, 112, 163, 208, 211 | 15:2 | 86 |
| | | 15:10 | 75n30 |
| 11:14-16, 29 | 188 | 15:3-10 | 78, 181 |
| 11:20 | 42, 44, 47, 55, 61, 223 | 15:4-7 | 75 |
| 11:21-22 | 46n3 | 15:5-6, 9 | 81 |
| 11:23 | 107, 114n59 | 15:7 | 77 |
| 11:28 | 229 | **15:8-10** | 75, **77–79**, 207 |
| 11:31-32 | 47, 78 | 15:8 | 216 |
| 11:33 | 187, 188 | 15:10 | 75n30 |
| 12:8-9 | 186–87 | **15:11-32** | 49, **79–89**, 101n44, 131, 164, 207, 211, 214, 225, 235 |
| **12:16-20** | 131, **143–45**, 208, 227 | | |
| 12:19 | 131 | 15:11 | 13, 224 |
| 12:22 | 41 | 15:12-24 | 213 |
| 12:32 | 60 | 15:16 | 215 |
| **12:35-38** | **153–59**, 162, 164, 165, 208 | 15:20-24 | 212 |
| | | 15:24 | 81 |
| **12:39** | **42–44**, 45, 47, 157, 207 | 15:25-32 | 213 |
| 12:41 | 160n99 | 15:32 | 81 |
| 12:42-46 | 160 | 16:1-31 | 126 |
| 12:49 | 108 | **16:1-13** | **173–78** |
| 12:51 | 108 | 16:1-7 | 65, 175, 208, 213, 225 |
| 12:53 | 42 | 16:1 | 13, 224 |
| 12:54-57 | 143 | 16:1-8 | 114n58 |
| 12:58-59 | 141 | 16:1, 9, 13, 14, 19 | 126 |
| **13:6-9** | **136–39**, 207, 225 | | |
| 13:6 | 224 | **16:19-31** | **126–31**, 132, 207, 212, 214, 216, 223, 225, 226 |
| 13:18-19 | 57n11, 224 | | |
| **13:20-21** | 57, **61–62**, 207, 212, 224 | 16:19 | 13, 224 |
| 13:24-27 | 133 | 17:6 | 58 |
| 13:28-29 | 128 | | |

| | | | |
|---|---|---|---|
| **17:7-10** | **162–66**, 209, 225 | 11:1-3 | 113n51 |
| 17:20-21 | 55 | 12:1-8 | 73 |
| 17:33 | 191 | 12:20-36 | 189 |
| **18:1-8** | **95–98**, 101n44, 112, 131, 207, 214 | 12:20-22 | 190 |
| | | **12:24** | **189–91**, 209 |
| 18:2 | 13 | 12:29 | 190 |
| 18:6-8 | 98 | 12:35 | 191 |
| 18:6 | 177 | 14:9 | 238 |
| **18:10-14** | 101, **114–18**, 120n64, 131, 207, 212, 214, 236 | **15:1-8** | **22–24**, 27 |
| 18:10 | 13 | *Acts* | |
| 18:14 | 114, 236 | 22:14-15 | 125n71 |
| 18:29 | 223 | | |
| 19:1-10 | 85 | *Galatians* | |
| 19:12-27 | 168, 219 | 5:9 | 62 |
| 19:22 | 171 | | |
| 20:1-2 | 196 | *Ephesians* | |
| 20:9-19 | 191 | 1:3-14 | 125n71 |
| 20:9 | 196 | | |
| 20:16 | 196 | *1 Thessalonians* | |
| 20:19 | 196 | 5:2-4 | 43 |
| 21:23 | 55n10 | | |
| 21:27 | 55 | *2 Peter* | |
| 22:25-26 | 60 | 3:10 | 43 |
| 22:27 | 159 | | |
| *John* | | *Revelation* | |
| 3:1-13 | 113n54 | 3:3 | 43 |
| 3:29 | 16 | 16:15 | 43 |

# The Parables in the Church Year

Below are listed all the parables that are included in the readings of the Roman Catholic Lectionary on the Sundays of Years A, B, and C. (The daily liturgy is not in view.)

If on a given Sunday a parable is read from another of the Synoptic Gospels, for example in Matthew's version instead of the Lukan version discussed in this book, or vice versa, the line is in *italics*.

| A | 5th Sunday in Ordinary Time | Matt 5:15 | The lamp on the lampstand | Pages **187–89** |
|---|---|---|---|---|
| A | 6th Sunday in Ordinary Time | Matt 5:25-26 | Going to court | Pages **141-43** |
| A | 9th Sunday in Ordinary Time | Matt 7:24-27 | Building a house on rock or on sand | Pages **184-87** |
| A | *15th Sunday in Ordinary Time* | *Matt 13:1-9* | *The Abundant Harvest* | (See pp. **65–72**) |
| A | 16th Sunday in Ordinary Time | Matt 13:24-30 | The Weeds in the Wheat | Pages **109–14** |
| A | *16th Sunday in Ordinary Time* | *Matt 13:33* | *The Leaven* | (See pp. **61–62**) |
| A | 17th Sunday in Ordinary Time | Matt 13:44-46 | The Treasure in the Field and the Pearl | Pages **47–54** |
| A | 24th Sunday in Ordinary Time | Matt 18:23-34 | The unforgiving servant | Pages **147–53** |
| A | 25th Sunday in Ordinary Time | Matt 20:1-16 | The Workers in the Vineyard | Pages **89–95** |
| A | 26th Sunday in Ordinary Time | Matt 21:28-31 | The different sons | Pages **122–26** |
| A | 27th Sunday in Ordinary Time | Isa 5:1-7 | The Song of the Vineyard | Pages **14–18** |
| A | *27th Sunday in Ordinary Time* | *Matt 21:33-43* | *The violent farmworkers* | (See pp. **191–203**) |
| A | *28th Sunday in Ordinary Time* | *Matt 22:1-13* | *The Great Banquet* | (See pp. **101–6**) |
| A | 28th Sunday in Ordinary Time | Matt 22:11-13 | The Guest without a Wedding Garment | Pages **145–47** |
| A | 32nd Sunday in Ordinary Time | Matt 25:1-13 | The ten bridesmaids | Pages **131–36** |
| A | 33rd Sunday in Ordinary Time | Matt 25:14-30 | The money given in trust | Pages **166–73** |

| | | | | |
|---|---|---|---|---|
| B | 5th Sunday in Lent | John 12:24 | The wheat seed falls into the ground and dies | Pages **189–91** |
| B | 6th Sunday of Easter | John 15:1-8 | The vine and the branches | Pages **22–24** |
| B | 10th Sunday in Ordinary Time | Mark 3:27 | The conquest of the "strong one" | Pages **45–47** |
| B | 11th Sunday in Ordinary Time | Mark 4:26-29 | The seed growing secretly | Pages **63–65** |
| B | 11th Sunday in Ordinary Time | Mark 4:30-32 | The mustard seed | Pages **56–61** |
| B | 33rd Sunday in Ordinary Time | Mark 13:28-29 | The budding fig tree | Pages **54–56** |

| | | | | |
|---|---|---|---|---|
| C | 3rd Sunday in Lent | Luke 13:6-9 | The barren fig tree | Pages **136–39** |
| C | 11th Sunday in Ordinary Time | Luke 7:41-42 | The two debtors | Pages **73–74** |
| C | 15th Sunday in Ordinary Time | Luke 10:30-35 | The merciful Samaritan | Pages **118–22** |
| C | 17th Sunday in Ordinary Time | Luke 11:5-8 | The friend at midnight | Pages **99–101** |
| C | 18th Sunday in Ordinary Time | Luke 12:16-20 | The crazy wheat farmer | Pages **143–45** |
| C | 19th Sunday in Ordinary Time | Luke 12:35-38 | The watchful slaves | Pages **153–59** |
| C | 19th Sunday in Ordinary Time | Luke 12:39 | The successful break-in | Pages **42–44** |
| C | 23rd Sunday in Ordinary Time | Luke 14:28-32 | Building a tower and making war | Pages **181–84** |
| C | *24th Sunday in Ordinary Time* | *Luke 15:1-7* | *The lost sheep* | (See pp. **75–77**) |
| C | 24th Sunday in Ordinary Time | Luke 15:8-10 | The lost coin | Pages **77–79** |
| C | 24th Sunday in Ordinary Time | Luke 15:11-32 | The lost son | Pages **79–89** |
| C | 25th Sunday in Ordinary Time | Luke 16:1-13 | The dishonest manager | Pages **173–78** |
| C | 26th Sunday in Ordinary Time | Luke 16:19-31 | The rich man and the poor man | Pages **126–31** |
| C | 27th Sunday in Ordinary Time | Luke 17:7-10 | A slave's wages | Pages **162–66** |
| C | 29th Sunday in Ordinary Time | Luke 18:1-8 | The judge and the widow | Pages **95–98** |
| C | 30th Sunday in Ordinary Time | Luke 18:10-14 | The Pharisee and the tax collector | Pages **114–18** |

www.ingramcontent.com/pod-product-compliance
Lightning Source LLC
Chambersburg PA
CBHW060647150426
42811CB00086B/2448/J